IMAGES
of America

HAYWOOD COUNTY

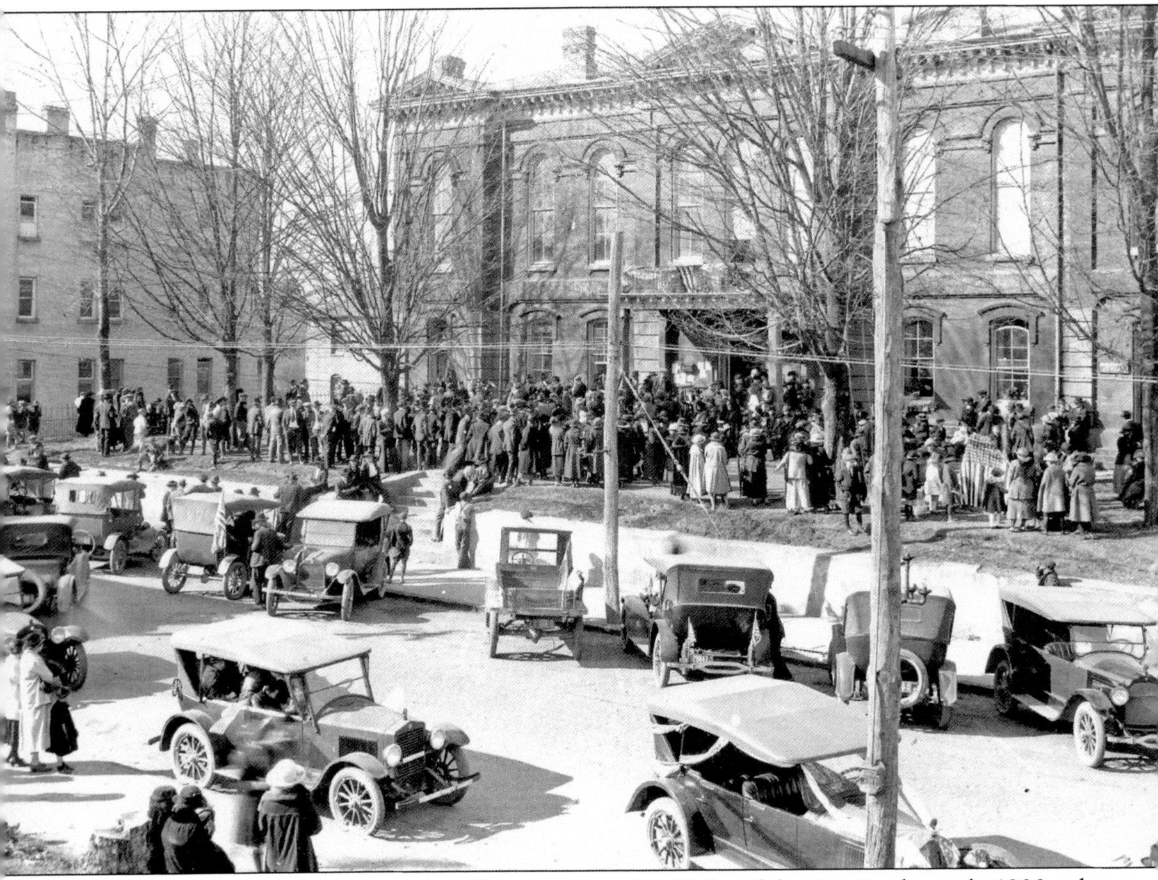

Haywood County Courthouse. During a Fourth of July celebration in the early 1900s, the Daughters of the American Revolution unveiled a marker erected on the courthouse lawn in Waynesville to honor the county's Revolutionary War veterans. (Courtesy of Henry Foy.)

On the Cover: Judy Alexander (left) on her horse, Target, and Edith Begni (right) on her horse, Babe Ruth, found this breathtaking view on Walker Bald overlooking Dellwood, Waynesville, and eastern Haywood County. (Courtesy of Cataloochee Ranch.)

IMAGES
of America

HAYWOOD COUNTY

Michael Beadle

ARCADIA
PUBLISHING

ISBN 978-0-7385-8558-1

Published by Arcadia Publishing
Charleston, South Carolina

Printed in the United States of America

Library of Congress Control Number: 2009937914

For all general information contact Arcadia Publishing at:
Telephone 843-853-2070
Fax 843-853-0044
E-mail sales@arcadiapublishing.com
For customer service and orders:
Toll-Free 1-888-313-2665

Visit us on the Internet at www.arcadiapublishing.com

To all students of history who explore the past
and find a new chapter of an old story

Contents

Acknowledgments

This book is dedicated to the generations of families and individuals who helped make Haywood County what it is today. These chapters contain a mix of previously published photographs and new photographs many in the general public have not seen. The images help to tell the story of a mountain county that I am proud to call home. My hope is that people who live in and visit Haywood County will have a better understanding of the landscapes, landmarks, and people who are honored in these pages.

Many thanks go to all those who assisted in helping make this book a reality—to Kay Miller for steering me toward Arcadia Publishing; to my patient and guiding editor at Arcadia, Lindsay Harris; to Haywood County Library director Robert Busko and all the library staff who were so gracious and helpful, especially the amazing Joyce Cope for her diligence and limitless patience in scanning hundreds of photographs; to Henry Foy for his expertise in passing along the history of Waynesville; to Clarine Best for maintaining and sharing a wealth of information about the Crabtree community; to Betty Ferguson and Judy Alexander Coker for imparting many photographs of their respective families' history; to Joy Garland and Sara Queen Brown for providing so many wonderful images of Clyde; to Wayne Carson at the Canton Historical Museum, who supplied a treasure trove of pictures and literature on Canton and the Champion paper mill (now known as Evergreen); and to Bruce Briggs, Kathy Ross, Vicki Hyatt, Doris Cathey, Jackie Stephens, Roland Osborne, and all the dedicated Haywood County citizens who continue to protect priceless photographs and historical records so we may never forget this county's legacy. Most of all, I would like to thank my wife, Nicole, and my family, who have supported my writing endeavors every step of the way.

INTRODUCTION

According to the ancient tales of the Cherokee, Haywood County was once the home of Kanati, the first man, and Selu, the first woman. They lived in what is now the Shining Rock Wilderness Area on the southern end of Haywood County. In this wilderness, Kanati thrived as a great hunter while Selu was a corn maiden associated with growing bountiful yields. For centuries, the Cherokee hunted, farmed, and lived on this land of mountains and river valleys until white Europeans came.

As tensions grew between the Cherokee and encroaching white settlers moving west, attacks erupted on both sides. When the American Revolutionary War broke out in 1775, some Cherokee villages, which ruled themselves autonomously, sided with the British. Some warriors attacked white settlements along the frontier. Worried that further attacks could ruin the patriot cause, these frontier settlements quickly formed militias to launch an assault against the Cherokee. A colonial militia of about 2,400 led by Gen. Griffith Rutherford marched from Old Fort over the Blue Ridge Mountains and into present-day Haywood County in September 1776.

The "Rutherford Trace," as it would later be known, crossed the Ford of Pigeon (Canton) and stopped at Locust Old Fields. The soldiers marched south through Pigeon Valley and on to Richland Creek, where they camped in what would become Waynesville before continuing west. Beyond Haywood, they encountered their first Cherokee towns, burning dozens to the ground, trampling or cutting down corn fields, slaughtering livestock, taking Cherokee as prisoners, and destroying huge stores of food. The militia met little resistance before heading back east. Homeless and devastated, many Cherokee fled over the mountains into East Tennessee. After the war, some of these soldiers on the Rutherford Trace would later settle in the lands they had marched through.

In the years following the Revolutionary War, white settlers began pouring into Haywood County from all directions. They found fertile valley farmlands and plentiful game. Speculators and wealthy investors took advantage of new claims made by land surveys, dividing and selling off huge tracts as the Cherokee were pushed farther and farther west. By the early 1800s, enough settlers had moved into the region to warrant the formation of a new county west of Asheville. These settlers needed a courthouse to register deeds and conduct legal proceedings. For some, Asheville was too far a journey over the rugged terrain—especially in inclement weather or during winter months. Thomas Love, a North Carolina state representative from the area, proposed a bill in the state legislature in the fall of 1808 to create Haywood County, named after the state treasurer, John Haywood. The bill passed into law in late December of that year, and the leading men of the new county began meeting in March 1809 to elect county officials, plan out roads, and build a new courthouse.

Robert Love, a Revolutionary War veteran, wealthy landowner, and older brother of Thomas Love, donated 17 acres to create the town of Waynesville, named after Revolutionary War hero Gen. "Mad" Anthony Wayne, who supposedly earned his odd moniker for his brash charges in battle. Within the 17 acres that Robert Love donated was the Town Square (the intersection where the present-day Waynesville Town Hall and Waynesville Police Department now stand) and the stretch of both sides of Main Street down to the lot where First Presbyterian Church now stands.

Waynesville, as the site of the county courthouse, naturally became the county's political seat of power, but other Haywood communities emerged in Crabtree, Iron Duff, Fines Creek, White Oak, Ivy Hill, Pigeon Valley, and Beaverdam. Haywood's original size was much larger than its current shape and included much of what are present-day Swain, Jackson, Macon, and Transylvania Counties. By the middle of the 19th century, most of Haywood County was still rural, with farms laid out along Jonathan Creek, Richland Creek, and the Pigeon River. Political leaders from the region pleaded with the state legislature to build railroad lines into the western part of the state and improve the economy. The plan nearly became a reality when the Civil War broke out.

Many Haywood County farmers did business with South Carolina and strongly opposed Pres. Abraham Lincoln's call to issue troops to put down the Confederate rebellion. According to war records, at least 1,100 Haywood County men marched off to fight with the Confederacy while 33 served with the Union. Though no major battles were fought in Haywood County, the county was far from safe. Deserters, soldiers, and bands of men from various loyalties roamed the countryside. Bushwhackers took advantage of the lawlessness and formed their own gangs, stealing, killing, and dishing out their own brand of vigilante justice. In February 1865, Col. George Kirk led a raid of 600 Union men into Waynesville, where they burned the home of Robert Love, broke out prisoners from the county jail, and set it on fire before heading back to Tennessee. By May—a month after Gen. Robert E. Lee surrendered his Confederate army at Appomattox—Union troops swept into Western North Carolina to finish off the remaining Confederate forces that moved into Haywood County. In a brief skirmish between Confederate sharpshooters who came upon a raiding regiment of Federal troops near what is now Sulphur Springs Road in Waynesville, one Union soldier was killed. These shots would be the last fired in the Civil War east of the Mississippi River. With a possible battle impending, leaders from both sides met at the Battle House in downtown Waynesville the next day and signed a truce ending hostilities.

After the war, a devastated Southern economy struggled to emerge. Railroad lines finally came through Haywood County in the early 1880s, bringing a major economic boost. Lumber companies bought large tracts of forest timber. Waynesville fostered a growing tourist industry, and by 1907, Canton had a huge paper mill. Into the middle of the 20th century, more industries grew up in Hazelwood, to the west of Waynesville. Clyde became a hub for livestock shipping and an auction market. In 1913, Methodist leaders in the region founded Lake Junaluska, formed by a dam across Richland Creek. The scenic lake would become a popular site for religious conferences and retreats as well as the World Methodist Council. Large hotels and inns sprung up in Waynesville, offering the promise of high-altitude fresh air, healing mineral springs, fine dining, dance halls, hiking, and hunting. With the establishment of the Great Smoky Mountains National Park, which included the Cataloochee Valley of Haywood County, the area became a nationally recognized draw for tourists. Other federally protected areas, such as Pisgah National Forest, beckoned naturalists, hikers, and campers. The construction of the scenic Blue Ridge Parkway and the highway corridor of Interstate 40 came through Haywood, bringing even more traffic to and through the county.

The following photographs of Haywood County's history reveal many more stories from its agricultural traditions and growth of its communities to its strong legacy of industry and cultural expression. This is but a taste of what Haywood County once was and what it has become.

One

LANDSCAPES

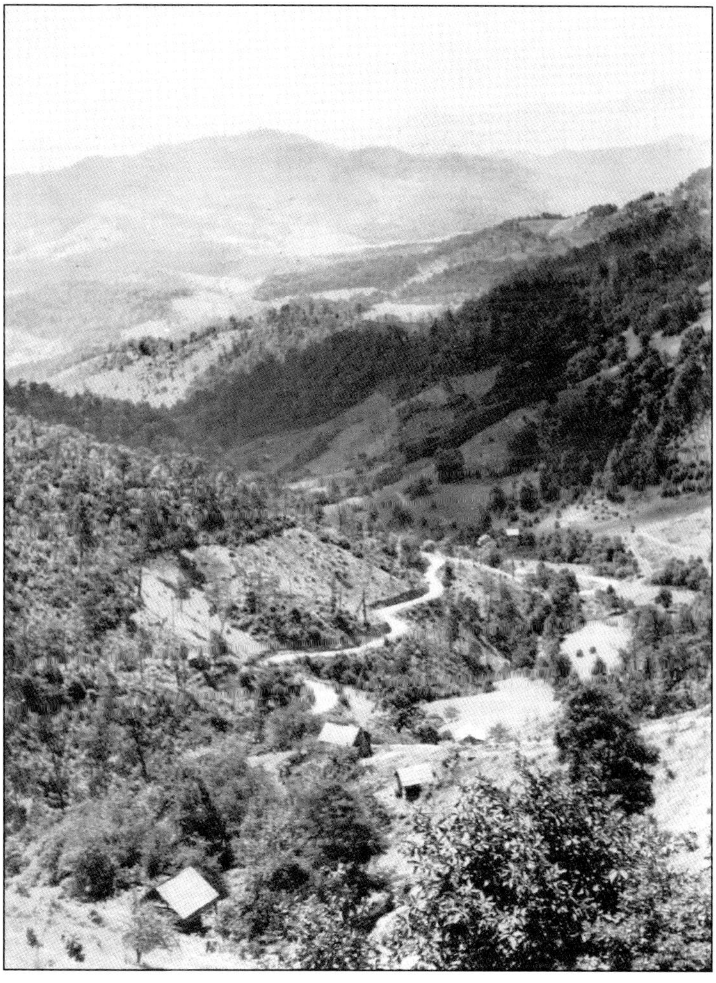

CATALOOCHEE VALLEY. Like Rivendell, the magical hidden valley of the elves in J. R. R. Tolkien's tales, Haywood County's Cataloochee Valley holds a mythical quality for many who have sought its breathtaking beauty and abundant wildlife in a remote location. It is accessible by way of a windy road from Jonathan Creek. (Courtesy of Cataloochee Ranch.)

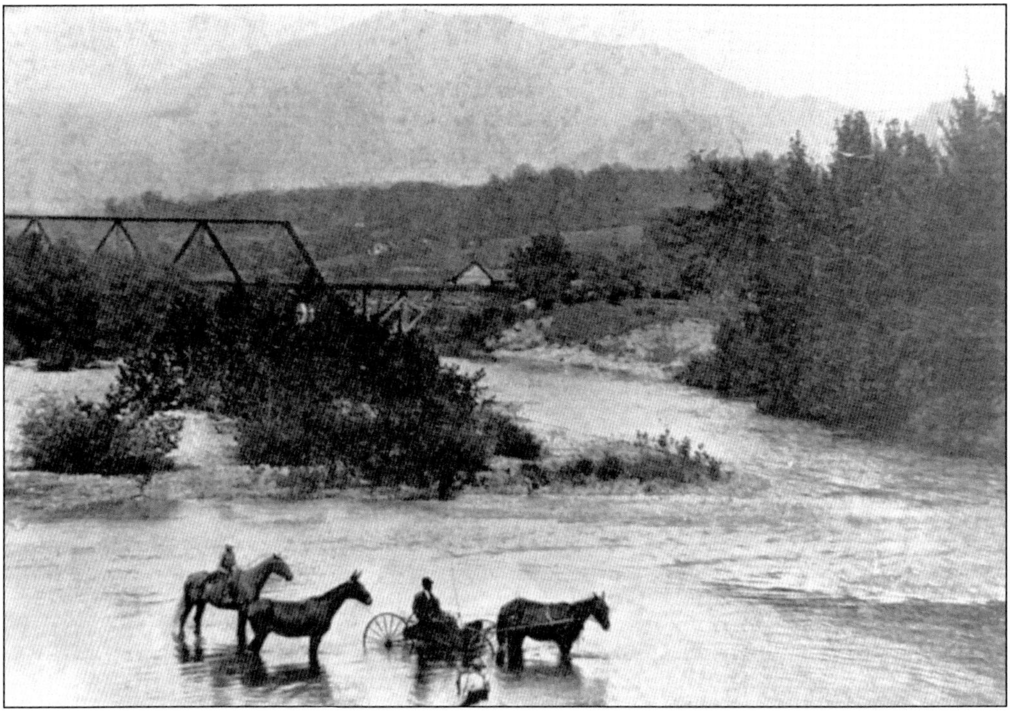

FORD OF PIGEON. One of Canton's original names came from the fact that horses and wagons used to wade across, or ford, the Pigeon River, which ran through town. This *c.* 1895 view looks north toward a railroad bridge. Years later, a local resident named Cash Mingus suggested the name "Canton" after Canton, Ohio, which appeared on a town bridge that crossed the river. (Courtesy of Canton Historical Museum.)

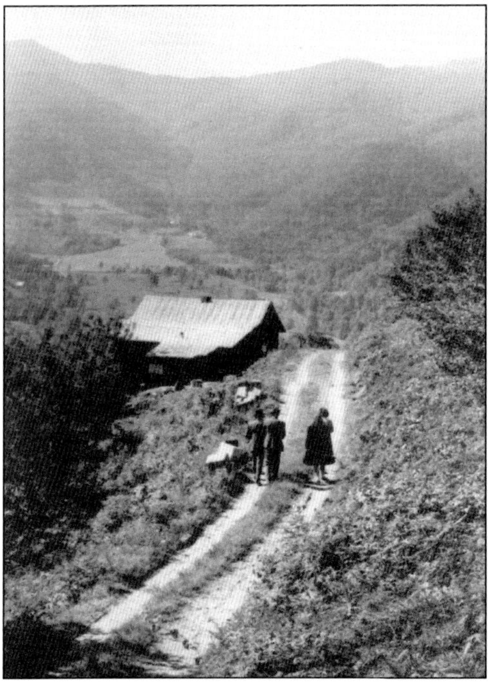

A SIMPLER TIME. This image, taken in the 1930s, features the farming community known as Barber's Orchard. The home on the left of the dirt path is where the Arrington family lived for many years. The Balsam Mountains loom in the horizon. (Courtesy of Louise Corbin.)

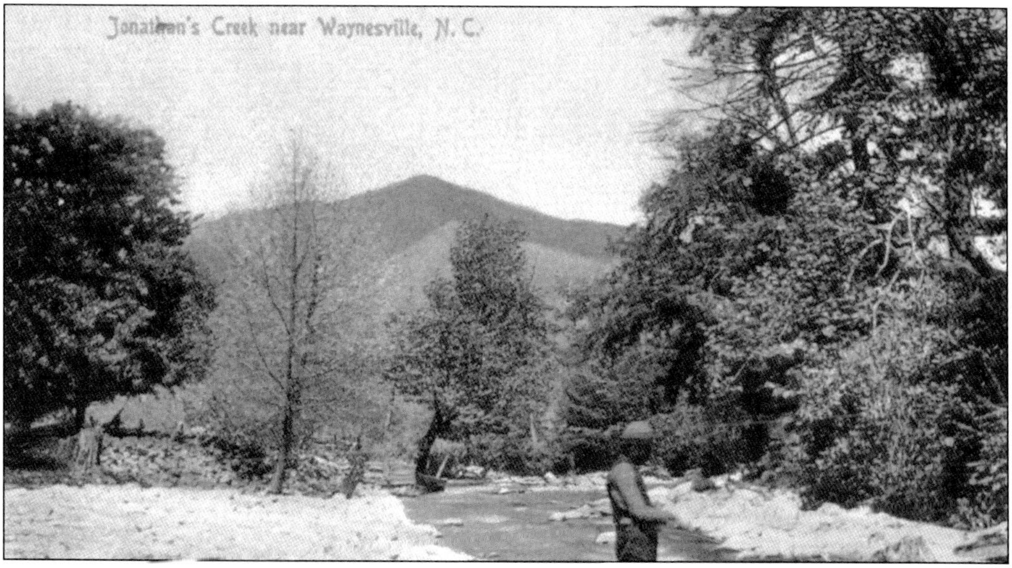

JONATHAN CREEK. This waterway on the western side of the county was named after one of the community's earliest settlers, Jonathan McPeters. "J-Creek," as it is called by many today, starts in Maggie Valley and turns north along Jonathan Valley before feeding into the Pigeon River. (Courtesy of Betty Ferguson.)

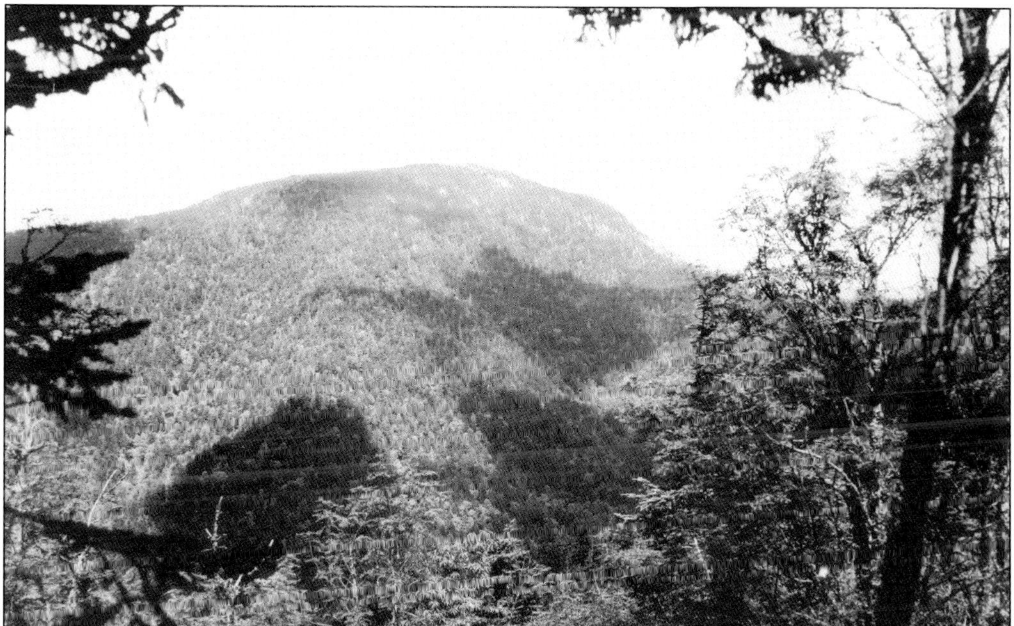

MOUNT GUYOT. Standing at 6,621 feet—the fourth tallest peak in the eastern United States and the highest in Haywood County—Mount Guyot rises majestically along the North Carolina/Tennessee border in the Great Smoky Mountains National Park. The Appalachian Trail runs across its southern slope. The mountain was named after Swiss geologist and geographer Arnold Guyot (1807–1884), who surveyed much of the Appalachian mountain range from Maine to Georgia and measured elevations using a glass barometer. (Photograph by George Masa; courtesy of Cataloochee Ranch.)

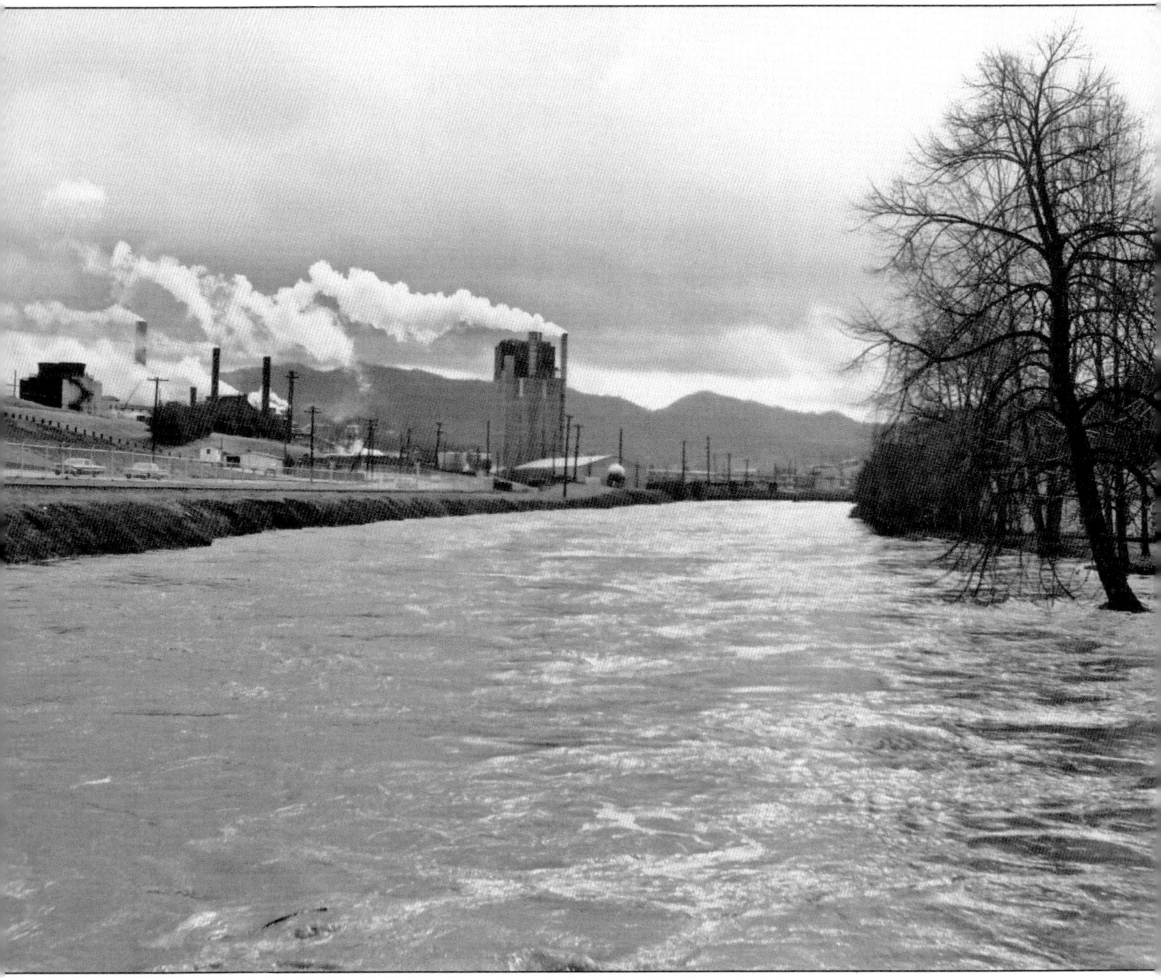

A River Runs through It. The Pigeon River, which originates in southeastern Haywood County, was one of the main reasons the Champion paper mill was built in Canton. Company president Peter G. Thomson envisioned floating logs downstream to the mill, but the river was not deep or sloped well enough to carry logs that far. Instead, the river, which cuts through the mill's property, proved to be a costly burden when heavy rains caused flooding in areas of the mill, damaging machinery, pulpwood, and paper. As part of the paper-making process, chemicals were dumped into the river for decades. By the late 20th century, the river had become so heavily polluted and coffee-stained that environmental efforts to clean it up nearly shut down the mill, which has long been the county's largest employer. After a string of lawsuits, hundreds of millions of dollars in mill renovations, and tougher pollution regulations, the Pigeon has become much cleaner in recent years. Whitewater rafting companies in East Tennessee now operate downstream on its scenic rapids. (Courtesy of Canton Historical Museum.)

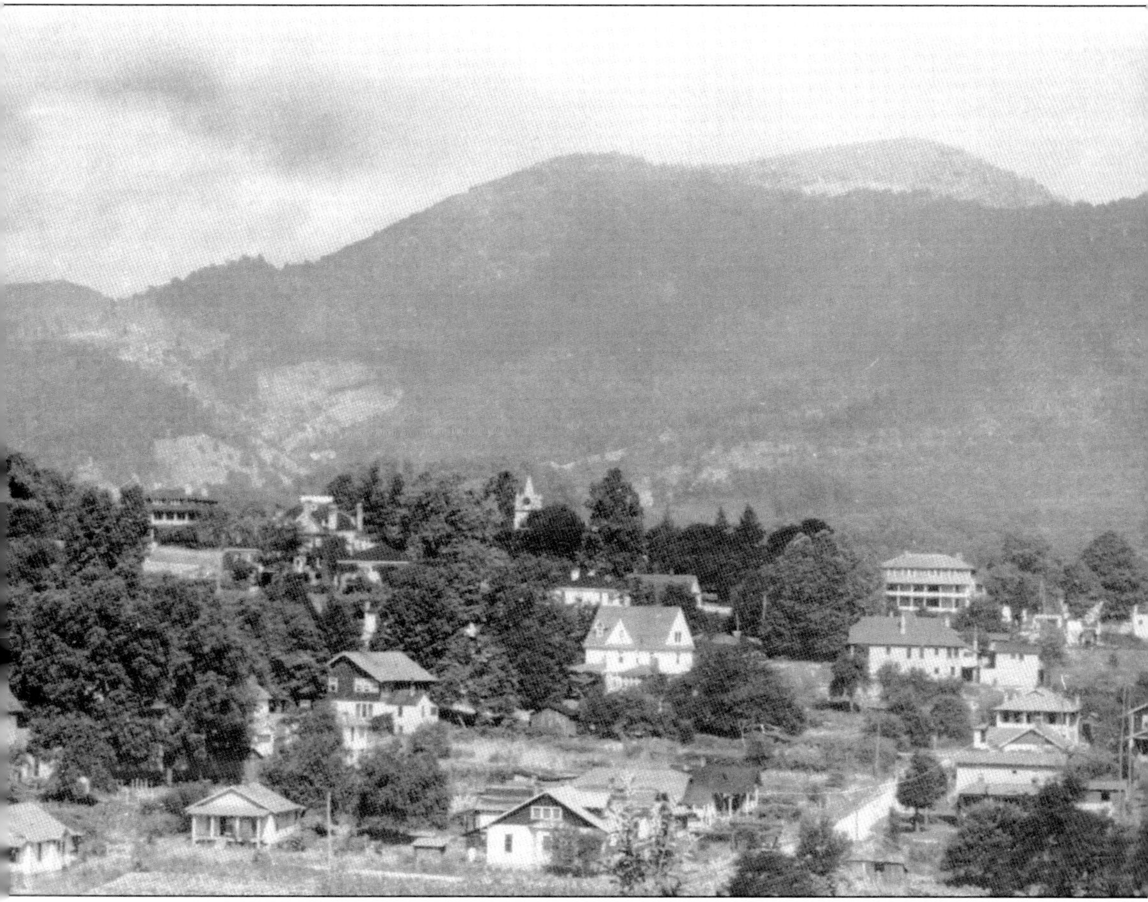

WAYNESVILLE. This vista of Waynesville overlooks Main Street in the 1920s. Mountains surround the town to create a bowl-like effect. This terrain proved noteworthy, as Waynesville became the site of the last shot fired in the Civil War east of the Mississippi River. In early May 1865—a month after Gen. Robert E. Lee's surrender—Union troops poured into Western North Carolina to snuff out the last remaining pockets of Confederate resistance. Haywood County–born Confederate colonel William Holland Thomas hoped to catch the advancing enemy off guard. After a brief skirmish near present-day Sulphur Springs Road, one Union soldier was killed. That night, Thomas had his men start dozens of campfires and make noise on the mountainside so it would appear there was a large army encamped outside the town. By dawn, the Union commander Col. William Bartlett offered a white flag of truce to Thomas and his commanding officer, Gen. James G. Martin. They all met in Waynesville at the Battle House (next to the present-day town hall building). Thomas and his men agreed to disband but were allowed to keep their weapons. Bartlett and his men agreed to end hostilities and leave the area. (Courtesy of Henry Foy.)

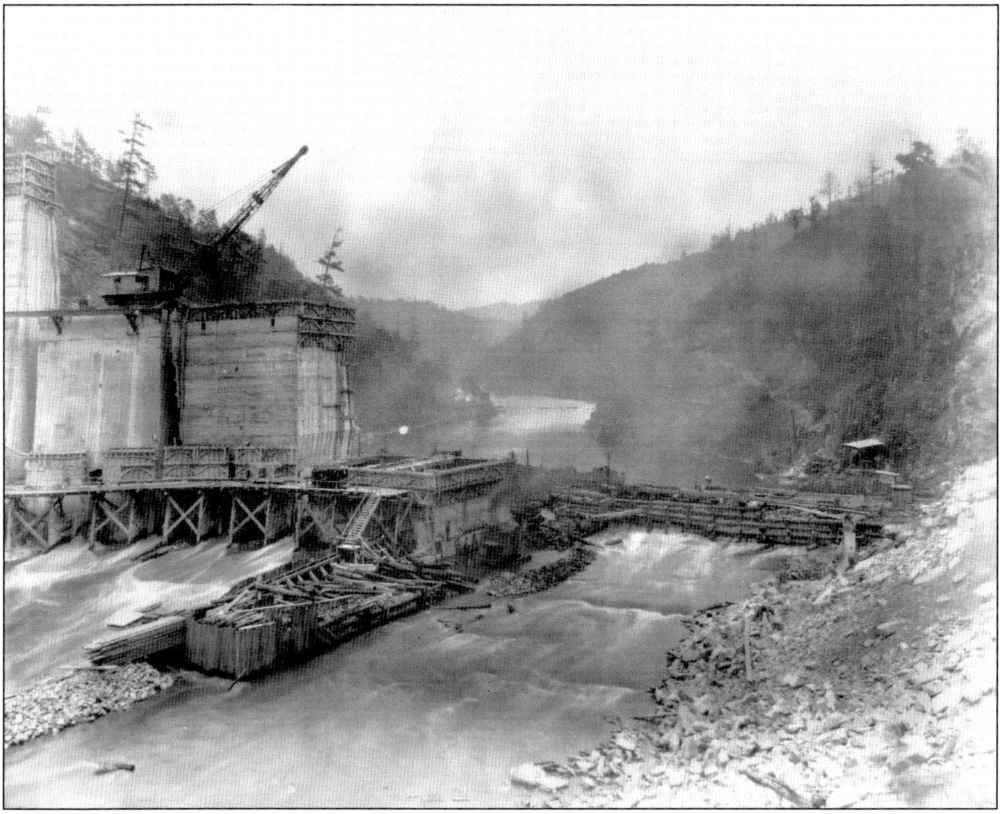

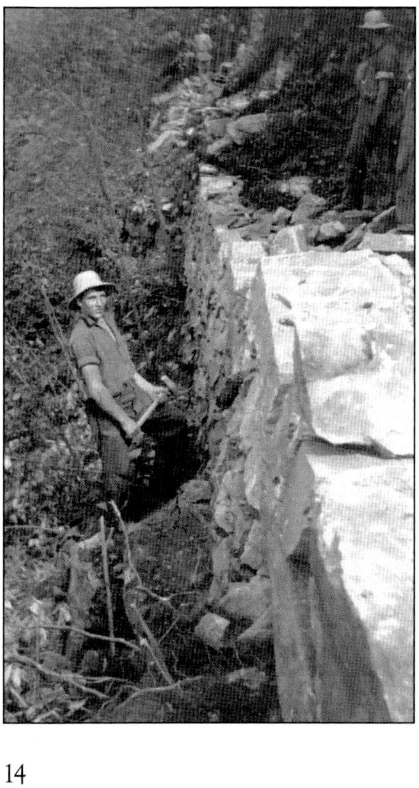

Walters Dam. Considered an engineering feat when it was completed in 1930 at Waterville near the Tennessee line, this concrete, concave dam stood 180 feet high, 870 feet wide, and 4.5 feet thick. Holding back the Pigeon River, its floodgates can discharge 60,000 cubic feet per second. During the 1930s, it was the highest hydroelectric dam east of the Rocky Mountains. (Courtesy of the *Mountaineer.*)

CCC Wall. Members of the Civilian Conservation Corps, a Depression-era work relief program that provided vocational training and labor for about three million Americans, built this wall in northern Haywood County near the Tennessee state line. The stone was taken from mountainsides along the trail, as there was no motorized equipment to haul rocks into the area back then. (Courtesy of Cataloochee Ranch.)

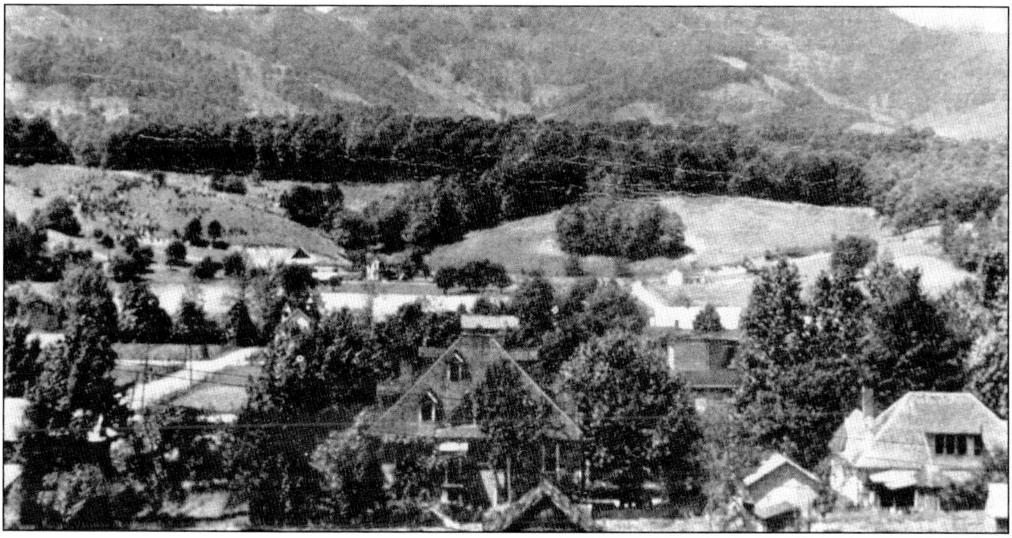

CLYDE. Located in the center of the county, the town of Clyde was once home to a busy stockyard and train station. In this 1900 photograph, Chambers Mountain rises in the distance. Two seemingly contradictory signs were placed on either end of the town limits—"Watch Clyde Grow," the slogan for an optimistic business community, and "Have Your Eyes Examined," an advertisement from a local eye doctor. (Courtesy of Sara Queen Brown.)

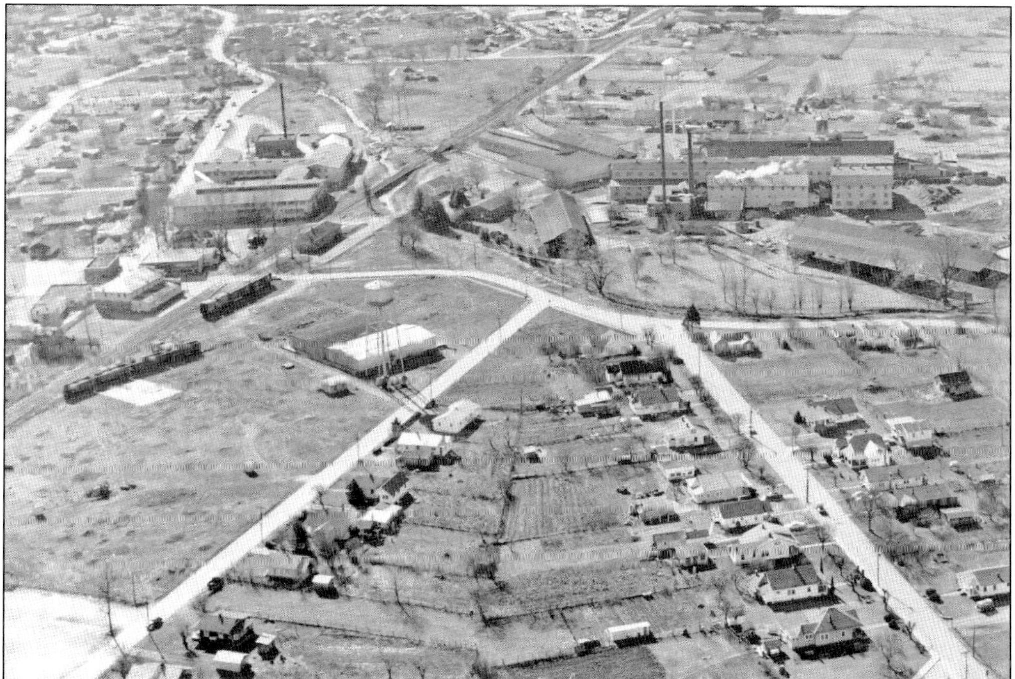

HAZELWOOD. This 1955 bird's-eye view of Hazelwood shows some of its once thriving industries, including the A. C. Lawrence Leather Company (upper middle right), Unagusta Furniture Company (upper middle left), and its lumber operation (upper right corner). Wellco Enterprises, which made boots for the military, and the Dayton Rubber Company, which made automotive hoses, fan belts, and rubber products, were also major players in Hazelwood's economy. (Courtesy of Henry Foy.)

LAKE JUNALUSKA. An internationally recognized center for religious conferences and retreats since its opening in 1913, this man-made lake has welcomed such dignitaries as First Lady Eleanor Roosevelt, Pres. Jimmy Carter, evangelist Billy Graham, and legendary musician "Doc" Watson. At center is the Terrace Hotel. To its left is the World Methodist Council building, headquarters for a consultative body linking most of the world's Methodist churches.

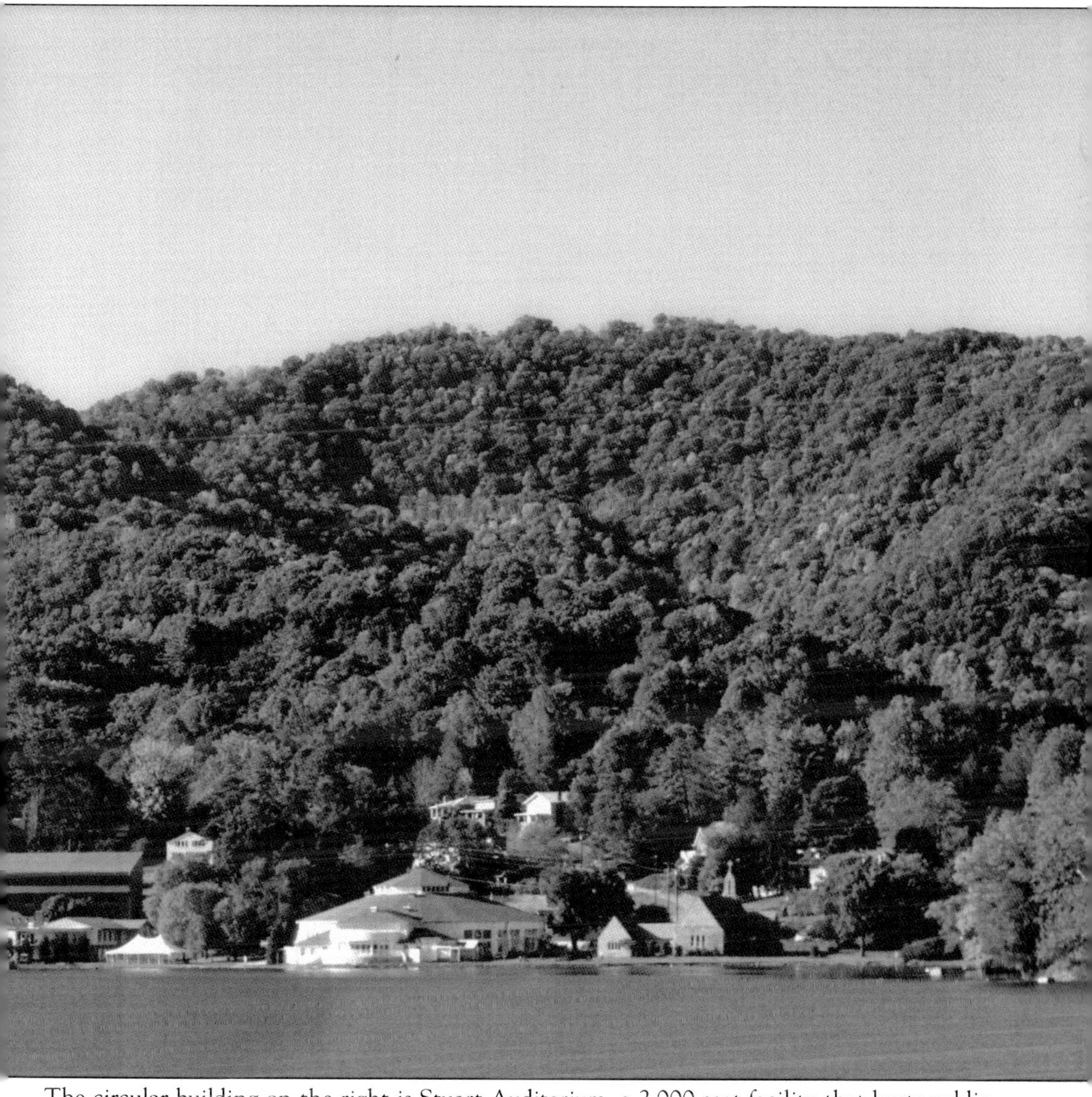

The circular building on the right is Stuart Auditorium, a 2,000-seat facility that hosts public speakers and performances. To its right is Memorial Chapel, a charming stone church that is a popular site for weddings. The scenic lake attracts visitors year-round who walk, run, or bike around its looping 2.5-mile Asbury Trail, which includes a lovely rose garden walkway, a small waterfall, and a footbridge. (Courtesy of Roland Osborne.)

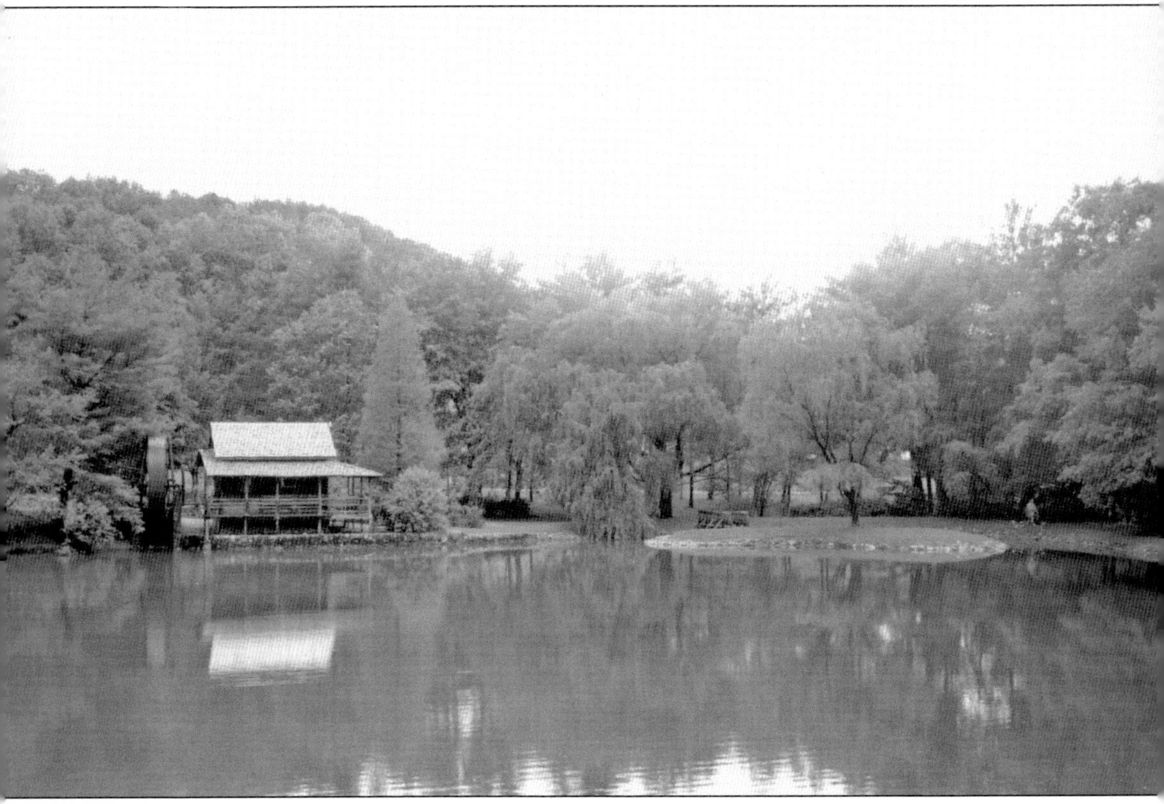

MILL POND. This peaceful setting on the campus of Haywood Community College near Clyde serves as a reminder of the county's Appalachian heritage. The waterwheel was erected on this property in 1980. The mill house was dedicated in 1987. David Crocket Campbell of Maggie Valley bought the waterwheel from a Pennsylvania company in 1908 to power a gristmill and sawmill. It was also used to power Maggie Valley's first electric icebox. The waterwheel was later sold to A. L. Freedlander, a Dayco executive and philanthropist who provided a sizeable donation to purchase the property for HCC's campus. After Freedlander's death, the waterwheel was donated to the college. HCC opened in August 1965 with one curriculum program and 39 students and has since expanded to include more than 50 programs and nearly 9,000 students. In 1986, HCC opened the first advanced technology center of its kind in the state. The college's Production and Crafts Department provides art degrees in the areas of clay, fiber, jewelry, and wood, as well as business training to allow students to sell and market their artwork. (Courtesy of Roland Osborne.)

Two

FARM LIFE

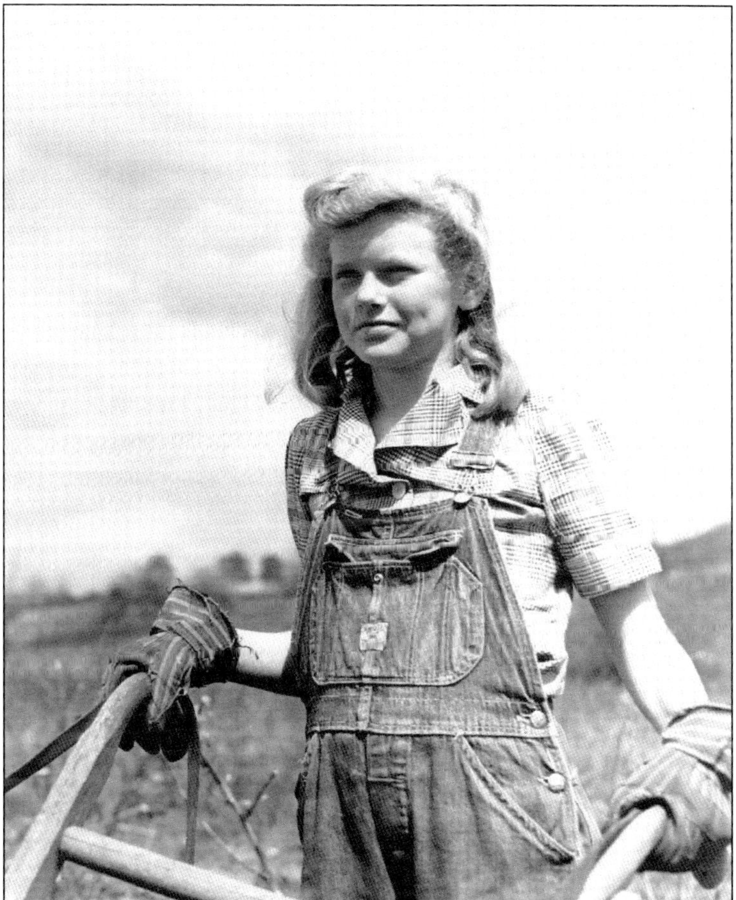

FIELD WORK. During World War II, Bessie Sue Francis spent her spare time plowing the raspberry patch on her family's farm in Allens Creek. Local labor was scarce because so many were serving in the military. Throughout the war, Haywood County families planted "victory gardens" and increased agricultural productivity to help feed soldiers overseas. (Courtesy of Ellene Francis.)

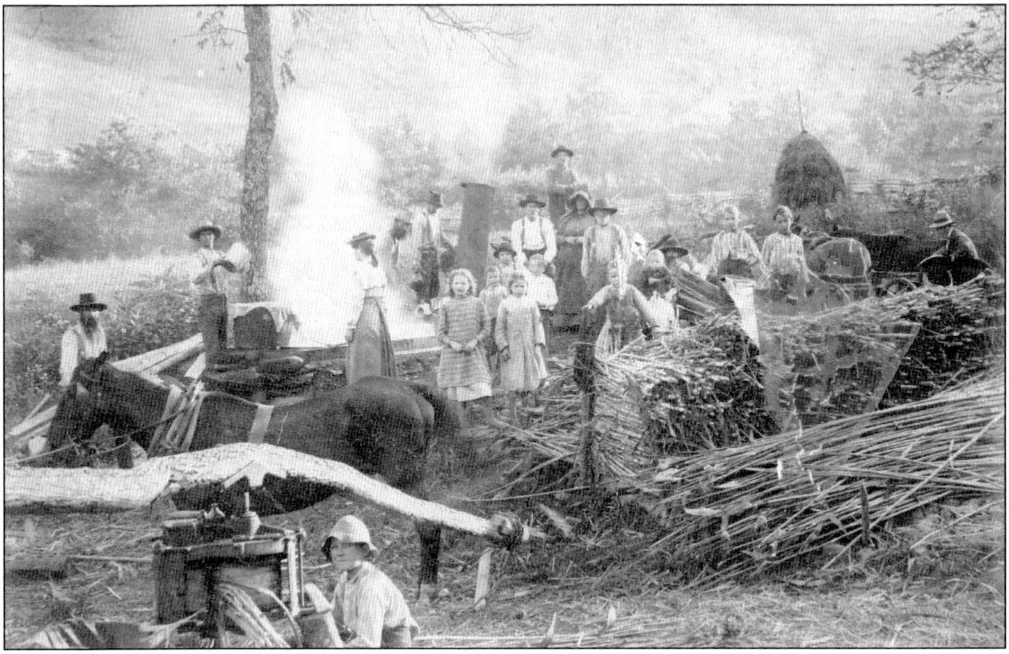

Sweet Memories. For families like this one in the Newfound community (around 1890), making molasses took a group effort. Stalks of sorghum cane were cut and squeezed through a roller mill turned by a mule or a hit-and-miss gas engine. Cane juice was collected in a pan and cooked over a fire until the juice boiled out, leaving syrupy molasses. (Photograph by S. A. McCanless; courtesy of Canton Historical Museum.)

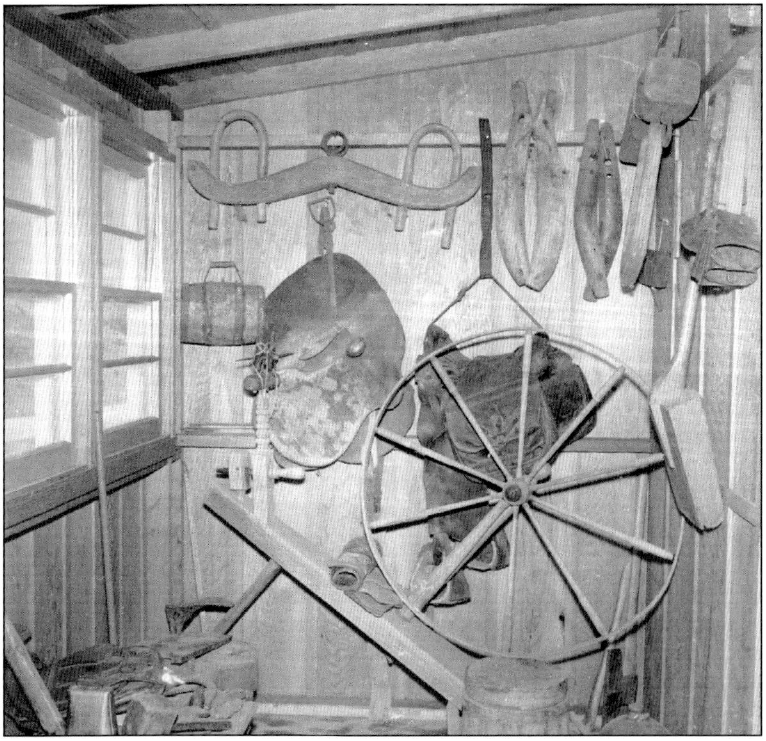

Farm Tools. These antique items—a spinning wheel, saddles, oxen yokes, mallets, and a shovel—were collected by Austin Carroll McCracken and kept in a small house he built off U.S. Highway 209, which runs through the farming communities of Iron Duff, Crabtree, and Fines Creek. (Courtesy of the *Mountaineer.*)

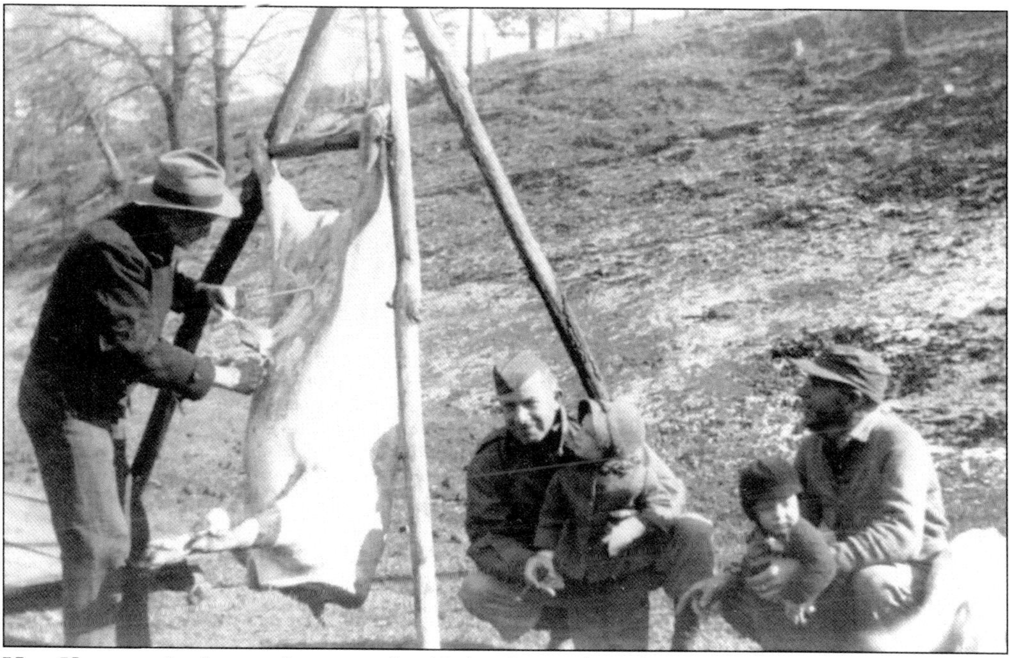

HOG KILLING. As the weather turned cold, families such as this one at the John Rogers farm on upper Crabtree would often kill a hog to prepare for those long winter months. The dead hog's body was dipped in a vat of boiling water so its hair would turn loose and could be scraped off with a dull knife. Once its entrails were removed, it was sectioned into pieces and salted for storage in a smokehouse. (Courtesy of Clarine Best.)

BEEF CATTLE. Raising livestock has long been a farming tradition in Haywood County as these prize steers from the 1950s illustrate. Despite the loss of farms in Western North Carolina in recent years, the county continues to lead the region in beef cattle production, with about 500 farmers producing nearly a quarter of its cattle. (Courtesy of Henry Foy.)

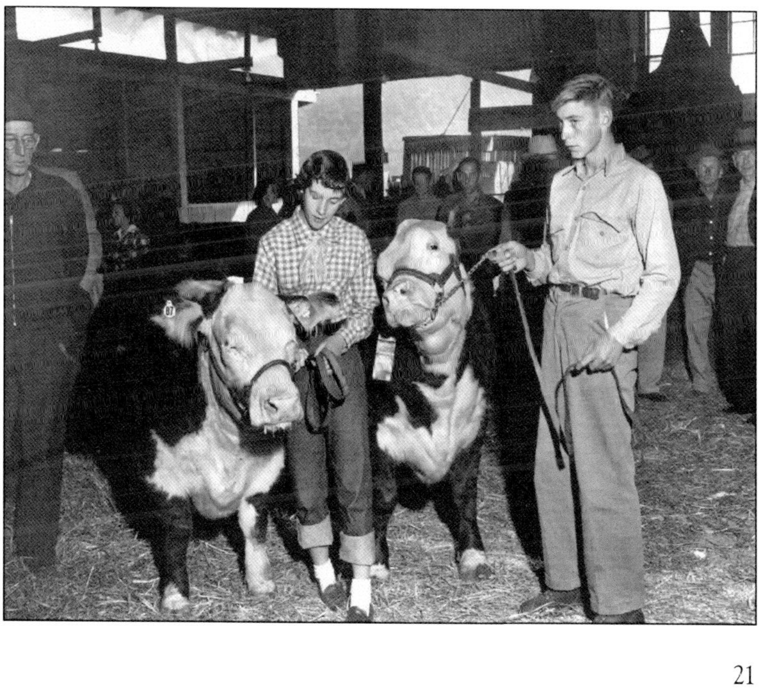

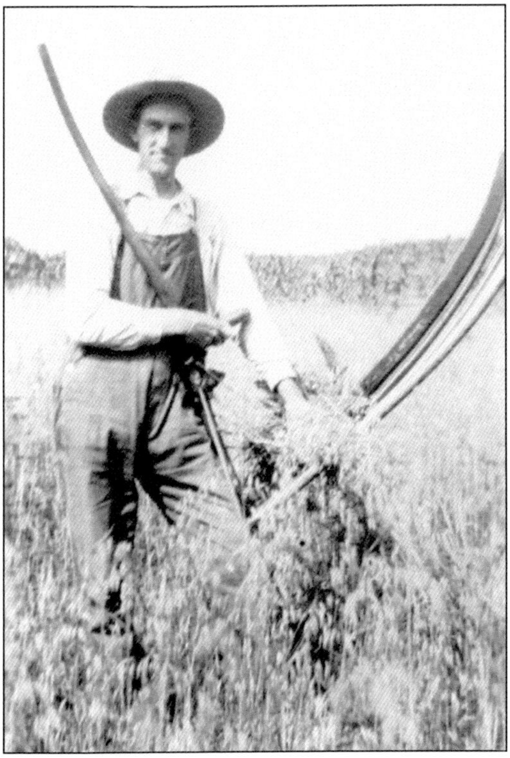

CRADLING WHEAT. The strength and dexterity it took to cradle wheat was highly prized in farming communities if one could do it well. John M. McClure (left), a barber in Waynesville, was one such man. Using a bladed tool that weighed about 25–30 pounds, he would cut the wheat in a long sweeping motion and, as it fell, scoop it up in an armful from the cradle in a twisting motion. (Courtesy of Clarine Best.)

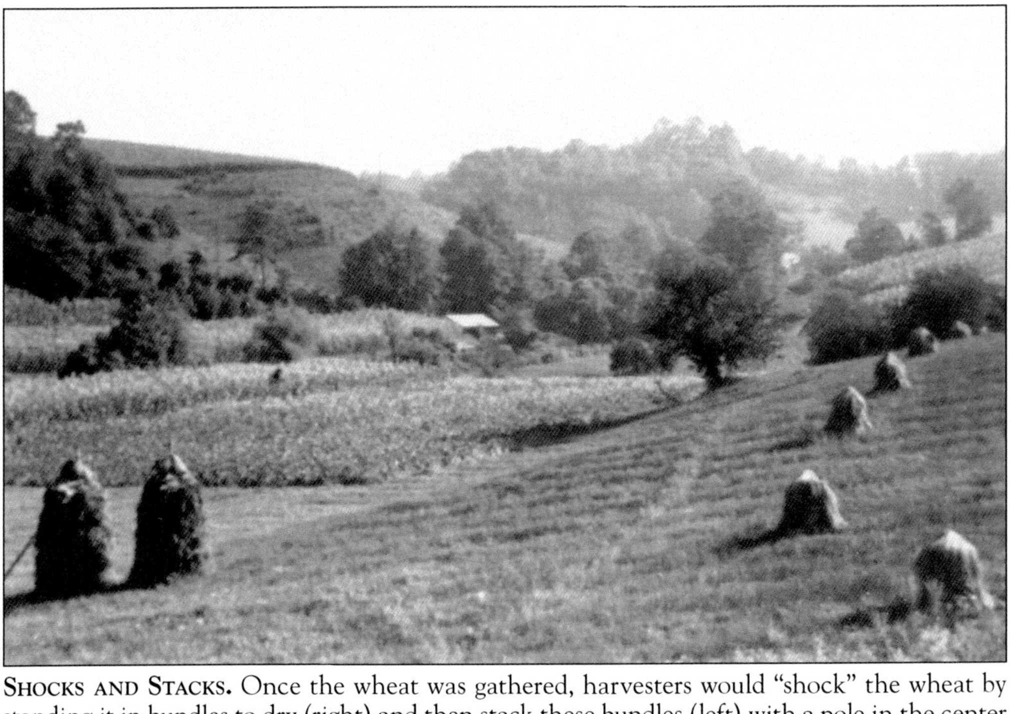

SHOCKS AND STACKS. Once the wheat was gathered, harvesters would "shock" the wheat by standing it in bundles to dry (right) and then stack these bundles (left) with a pole in the center to keep it from leaning over. A cap over the stacks would protect it from the elements. This c. 1945 photograph is of Sam Green's farm in Crabtree. (Courtesy of Clarine Best.)

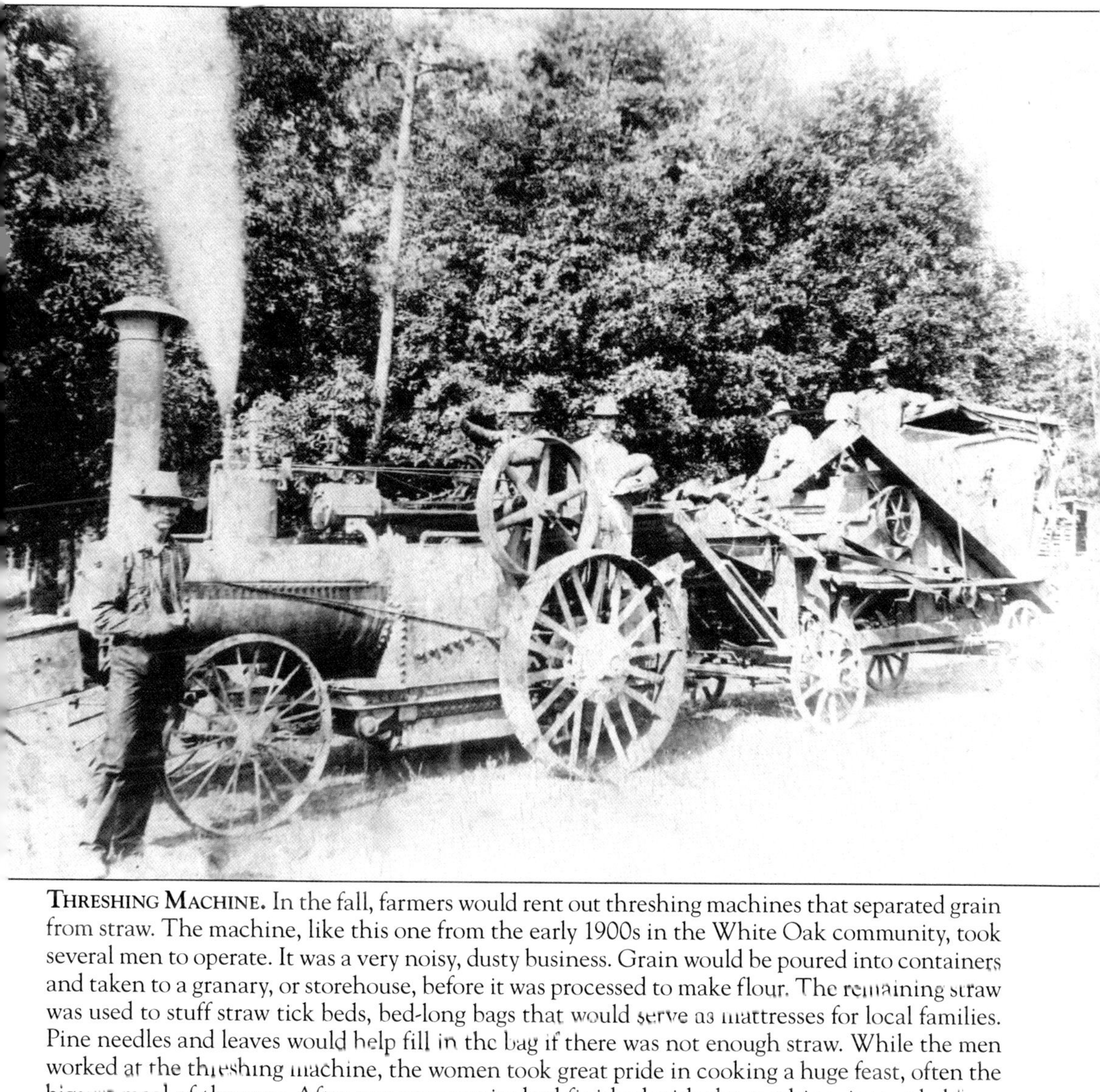

THRESHING MACHINE. In the fall, farmers would rent out threshing machines that separated grain from straw. The machine, like this one from the early 1900s in the White Oak community, took several men to operate. It was a very noisy, dusty business. Grain would be poured into containers and taken to a granary, or storehouse, before it was processed to make flour. The remaining straw was used to stuff straw tick beds, bed-long bags that would serve as mattresses for local families. Pine needles and leaves would help fill in the bag if there was not enough straw. While the men worked at the threshing machine, the women took great pride in cooking a huge feast, often the biggest meal of the year. After one community had finished with the machine, it traveled from farm to farm until the harvest was complete. (Courtesy of Clarine Best.)

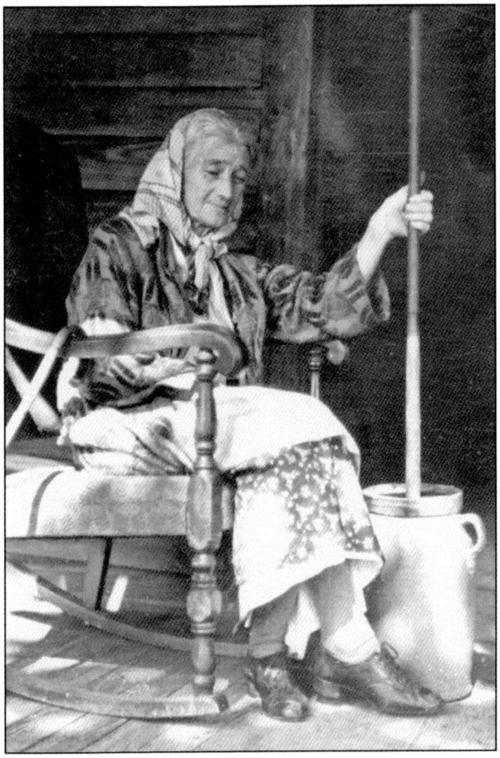

Churning Butter. Frances Evans of Cove Creek makes butter using a churn dash, a stick with a fan-like paddle on the end. It was stuck through a container's lid that had a hole in the middle. After moving the stick up and down hundreds of times splashing the liquid, it would solidify into butter, which was squeezed into molds to form block shapes. Before the days of refrigeration, butter sticks were floated on the cool, fresh water of a springhouse. (Courtesy of Clarine Best.)

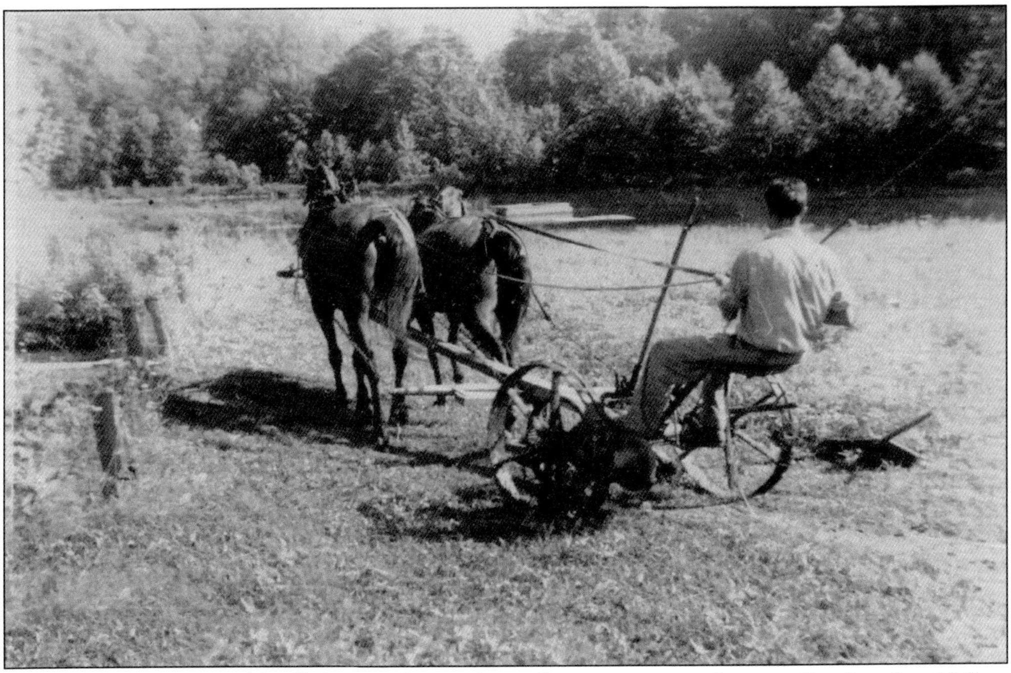

Hay Mower. Larry Caldwell drives a horse-drawn hay mower at a farm in Cataloochee Valley. Once mowed, the hay was raked into piles around a stack pole. It would look like a hut with a thatched roof. Sheep or livestock could then eat around the sides of the haystack. (Courtesy of Cataloochee Ranch.)

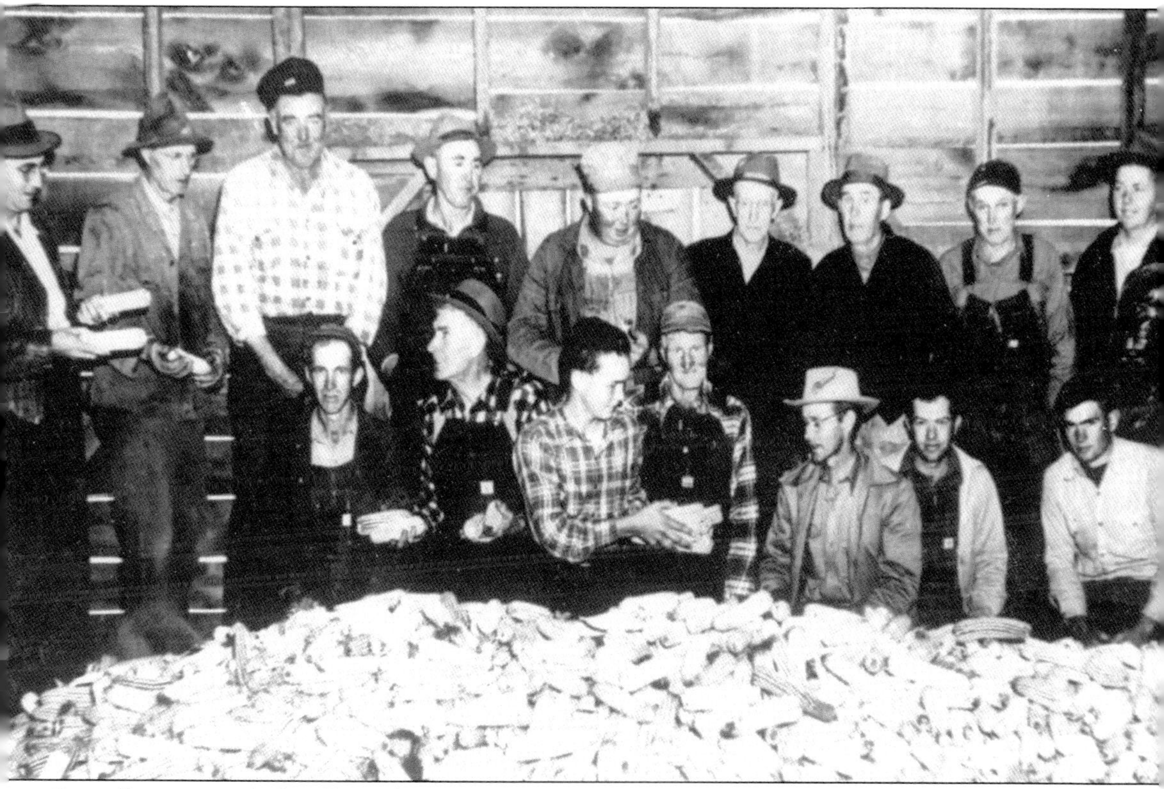

Corn Shucking. At Ray Best's farm on upper Crabtree, neighbors gathered for an annual corn shucking. These affairs were great social events. Neighboring farmers would help with each other's harvest. Men would compete to see who could shuck the fastest. Prizes might be hidden in the piles of corn. If a boy happened to pick out a rare, red-colored corncob, he got to kiss the prettiest girl there. This photograph from the 1950s shows Ray Best's son, Bill (center, with a handful of corn), who was the first in Haywood County to grow 100 bushels of corn to an acre. He grew up to become a professor at Berea College in Kentucky and earned his doctorate in Appalachian studies. He taught, coached swimming, helped disadvantaged students prepare for college, authored five books, and is now a nationally recognized leader in sustainable agriculture and preserving heirloom fruits and vegetables. (Courtesy of Clarine Best.)

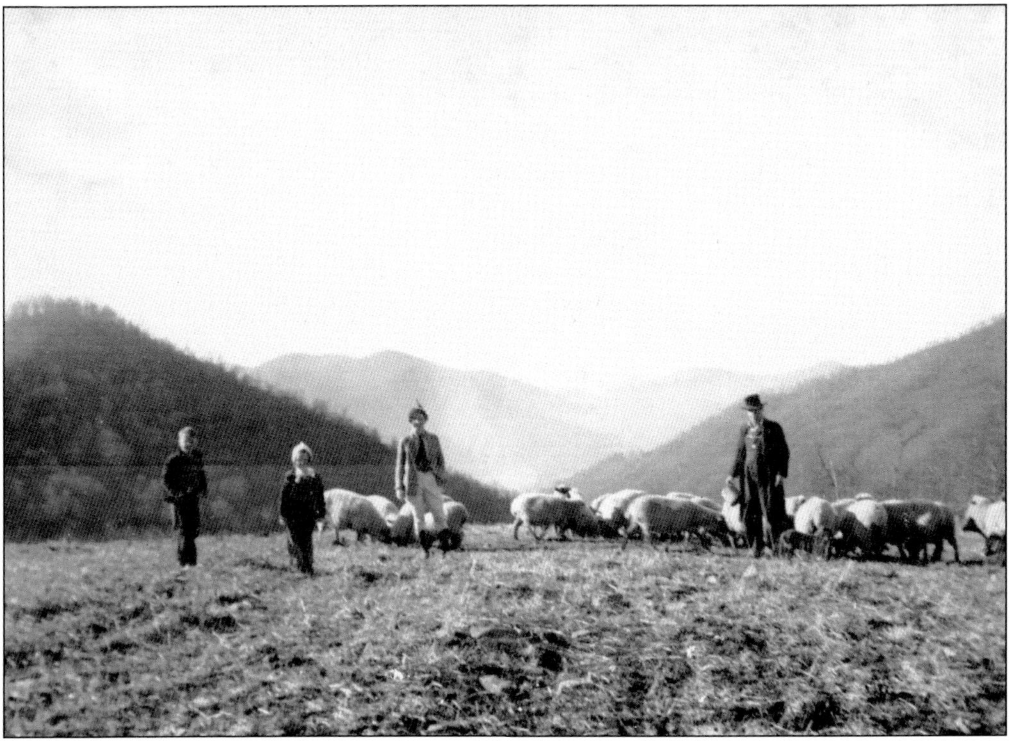

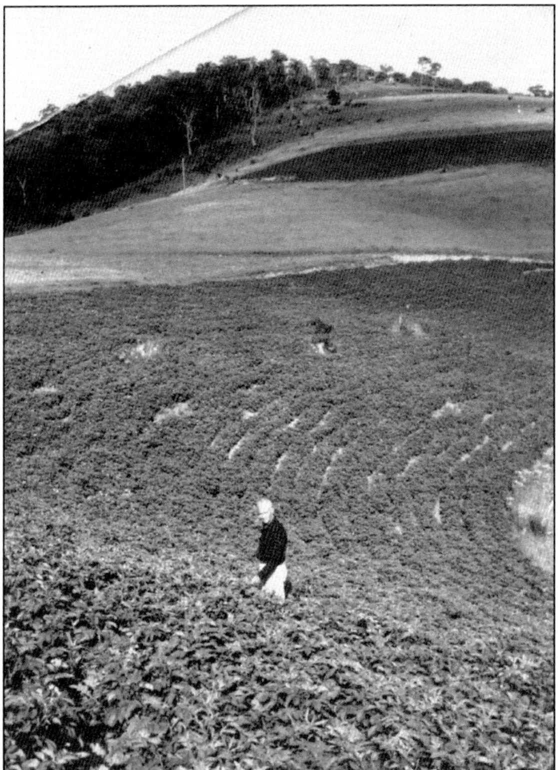

POTATO KING OF HAYWOOD COUNTY. Verlin Campbell (above, far right) herded sheep and grew potatoes in such quantities that he earned this distinguished title as a farmer. A large man with a booming voice, Campbell sometimes used outlaws from Tennessee as hired labor. In lieu of payment, he offered them meals and a place to stay in his bunkhouse. In 1935, Campbell sold about 900 acres of land on Fie Top Mountain to Tom Alexander, who converted Verlin's barn into a house and created a dude ranch known as Cataloochee Ranch. The building still stands as the main office and dining hall for guests who come from all over the world to go horseback riding, hiking, and sightseeing. Alexander (at left in a potato field) continued to carry on Campbell's farming tradition, raising livestock and growing crops such as hay and potatoes. (Both courtesy of Cataloochee Ranch.)

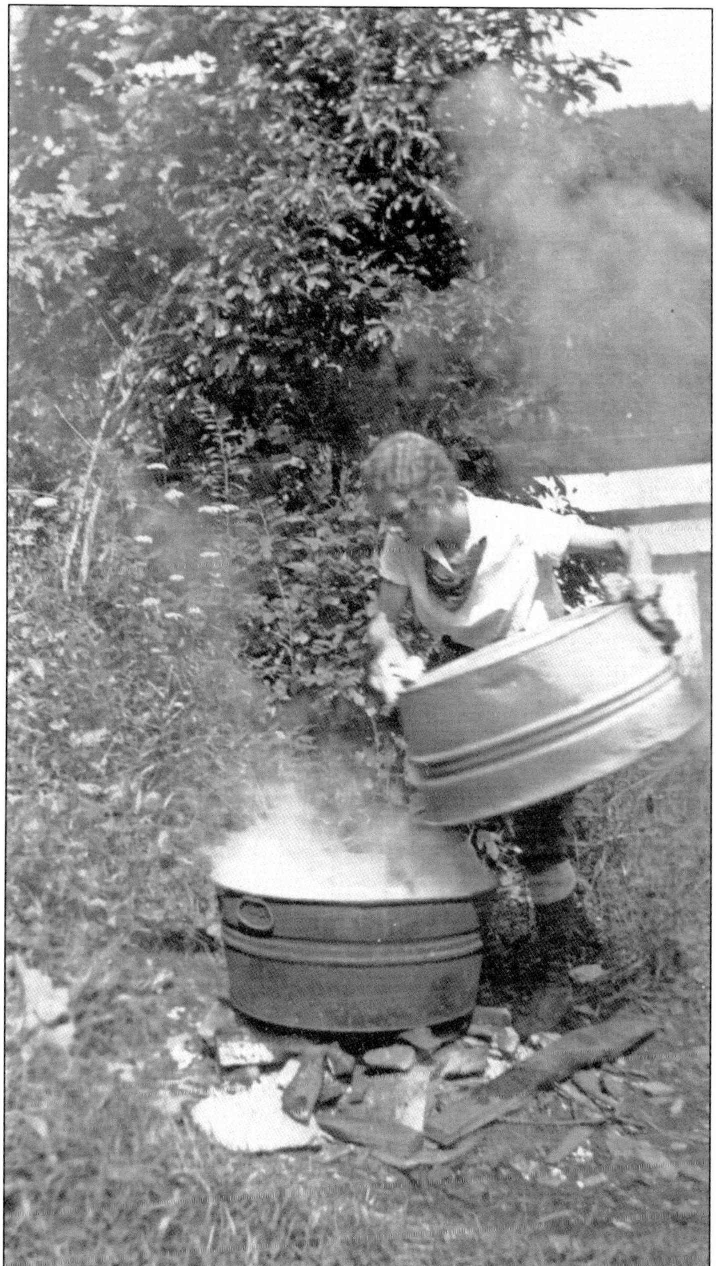

Canning in Cataloochee. Judy Alexander, a Richmond, Virginia–born doctor's daughter, honed many new skills while living in a remote section of Cataloochee Valley in the early 1930s during the first years of her marriage. To can beans, she would fill glass jars with beans and water and then place a lid and a ring around the top. Towels were placed over the jars, which were set in a washtub to boil in water over a fire for about three hours. The washtub would be covered with another tub to seal in the heat. After simmering long enough, the washtub top came off, and the jars were allowed to cool. When the vacuum seal on the container formed, it made a popping sound. This signaled that the jar was properly sealed and could be stored for months. (Courtesy of Cataloochee Ranch.)

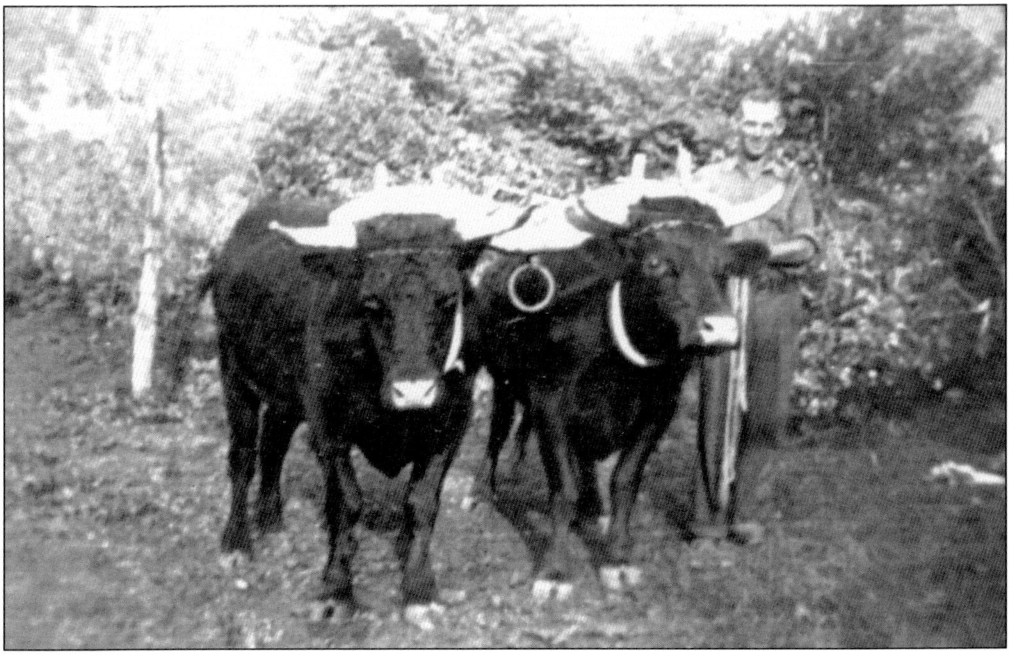

Beasts of Burden. Jack Best in Rogers Cove on upper Crabtree trained teams of yoked oxen to plow fields and haul just about anything. With a yoke, a wooden bow underneath their necks, and a rope or chain used to steer them, they were the precursor to the modern-day tractor. (Courtesy of Clarine Best.)

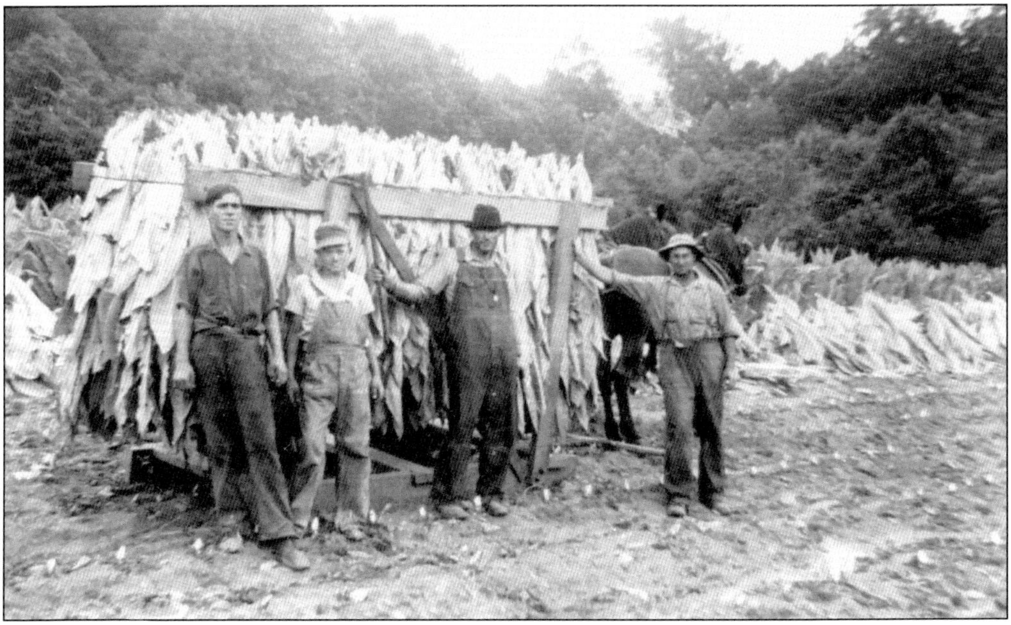

Tobacco. In the early 1900s, farmers in Haywood County tried growing flue-cured tobacco, but it became too expensive to ship to Virginia, so farmers later switched to burley tobacco, which is harvested in the fall by taking all the leaves off the stalk at once, stringing it up on sticks, and curing it in open barns. This tobacco yield came from the Kelleys' farm in Waynesville. (Courtesy of Clarine Best.)

Three

COMMUNITIES

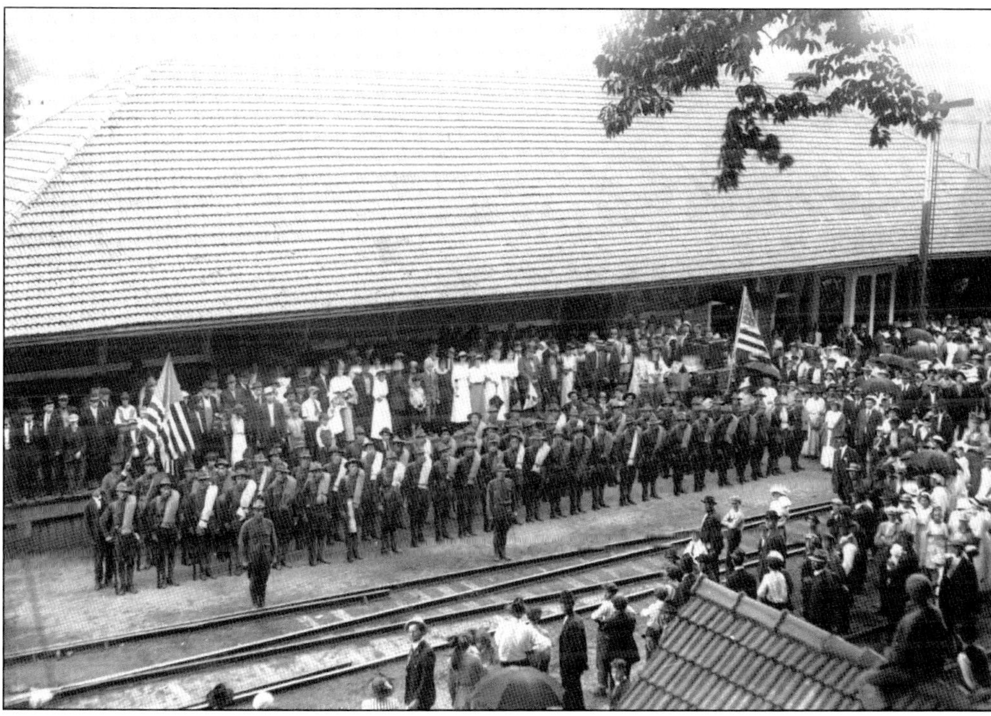

WORLD WAR I. On June 26, 1916, Haywood County's Company H, 1st North Carolina Infantry of the National Guard, departed Waynesville's train depot. These troops guarded the Mexican border and returned to Waynesville in February 1917, only to be mustered into service once more in July 1917 and sent to France during World War I. (Courtesy of Henry Foy.)

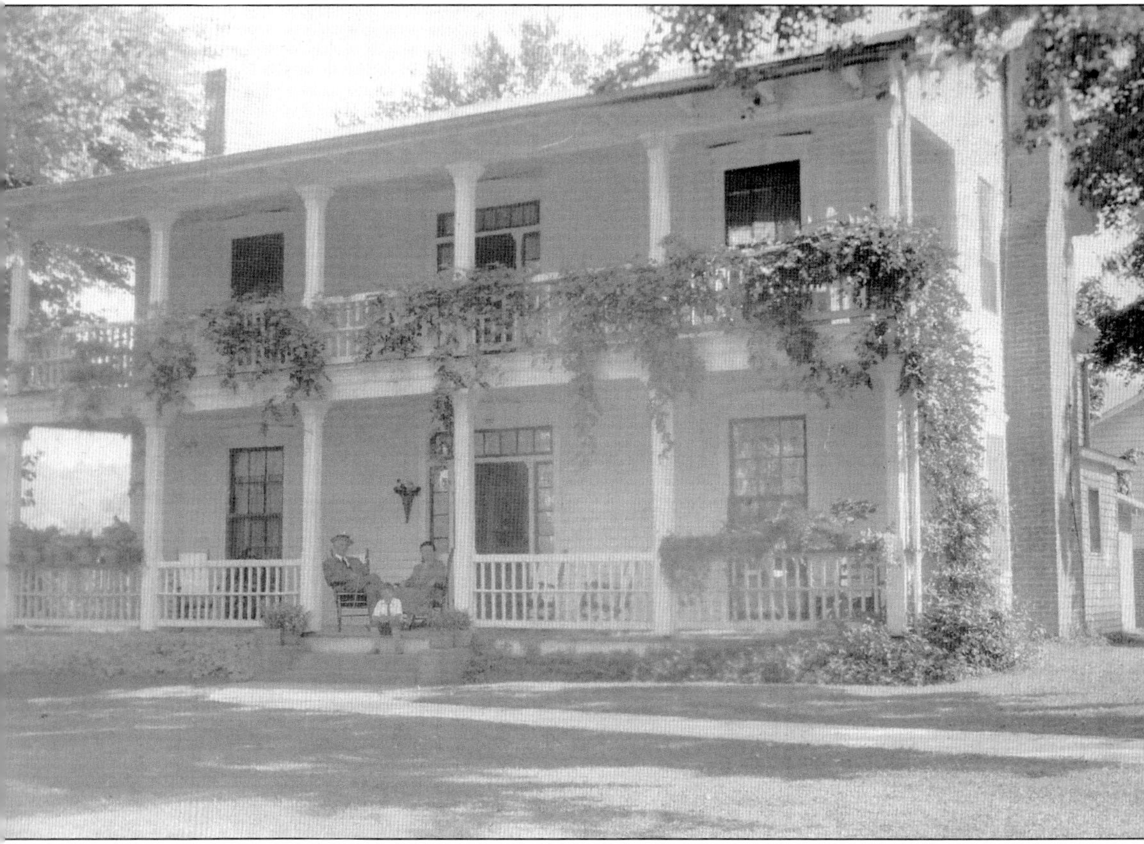

SHELTON HOUSE. Stephen Jehu Shelton, a Confederate veteran, businessman, and sheriff of Haywood County, built this two-story frame house in Waynesville for his family. It took about five years to build and was finished around 1880. He used black walnut trees on his 67-acre property to make the doorways, mantels, wardrobe closet, bed frame, and stair railing. Among its notable features are double-stacked front porches, jib doors, and a wallpaper frieze in the dining room. After 1919, Stephen's son, William Shelton, sitting on the porch (left) with his wife, Hattie (right), and their nephew Henry Tuttle, occupied the house. Will left town to work as an agricultural agent and superintendent of a Navajo training school in New Mexico. When he retired, he returned to this house, which is now listed on the National Register of Historic Places. It serves as the Museum of North Carolina Handicrafts, with one of the finest folk art craft collections in the Southeast. (Courtesy of Shelton House.)

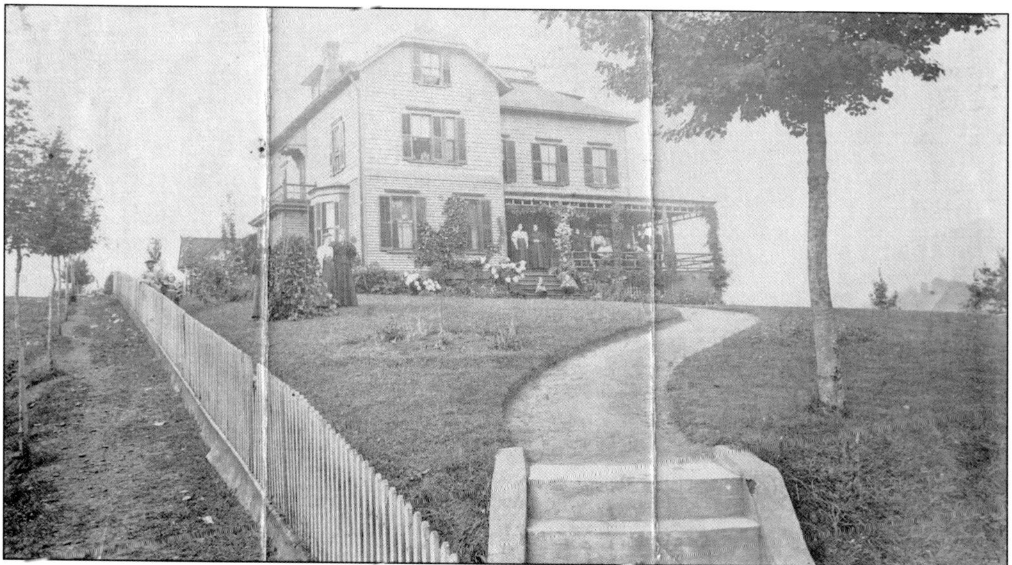

Goodyear Home. This house, which no longer stands on the corner of Tate and Church Streets in Waynesville, was once the home of Charles Goodyear, son of the inventor who first vulcanized rubber in America and whose name would lend itself to one of the world's largest tire companies. After Goodyear's death in 1896, the property eventually came under the ownership of the Satterthwaite family. (Courtesy of Henry Foy.)

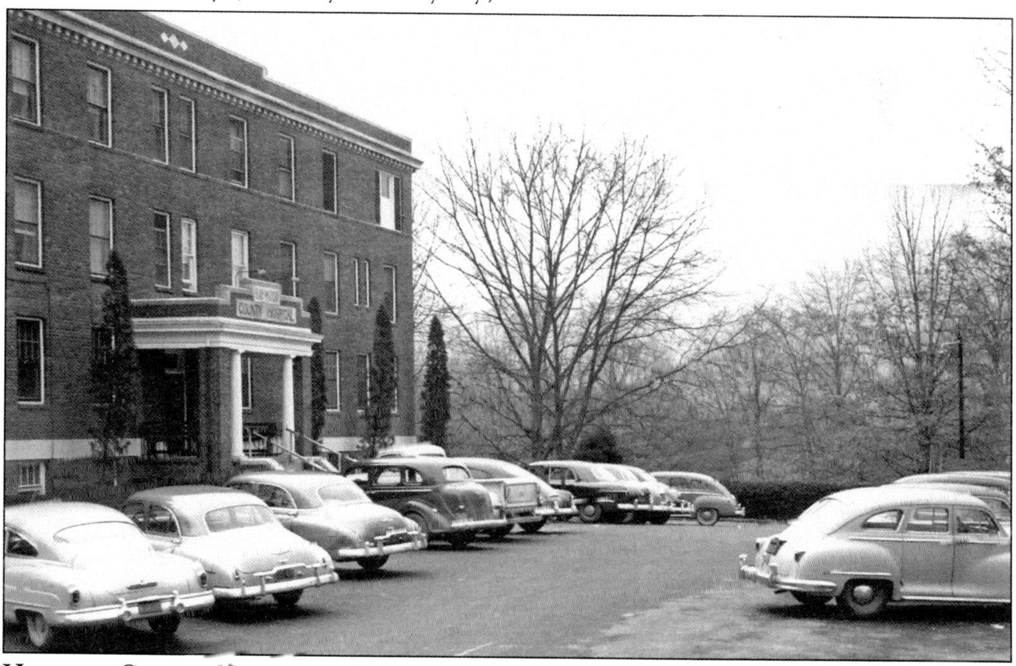

Haywood County Hospital. This hospital was the first in the state built with money approved by a county-wide bond referendum. The three-story building opened on December 31, 1927, on a 5-acre hillside about 2 miles from downtown Waynesville. The hospital moved to its present location in 1979 after another voter-approved bond referendum. The old county hospital building now houses the Haywood County Schools' administration offices and the county's Department of Social Services. (Courtesy of Henry Foy.)

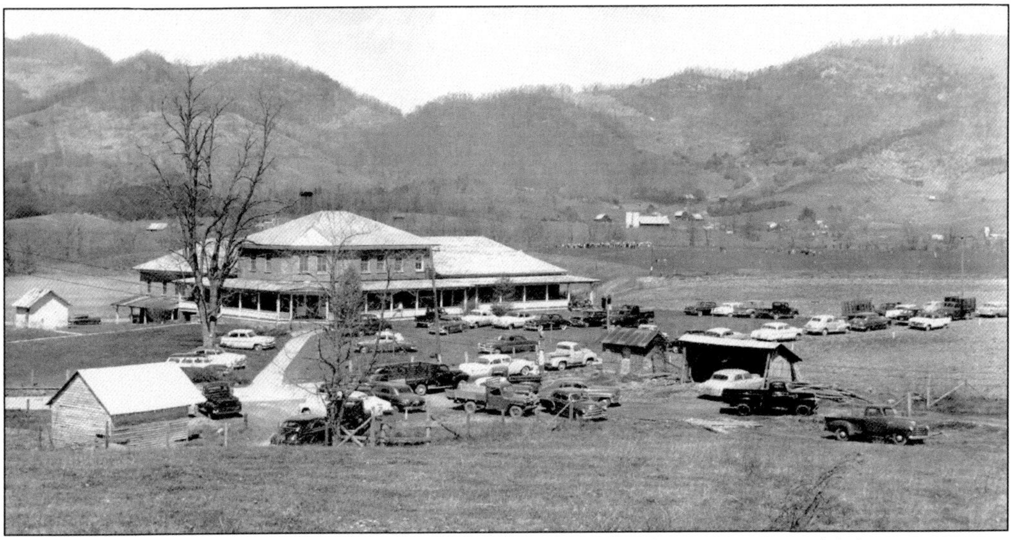

The County Home. In the early 1900s, state law required each county to establish a site to care for the poor, elderly, mentally ill, and physically disabled. Haywood leaders bought a 140-acre farm in the Bethel community and built the County Home. Its residents farmed, cooked, cleaned, looked after each other, and maintained the property until it was shut down in 1954. County Home residents were placed into foster homes and nursing homes. (Courtesy of the *Mountaineer.*)

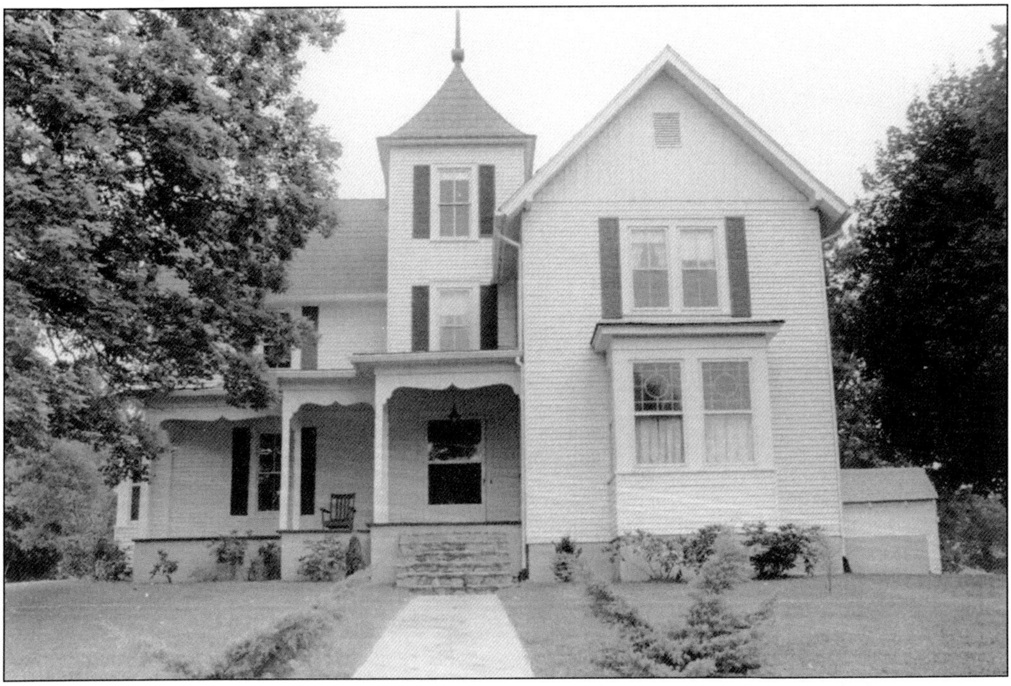

Blaylock House. This L-shaped frame house, built around 1890 in the Bethel community, features a combination of Italian Villa and Queen Anne–style architecture, a three-story tower, curvy skirts along the top of its front porch posts, bay windows with circular paned glass, interior matchboard walls, and unique mantelpieces with scroll brackets. It was once the home of Civil War Confederate officer Capt. James Blaylock and his wife, Nancy Louisa Cathey Blaylock. (Courtesy of the *Mountaineer.*)

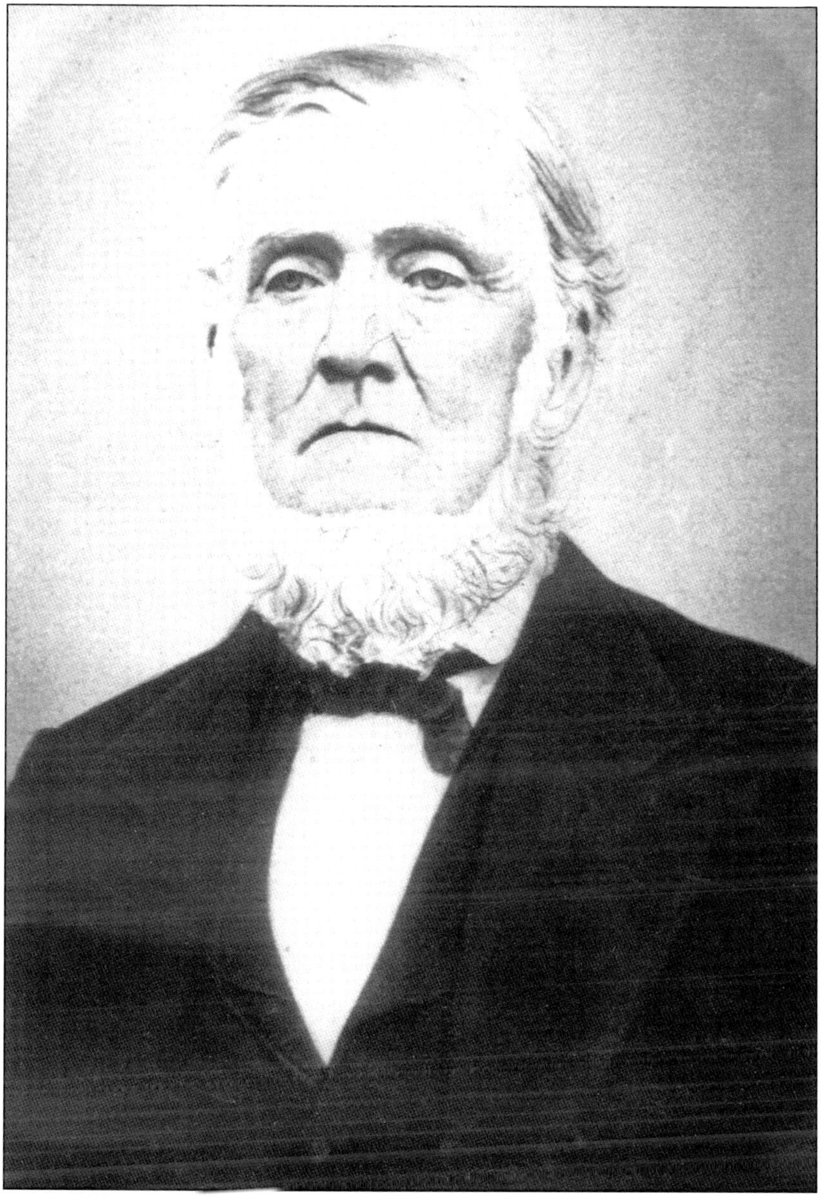

CATHEY FAMILY. The Catheys have lived in the Bethel community for more than two centuries. William Cathey was one of the earliest white settlers in what was then called Pigeon Valley. He moved to Haywood County from Virginia. His son, Col. Joseph Cathey (1803–1874), pictured here, was something of a Renaissance man. He studied law, economics, medicine, and theology and was a miller, merchant, farmer, state legislator, and family physician. For more than 30 years, he ran Cathey's Store and a mill at the forks of the Pigeon River. The store sold and bartered food, medicine, hats, coats, shoes, books, combs, tools, and farming equipment. For all his success, he also endured heartbreak. Two of his four sons died in the Civil War while serving in the Confederate army—Capt. James Madison Cathey, who was killed in battle at Petersburg, Virginia, and Lt. Joseph Turner Cathey, who died of fever in a hospital in Wilson, North Carolina. (Courtesy of Doris Cathey.)

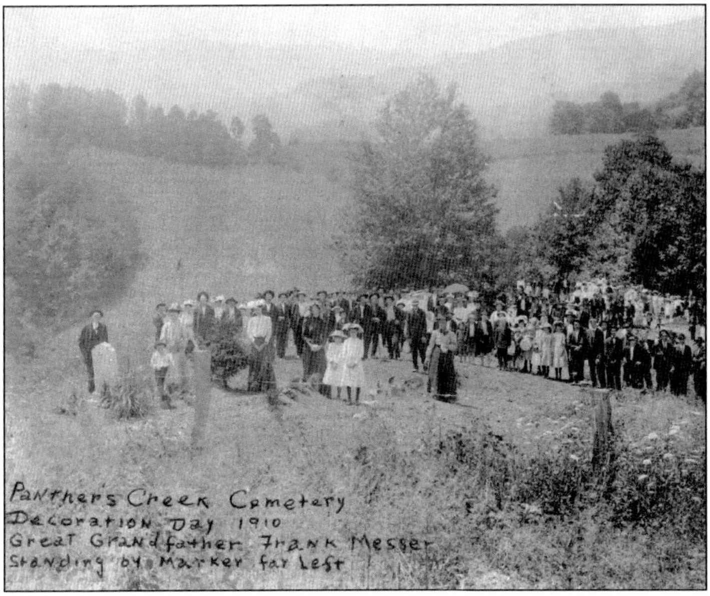

Decoration Day. After the Civil War, families in both Northern and Southern states would decorate the graves of soldiers with flowers. Decoration Day became an annual tradition honoring veterans and eventually became the holiday known as Memorial Day. In this 1910 photograph, Haywood County residents gathered at Panther Creek Cemetery for Decoration Day. (Courtesy of the Haywood County Public Library Digital Collection.)

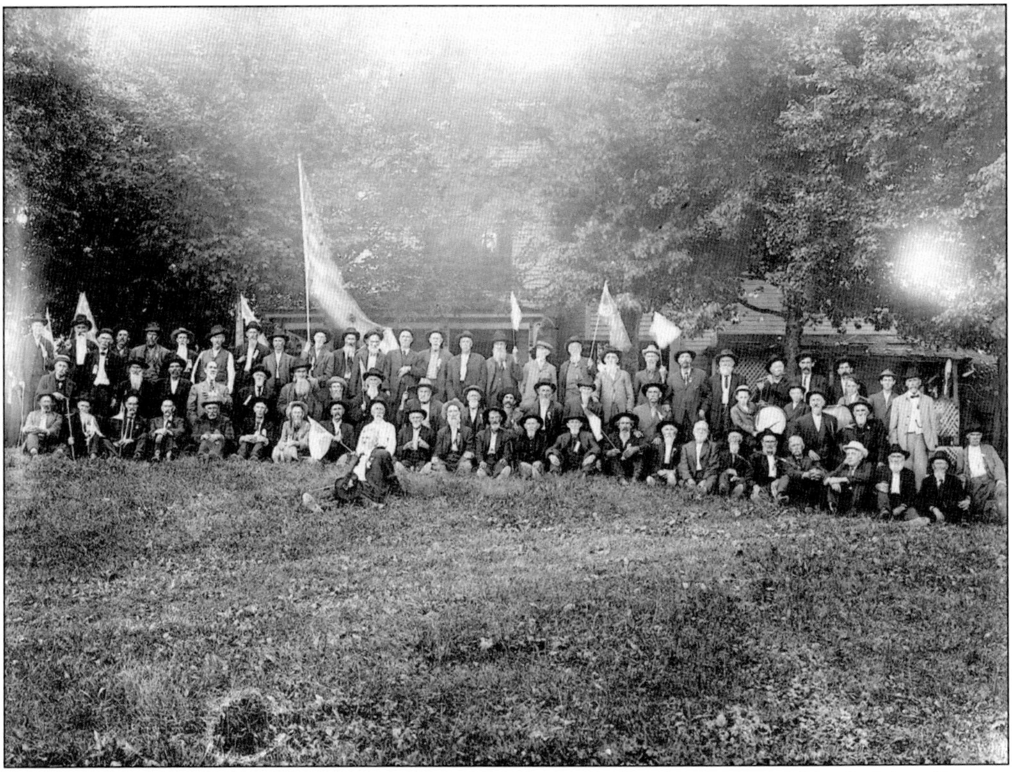

Confederate Reunion. Haywood County Confederate veterans met at the White Sulphur Springs Hotel on July 4, 1908. W. W. Stringfield, seated in front by himself, was the owner of the hotel and had been a Confederate officer. Originally from Strawberry Plains, Tennessee, he moved to Waynesville after the war, married Maria Love, earned a senate seat in the state legislature, and was an outspoken advocate for Confederate veterans. (Courtesy of the Haywood County Public Library Digital Collection.)

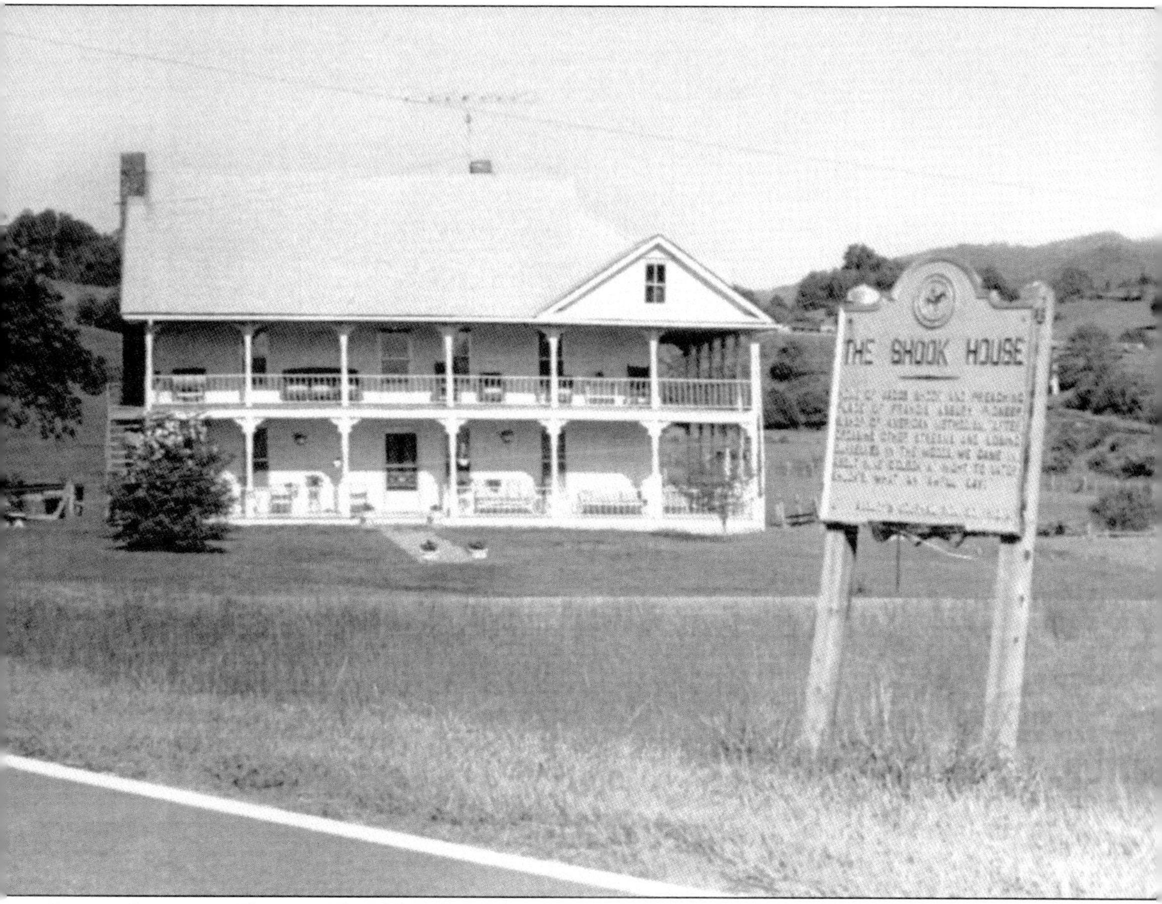

Shook-Smathers House. The oldest frame house in North Carolina west of Asheville still stands today as a testament to the fine craft skills of its original builder, Jacob Shook, who used hewn logs, wooden pegs, and iron nails he hammered out himself to construct a house for his son Peter. It was completed around 1800. Shook was a Revolutionary War veteran of German descent and one of Clyde's first white settlers. He owned much of what is present-day Clyde. On November 30, 1810, pioneer Methodist bishop Francis Asbury found brief respite at this house after an arduous journey in which he got lost in the wooded mountains. Levi Smathers later bought the home around 1850 and had it enlarged in the late 1800s. In addition to its fine Georgian-style doors and plain wide-board walls, the structure has a third-story chapel that once held religious services and music lessons. After falling into disrepair, the house was restored as a museum. (Courtesy of the *Mountaineer*.)

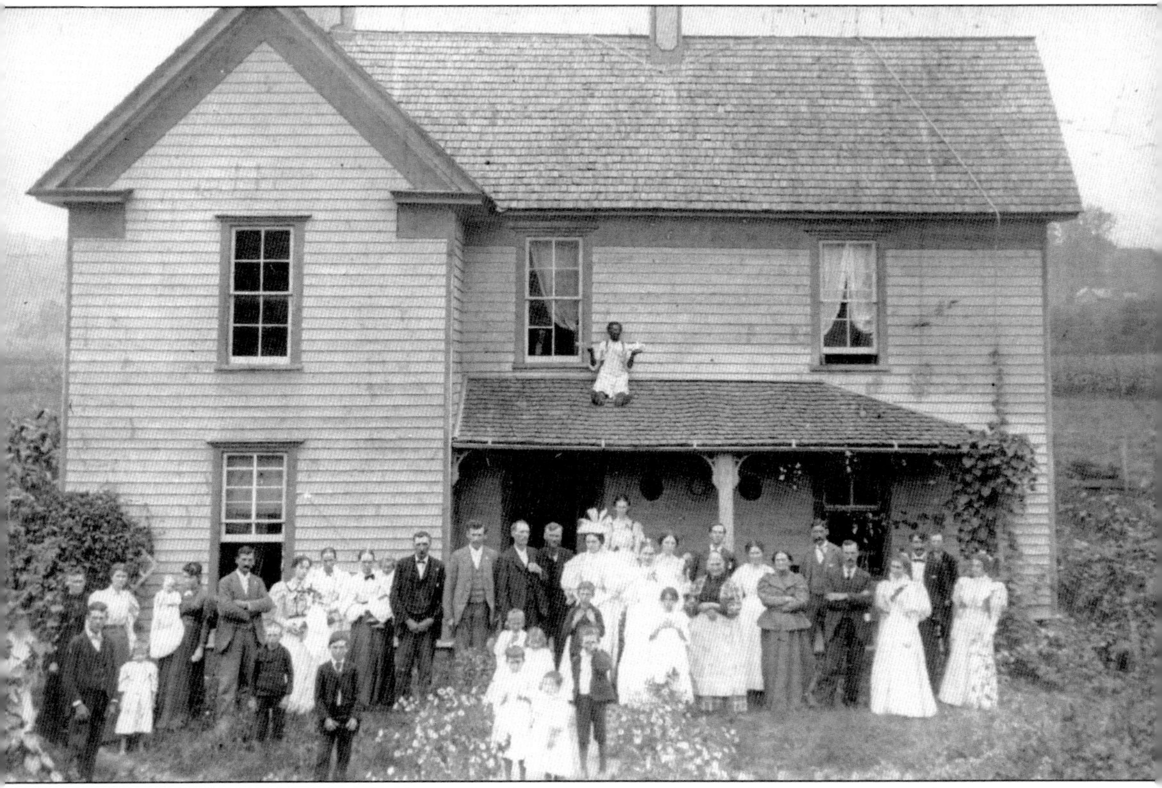

Infare. Mark P. Haynes, center with a hand on his jacket, and Joyce Westmoreland, center with a big white hat, married in 1898 in the Loving Place community between Clyde and Canton. After the wedding ceremony, another tradition began—the infare, or post-wedding reception. The bride would change into a new dress, and family and friends would get into their buggies or wagons and meet at the groom's house or the groom's parents' house for an evening of singing, dancing, feasting, and games in which the bride and groom were both playfully teased. On the first night after the party, friends and family would sneak up to the newlyweds' house and "serenade" the sleeping couple by banging on pots and pans, ringing bells, and perhaps firing off a gun. The racket continued until the couple welcomed in their guests for refreshments. At this particular infare, a young African American dwarf boy named "Little Hardy" sits on the roof holding a pie and a cake that he and his mother, the Haynes family cook, had baked for the festivities. (Courtesy of Sara Queen Brown.)

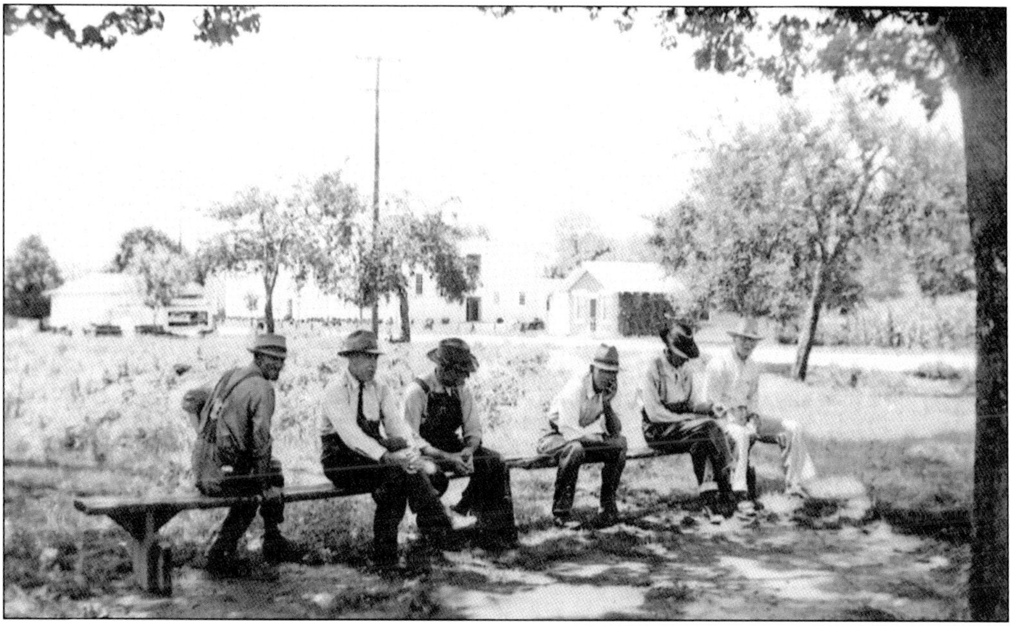

Passing Time. The Loafers and Whittlers Bench in Clyde was a popular gathering place for men to meet, swap stories, and socialize in the 1930s and 1940s. Present-day Old Clyde Highway runs through the back of this scene. From left to right are Pearson Clark, Mack Penland, Mark Haynes, ? Killian, Mark Leatherwood, and Cephus Shook. (Courtesy of Sara Queen Brown.)

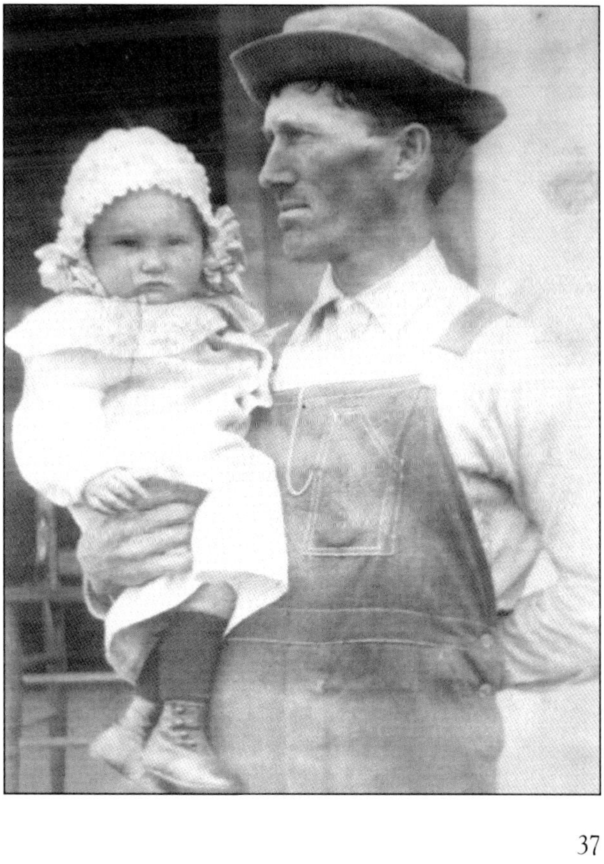

Investments. T. H. Haynes, holding his baby daughter Lois, was the first cashier at the Bank of Clyde and also served as the first secretary and treasurer of the Clyde Savings and Loan Association. Though dressed in overalls in this photograph, Haynes was regularly seen in suits. (Courtesy of the Town of Clyde.)

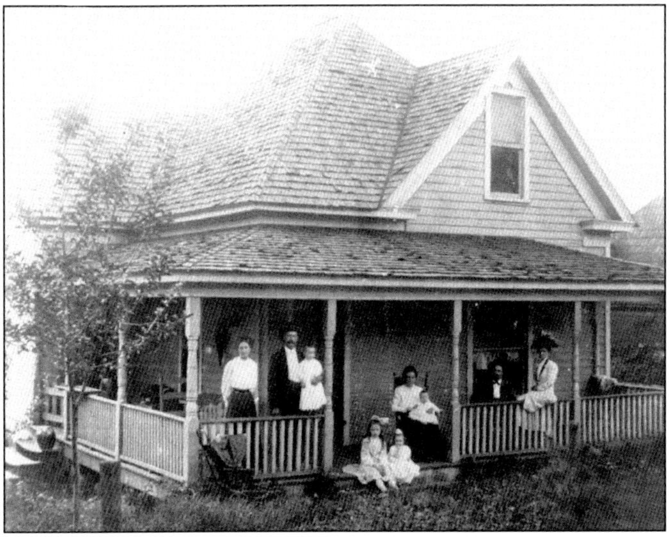

John Shook House. A great-grandson of Jacob Shook, John Shook, pictured here second from left at his Clyde home, served as the town's mayor and postmaster. He also worked for the U.S. Treasury Department's revenue division. As a sergeant in the Spanish-American War, he was part of Haywood County's Company H that marched into Havana, Cuba, to raise the American flag at the end of the war. (Courtesy of the Town of Clyde.)

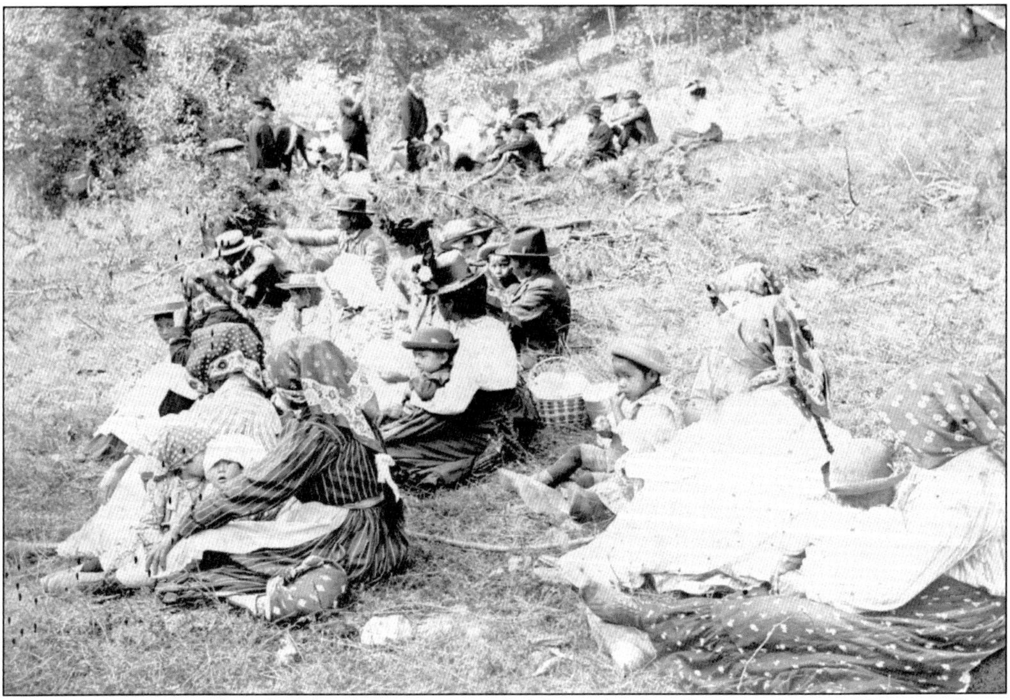

Cherokee Trade. Cherokee families once traveled from the Qualla Boundary to Waynesville—about 25 miles—in order to sell baskets and various crafts to Haywood County customers. Sometimes they would carry their wares door to door, according to former Waynesville mayor Henry Foy. In this photograph, taken in 1903, Cherokee rest in a wooded area just off present-day Russ Avenue where the Garrett Hillcrest Cemetery now stands. (Courtesy of the Haywood County Public Library Digital Collection.)

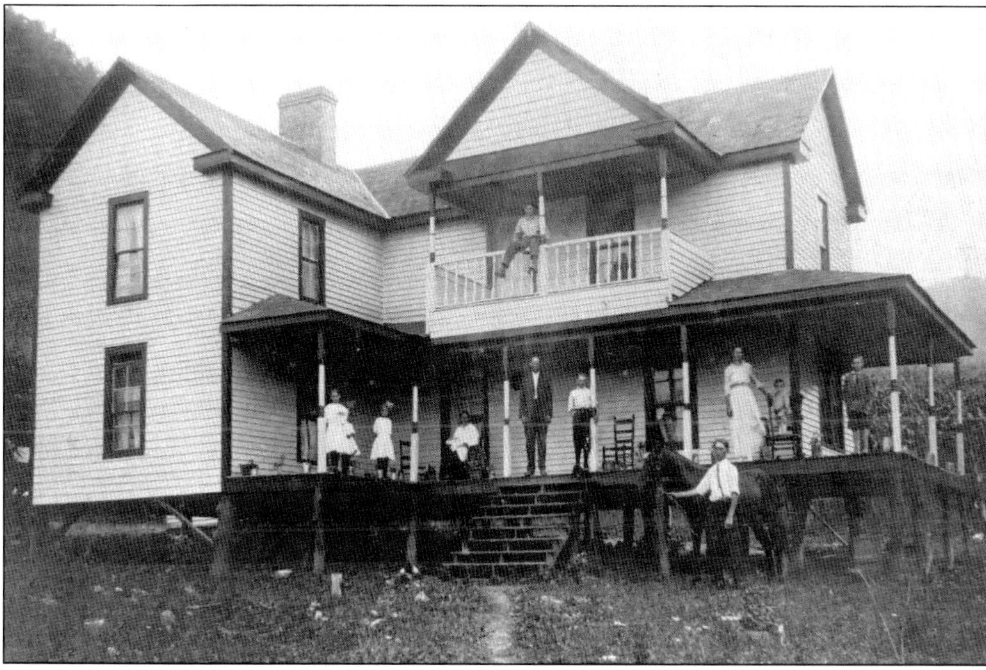

THE BEST HOUSE. Pinkney Best, a horse trader and farmer, and his wife, Eva Rogers Best, moved their family into this new home in Rogers Cove on upper Crabtree in 1914 after their previous house burned. The Bests had 14 children. The family name lives on in Crabtree, but the house no longer stands. (Courtesy of Clarine Best.)

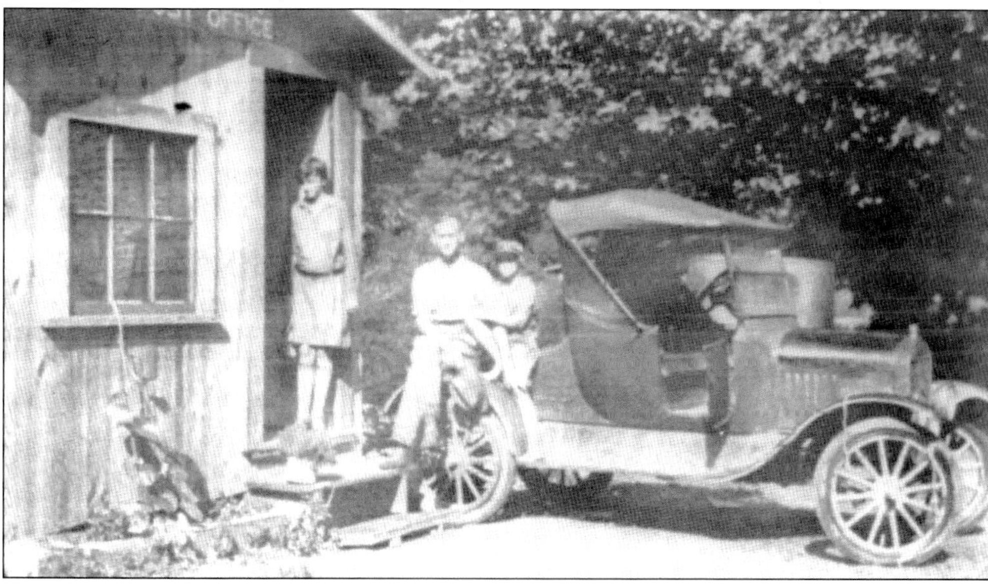

CRABTREE POST OFFICE. Coman Francis (center) was the mail carrier for Clyde, Fines Creek, and Crabtree from 1906 to the early 1940s. Over the years, he delivered mail by horseback, then buggy, then a two-wheeled cart, and finally a Model T Ford. Francis also served as chairman of the Haywood County Board of Education. His daughters Bonnie Francis (Shook), left, and Willie Eda Francis (Harris), right, join him in this photograph taken around 1920. (Courtesy of Sara Queen Brown.)

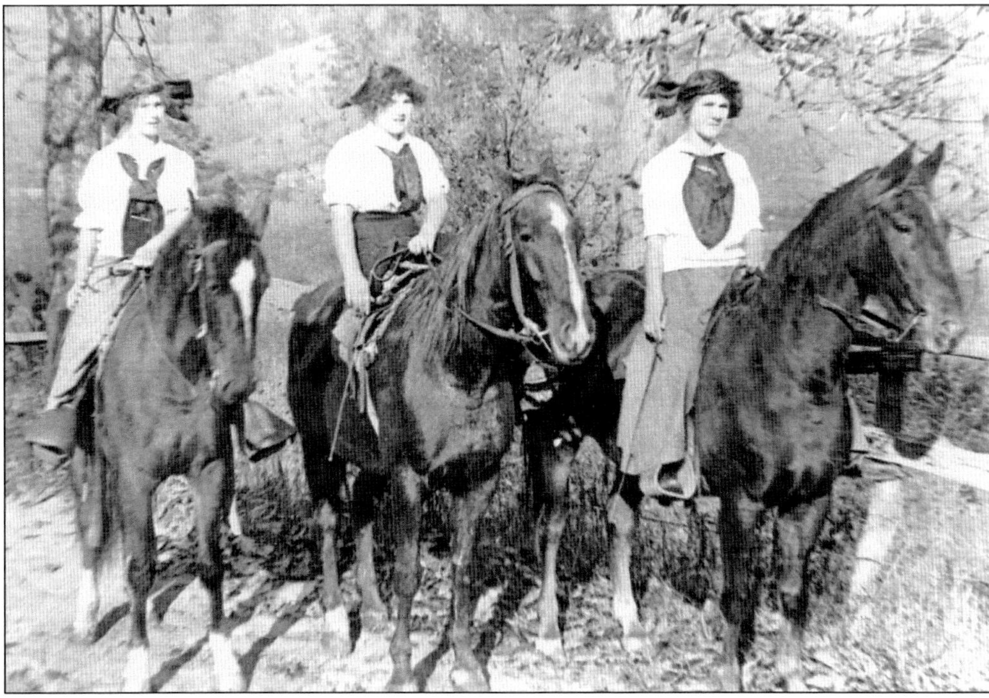

Back in the Saddle. From left to right, Essie Hill, her sister Mattie, and Gussie Medford ride their horses through Crabtree. The Hill family included 12 siblings—the first eight were girls and the next four were boys, born in that order. Note the different saddles they use. (Courtesy of Clarine Best.)

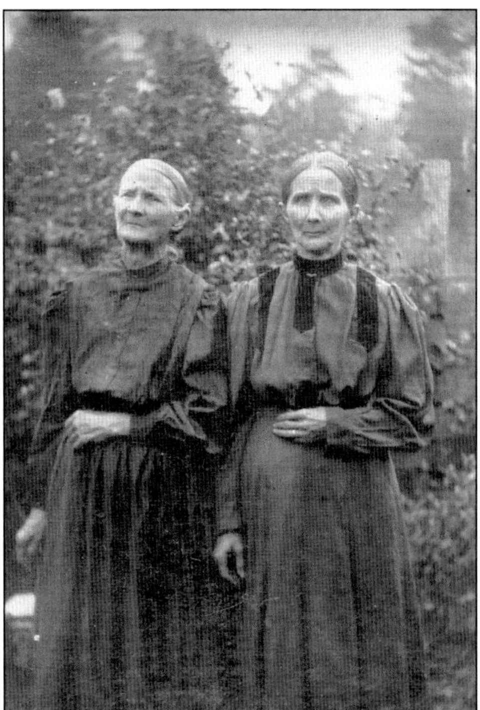

Mother and Daughter. Elizabeth Evans (left) married Adolphus Henry, who donated land for the first church in Maggie Valley (the present-day First United Methodist Church of Maggie Valley). Adolphus died in 1892 while cutting a tree behind his house. After his death, Elizabeth went to live with her daughter, Nancy Jane Henry Rathbone (right). (Courtesy of Betty Ferguson.)

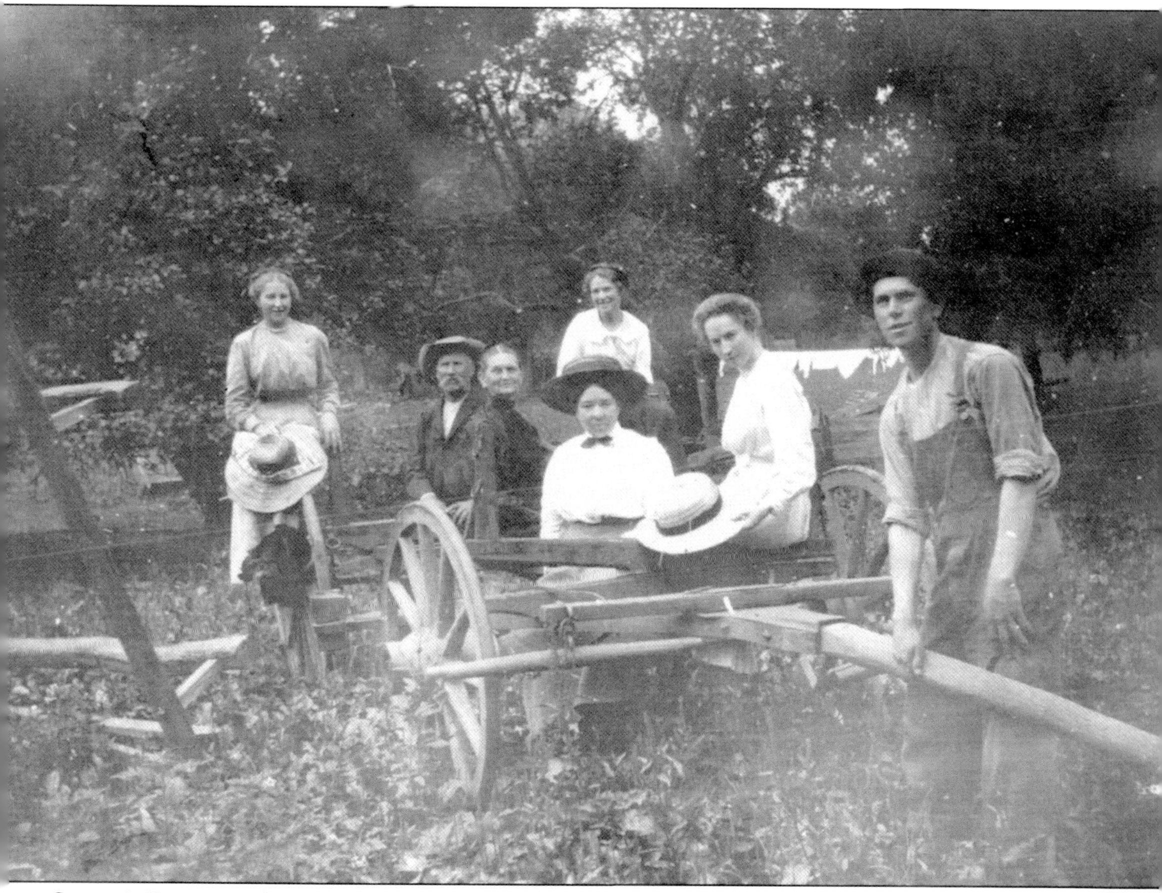

Queen's Farm. At this farm in Dellwood, James Queen, his wife, Mary, and their family raised chickens, hogs, sheep, and cattle; traded mules and sold livestock; grew and canned vegetables; and welcomed guests to their boardinghouse. From left to right are Jimmie, James and his wife, Mary, Mattie, Fannie (with hat on), Maggie, and Sam Love Queen. (Courtesy of Sara Queen Brown.)

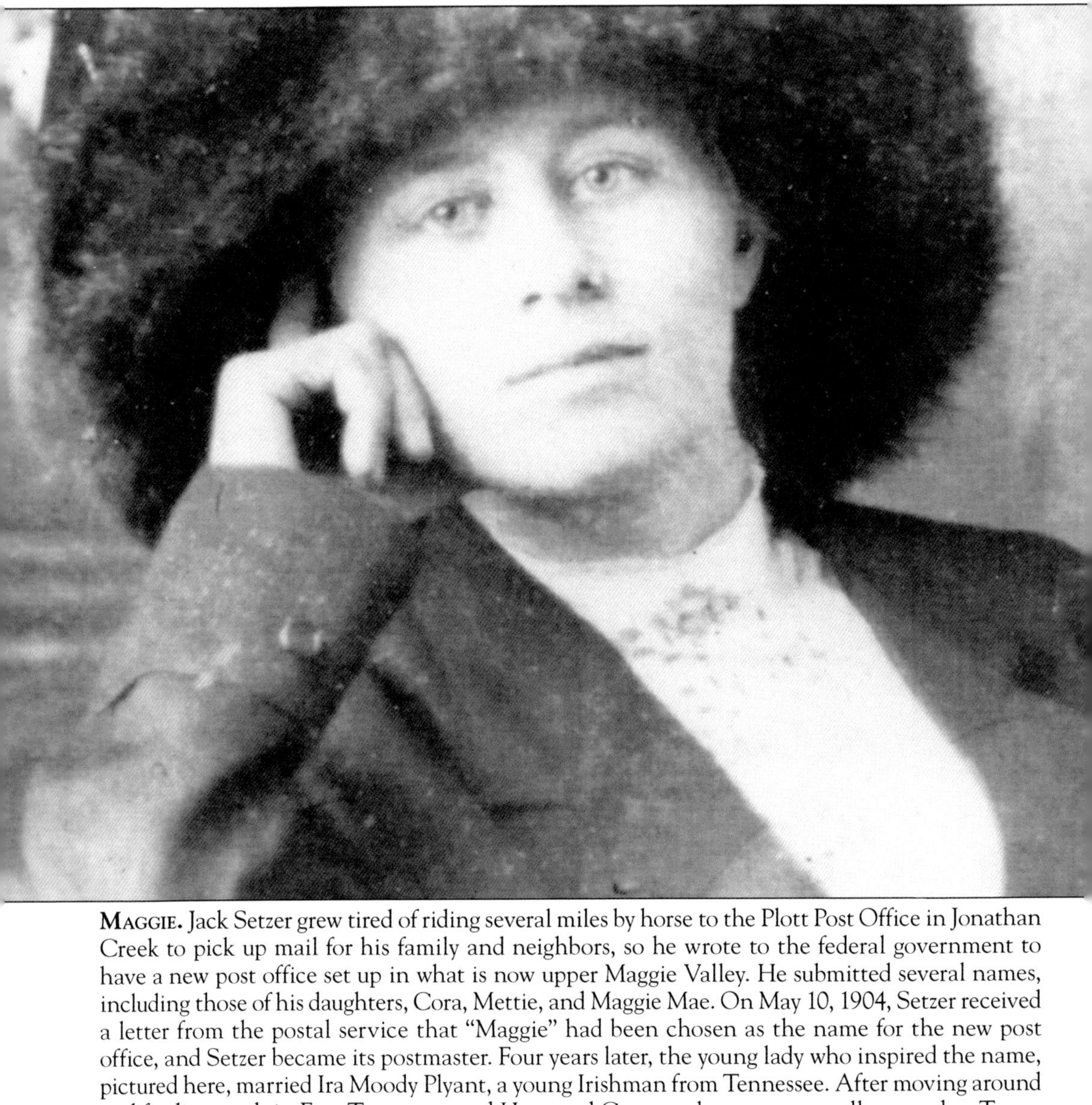

MAGGIE. Jack Setzer grew tired of riding several miles by horse to the Plott Post Office in Jonathan Creek to pick up mail for his family and neighbors, so he wrote to the federal government to have a new post office set up in what is now upper Maggie Valley. He submitted several names, including those of his daughters, Cora, Mettie, and Maggie Mae. On May 10, 1904, Setzer received a letter from the postal service that "Maggie" had been chosen as the name for the new post office, and Setzer became its postmaster. Four years later, the young lady who inspired the name, pictured here, married Ira Moody Plyant, a young Irishman from Tennessee. After moving around and finding work in East Tennessee and Haywood County, the two eventually moved to Texas, where they settled down to raise a family. In 1972, Maggie returned to Maggie Valley, where she received a celebrity welcome, signed autographs, and spoke to civic groups. She died in 1979 and was buried beside her husband in Houston, Texas. (Courtesy of Betty Ferguson.)

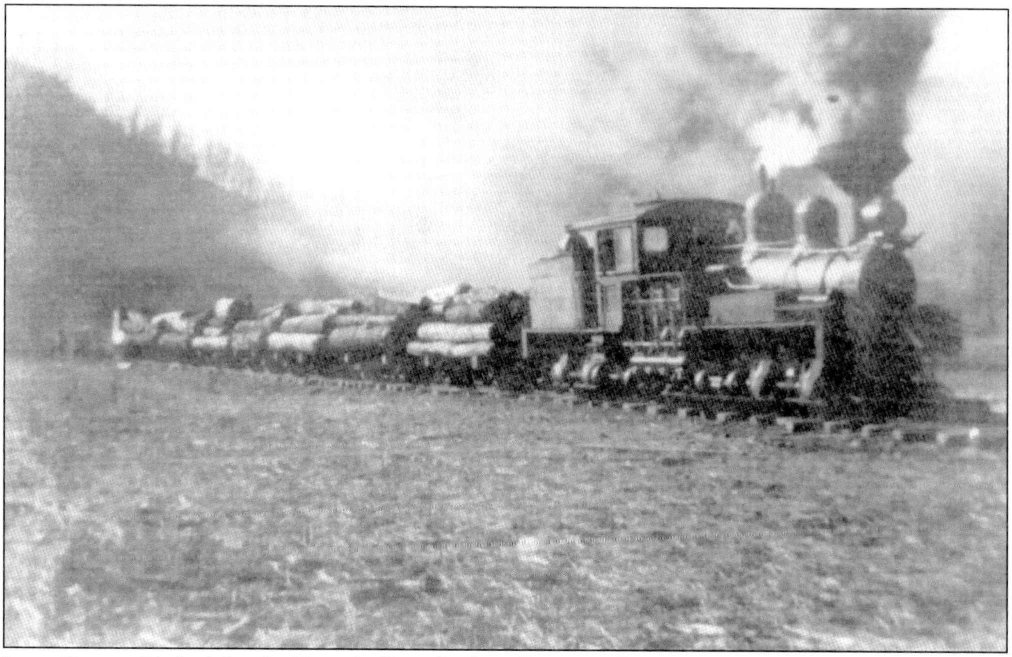

Log Train. Viola Moody Campbell took this photograph sometime between 1916 and 1918. Campbell developed and printed her own photographs in a darkroom, which she set up in her family's smokehouse. This log train probably came from the Flat Creek community. In the 1920s, Campbell had a house built behind what is now J. Arthur's Restaurant in Maggie Valley. (Courtesy of Betty Ferguson.)

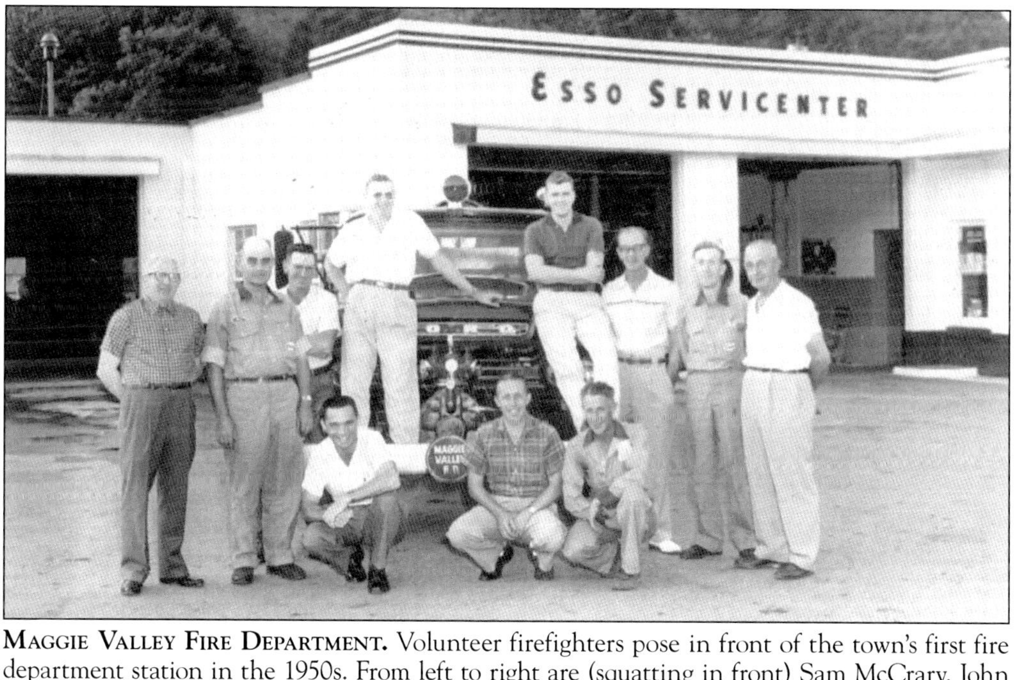

Maggie Valley Fire Department. Volunteer firefighters pose in front of the town's first fire department station in the 1950s. From left to right are (squatting in front) Sam McCrary, John Medford, and Wilson Fisher; (standing) Kim Parham, Harry Ward, Charles Ferguson, Robert Ferguson, Jimmy Plott, Fred Henry, Willard Setzer, and Hoxie Griswold. (Courtesy of Betty Ferguson.)

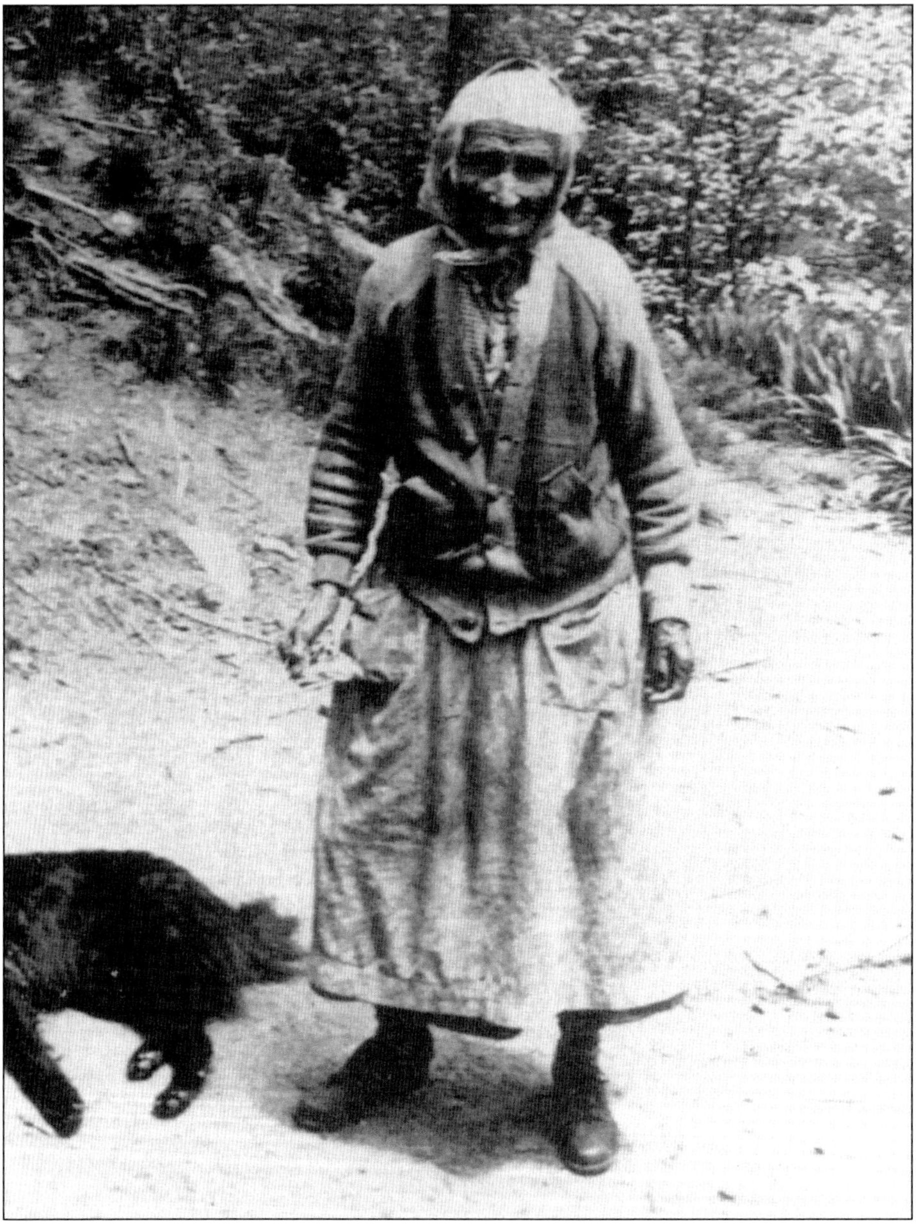

Nance Dude. In the winter of 1913, a 65-year-old woman named Nancy Ann Kerley, above, was found guilty of killing her two-year-old granddaughter, Roberta Putnam. It became one of Haywood County's most notorious—and puzzling—crimes. According to one account, Nancy's daughter was trying to get rid of her child after her common-law husband agreed to marriage as long as there was no child involved. So Nancy took the toddler and went up and down the road with the hopes of giving her away. When Roberta was found weeks later dead inside a cave, Nancy was immediately accused and arrested. A mob nearly burst into the local jail to lynch her. Poor and poorly defended, she wound up serving 15 years of hard labor at a Raleigh prison for a crime she never confessed to committing. At the age of 80, she was paroled and sent home. Children threw stones at her. Others called her a witch. Scorned by family and neighbors, she moved to Swain County, where she lived to be 104. (Courtesy of Betty Ferguson.)

Still Going. Law enforcement agencies continue to uncover secret locations where people make moonshine, an old mountain practice made popular since the days of Prohibition, when the federal government outlawed the production, sale, and distribution of alcohol. This still, broken up in Haywood County in 1972, was most likely found in a remote, wooded area near a mountain stream, as is often the case with such operations. (Courtesy of the *Mountaineer.*)

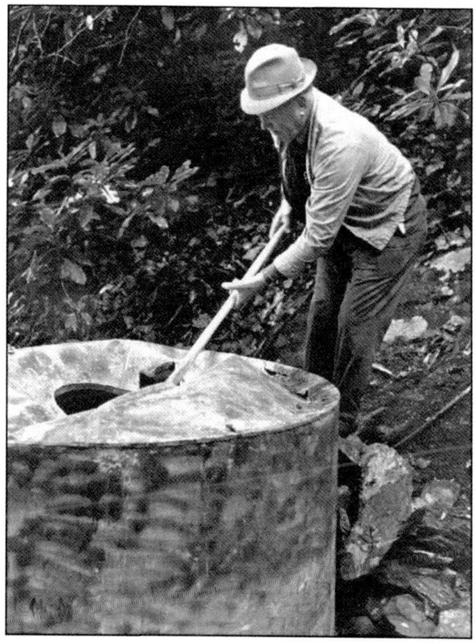

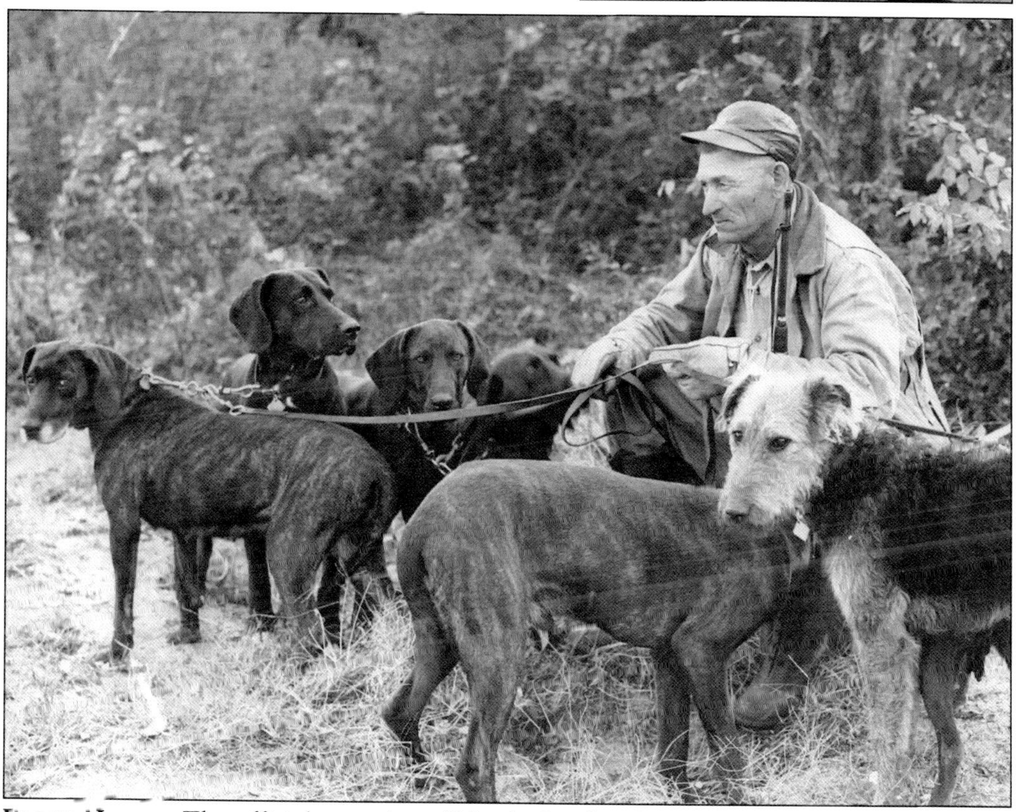

Plott Hound. The official state dog of North Carolina has its roots in Haywood County, thanks to the Plott family. Henry Vaughn "Von" Plott, pictured here, helped bring national attention to these brindle-coated dogs through careful breeding and training. They have become prized hunting dogs, known as expert trackers, tenacious fighters, and fiercely loyal companions. (Courtesy of the Plott family.)

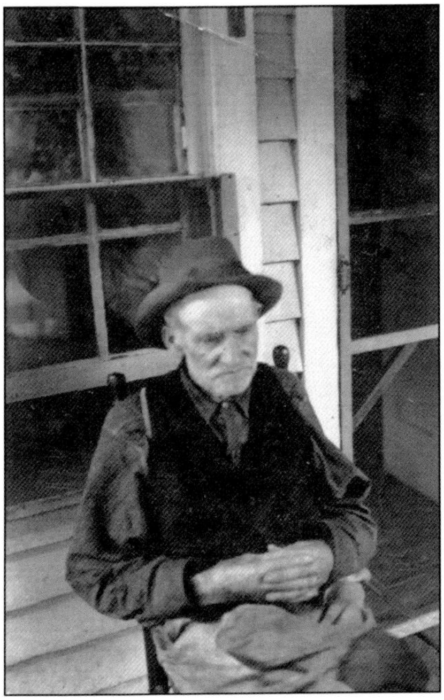

Turkey George. One of Haywood County's most famous bear hunters, "Turkey" George Palmer of Big Cataloochee was said to have killed 105 bears in his time. He apparently got his nickname after a tussle with several wild turkeys he had trapped in a pen. When he went to retrieve one, they attacked him with a flurry of flapping wings and stomping feet. (Courtesy of Haywood County Public Library Digital Collection.)

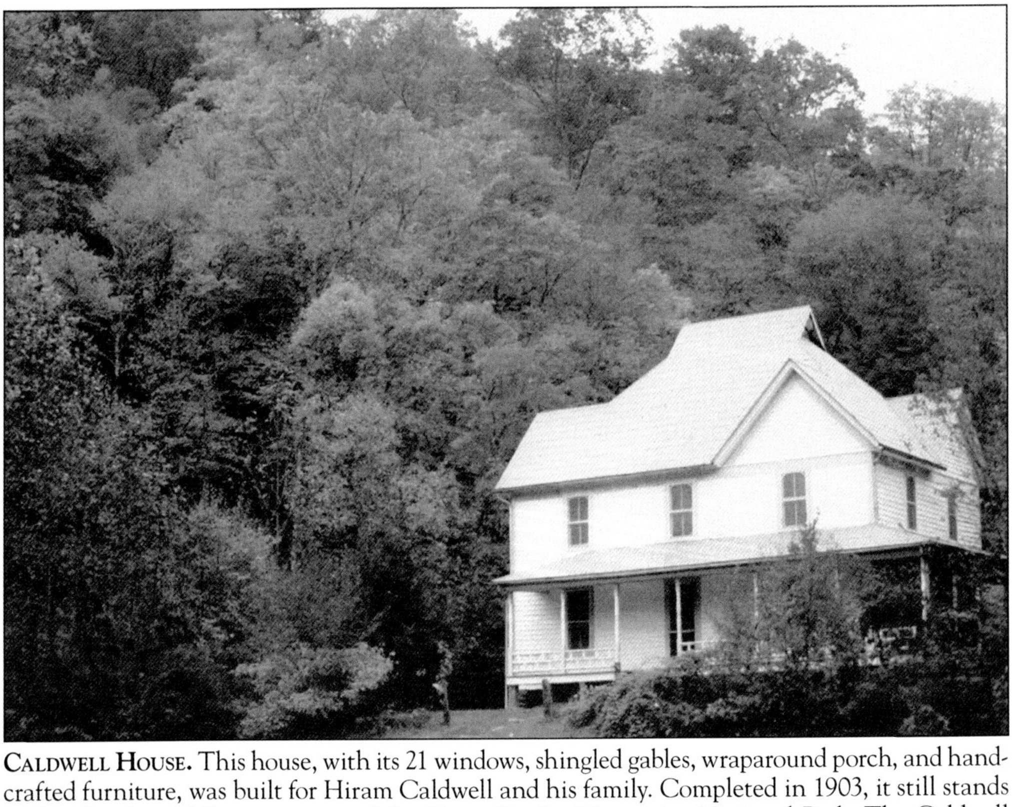

Caldwell House. This house, with its 21 windows, shingled gables, wraparound porch, and handcrafted furniture, was built for Hiram Caldwell and his family. Completed in 1903, it still stands in Cataloochee Valley, now part of the Great Smoky Mountains National Park. The Caldwell family raised sheep, wove sheep's wool into cloth, and made padded quilts that were traded and sold in local markets. (Courtesy of Betty Ferguson.)

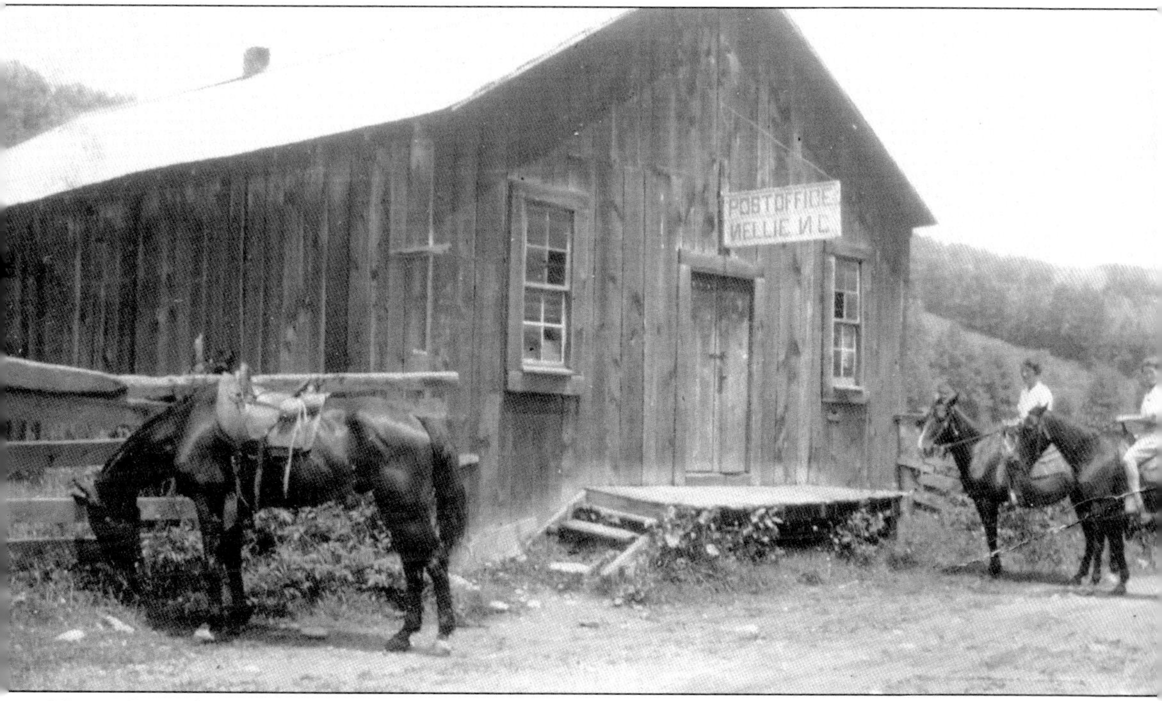

Nellie Post Office. One of four post offices in Cataloochee Valley in the early 1900s, Nellie was named after Turkey George Palmer's daughter. An elderly Native American supposedly painted the sign, drawing a backwards "N" twice. The postmistress, Millie Palmer, thought it added some character to the store, so she kept it. The Nellie office was actually part of a general store. Stamps cost 2¢ for letters and 1¢ for postcards. Mail carriers bid for contracts to deliver the mail. In the remote sections of Cataloochee Valley, the lone mode of transportation was a horse. As the federal government began setting aside land to create the Great Smoky Mountains National Park, Cataloochee residents were urged to sell their lands and move away. Some did, but others remained and fought the exodus for a time. The Nellie Post Office eventually closed in 1937. (Courtesy of Cataloochee Ranch.)

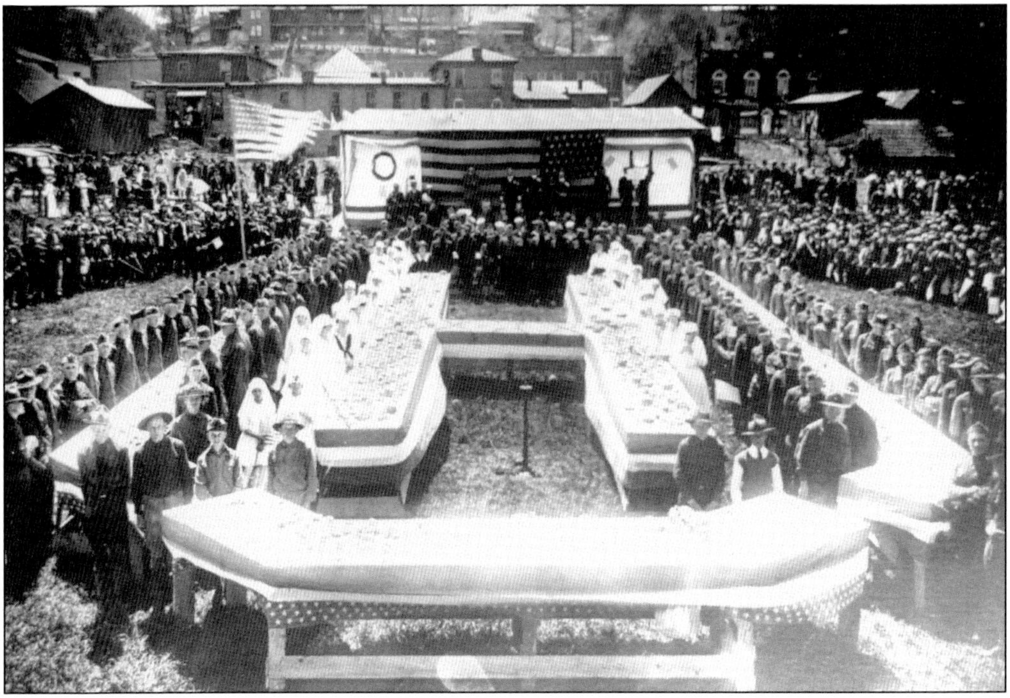

Welcome Home. Canton offered a festive celebration for its soldiers and nurses who returned after serving overseas in World War I. These veterans included members of a renowned ambulance corps that dodged bombs and gas attacks on the front lines to carry off wounded soldiers to makeshift hospitals. This photograph was taken on May 3, 1919, near where the present-day Canton Town Hall now stands. (Courtesy of Canton Historical Museum.)

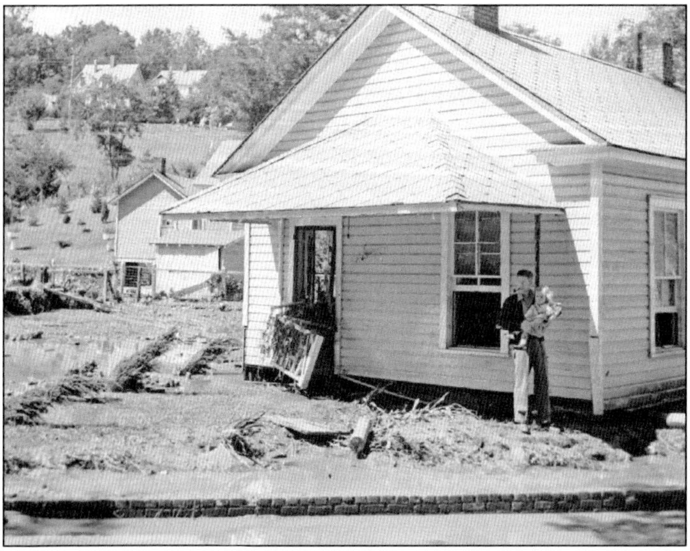

Flood Damage. Situated along the Pigeon River, Canton has endured some major floods over the years. Tropical storms bringing torrential rains over a short period of time can be especially hazardous. Twice in August 1940, heavy rains hit the county, and Canton received some of its worst flooding ever, especially for the Fiberville community, shown here, where mill workers lived in small houses next to the river. (Courtesy of Canton Historical Museum.)

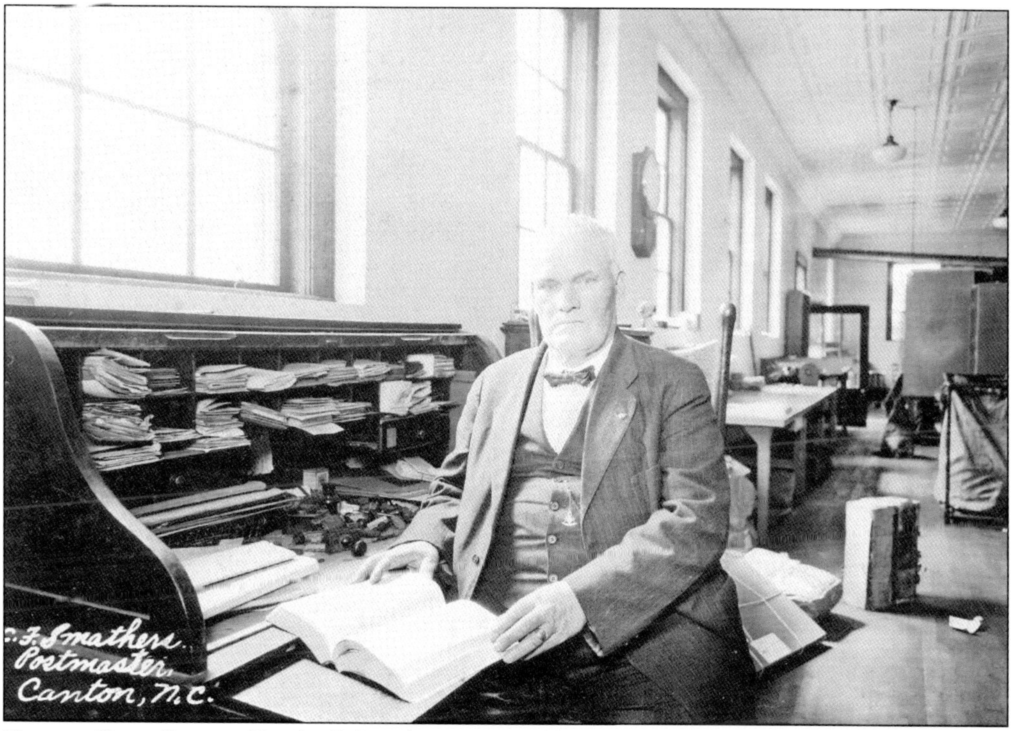

Canton Post Office. Charles F. Smathers, pictured here, served as postmaster for Canton in the early 1900s. Many of Haywood County's earliest communities were named after their postmaster or post office. Canton was once known as Vinson, the name of a postmaster. Likewise with the Ivy Hill community formerly called Plott. Present-day Bethel was referred to by its postal name of Woodrow. Dellwood's postal address was once Tito (pronounced TIE-toh), and Crabtree went by the name of Peru (pronounced PEE-roo). (Courtesy of Canton Historical Museum.)

Sharp-Owen House. This home was built in 1923 for W. Turner Sharp, an influential business leader in Canton at the time. Sharp ran a general store and oversaw the construction of several major buildings in downtown, including the Imperial Hotel, a post office, and the J. O. Plott wholesale grocery store. He was also a school board member, the town's mayor, and president of the board of trade. (Courtesy of Canton Historical Museum.)

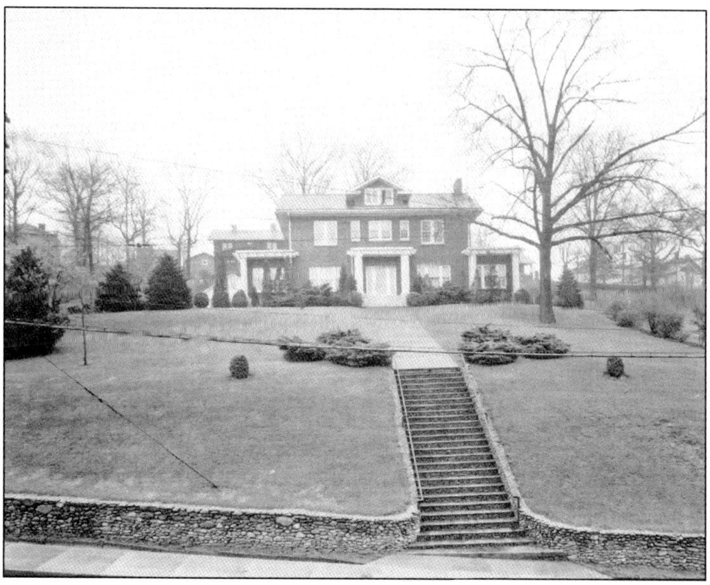

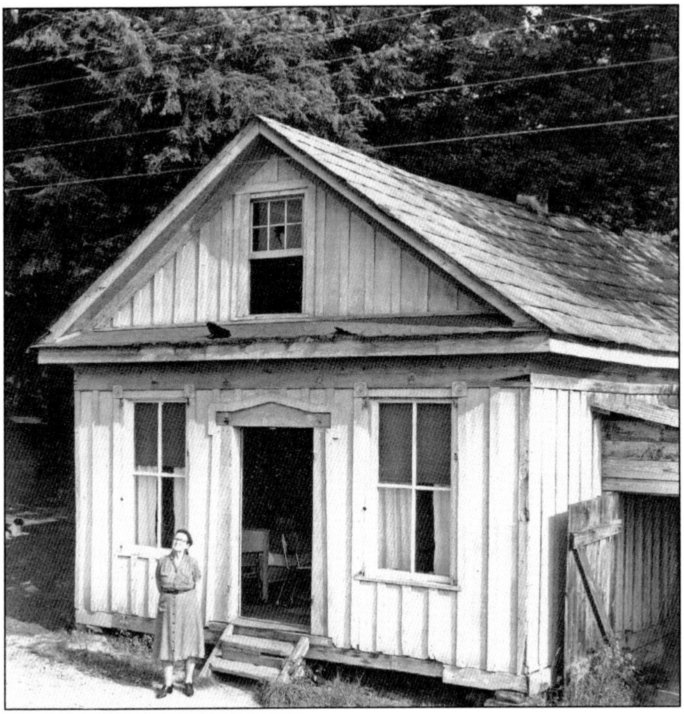

Tuscola Post Office. Before Lake Junaluska formed, the community was called Richland, a reference to the fertile valley farmland. It was also called Tuscola, which some claim to be a Cherokee term meaning "place where there is digging." Postmistress Maggie Kirkpatrick Long stands in front of the post office. Her husband, Rev. R. C. Long, also served as postmaster. He was a Methodist circuit preacher and missionary to the Cherokees and helped found Tuscola Academy in 1858. (Courtesy of the *Mountaineer.*)

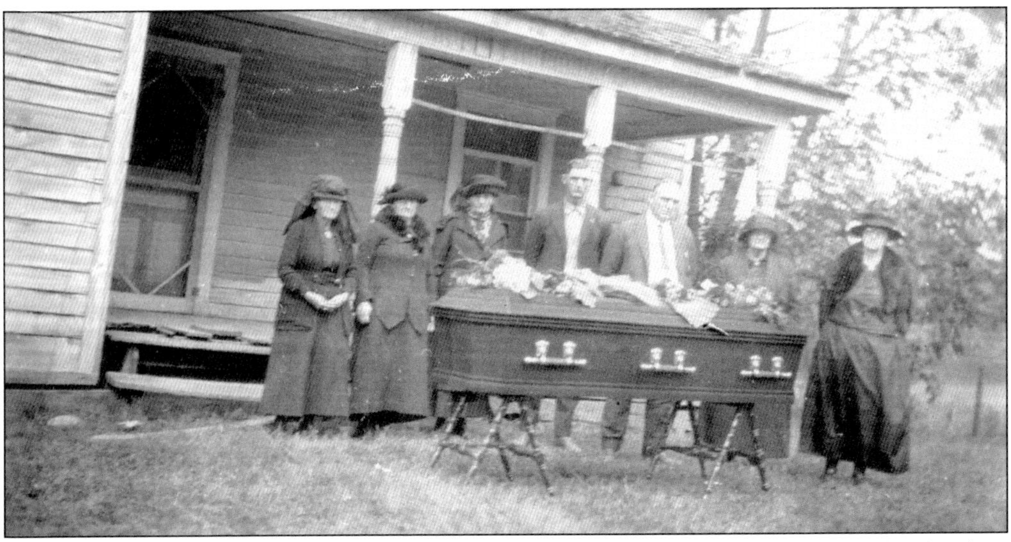

Funeral. Sarah Owen Ferguson (far left) and family members attend the funeral of her brother, Yule Owen. The Fergusons have long been a prominent family in the Crabtree community. One of the most famous was Homer Ferguson, who went on to become a longtime president of one of the nation's largest naval shipyards in Newport News, Virginia. During the Great Depression and war years, he welcomed scores of Haywood residents for jobs at his shipyard. (Courtesy of Betty Ferguson.)

Four

CHURCHES AND SCHOOLS

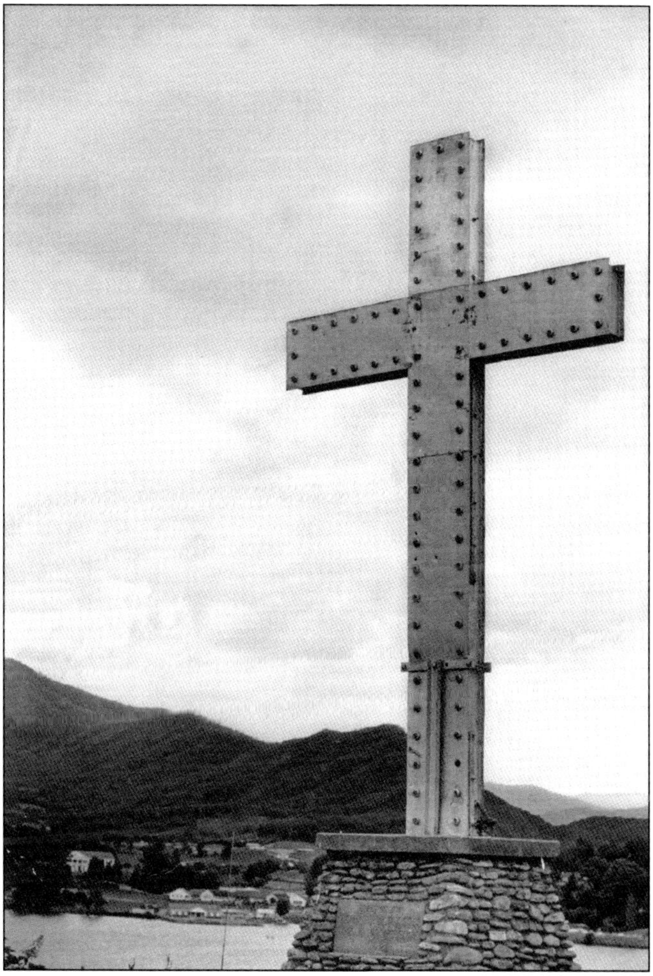

THE JUNALUSKA CROSS. This 25-foot-tall beacon of light, built in 1922, overlooks Lake Junaluska. Supported by a 5-foot-tall stone base, it includes about 200 lightbulbs. Only during the brownouts of World War II and when the cross was taken down in 1994—repaired and replaced—has it been out of operation. An amphitheater on the hillside just below holds vesper meetings and religious services, including an annual Easter sunrise service. (Courtesy of the *Mountaineer*.)

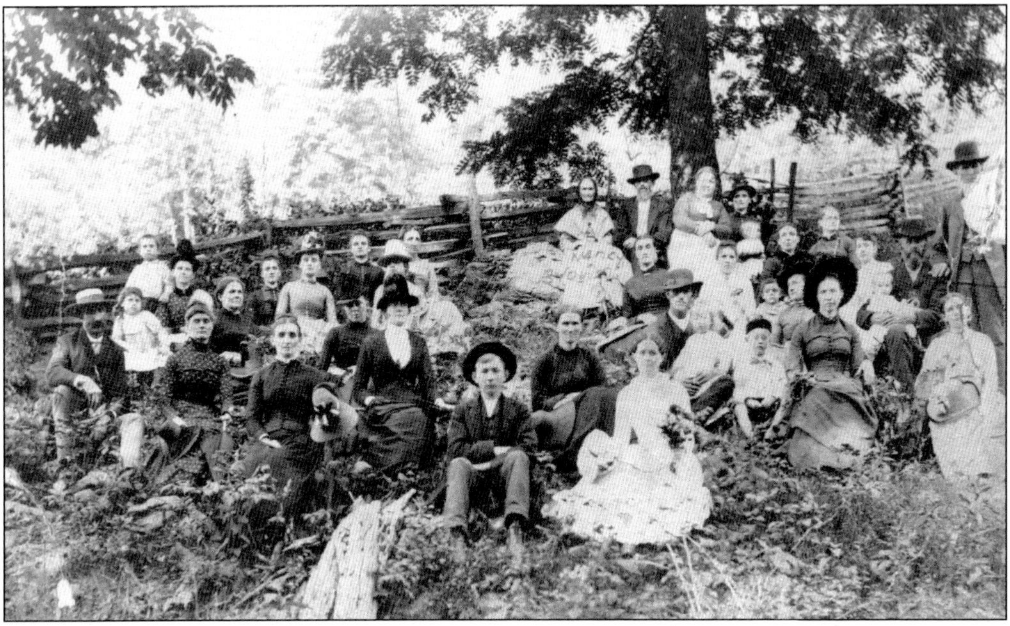

Fresh Air and Prayer. This missionary picnic group met in the Camp Branch community in 1890 at the home of Manson Tate. Many rural communities relied on missionaries and circuit preachers who toured around preaching on a circuit of different churches within a given county or region. (Courtesy of Shelton House.)

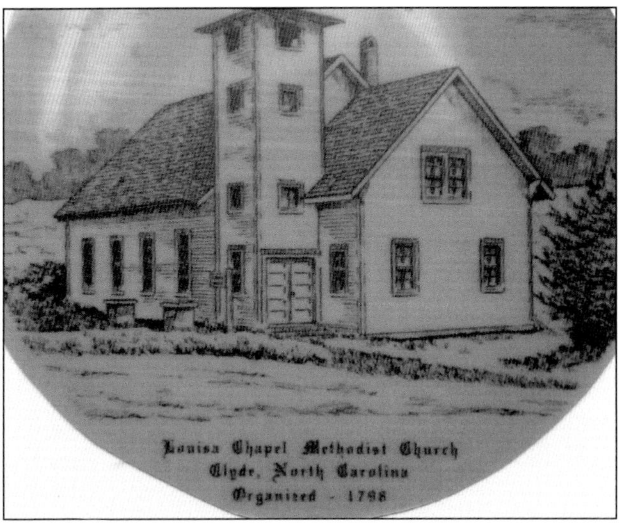

Louisa Chapel. This chapel in Clyde was named after Jacob Shook's granddaughter. It was organized in 1798 with help from Samuel Edney, the first Methodist minister in North Carolina appointed west of the Blue Ridge Mountains. Before the church was erected, the grounds were used for religious services. Local families would travel by horse and wagon to attend weeklong tent revivals. Brush arbors were constructed to offer shelter from the rain. Preaching and singing would go on both day and night. (Courtesy of Sara Queen Brown.)

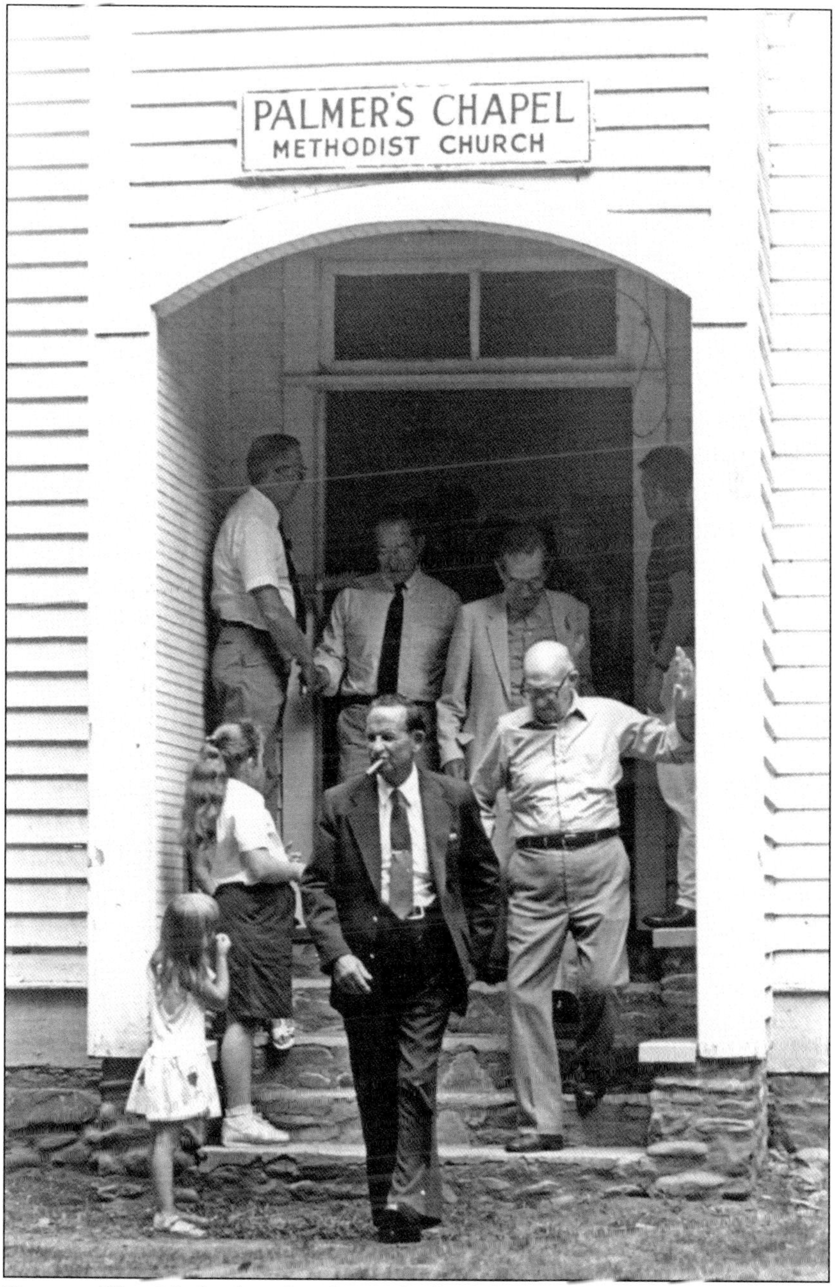

PALMER CHAPEL. This Methodist church was built in Big Cataloochee between 1898 and 1900 on land deeded by Mary Ann Palmer. In its early days, it had no permanent minister, so a circuit rider came to preach on the third Sunday of each month. He was often paid with food. The design of the chapel was quite simple—a framed rectangular box with a gabled roof and wooden shingles. Interior walls and the ceiling were once painted sky blue. They are now white. In 1929, the government bought the property for $1,150 as part of the effort to secure land for the Great Smoky Mountains National Park. The congregation continued to hold worship services there, though numbers dwindled as local property owners moved out of Cataloochee. Annual Cataloochee reunions still include church services in Palmer Chapel. (Courtesy of the *Mountaineer*.)

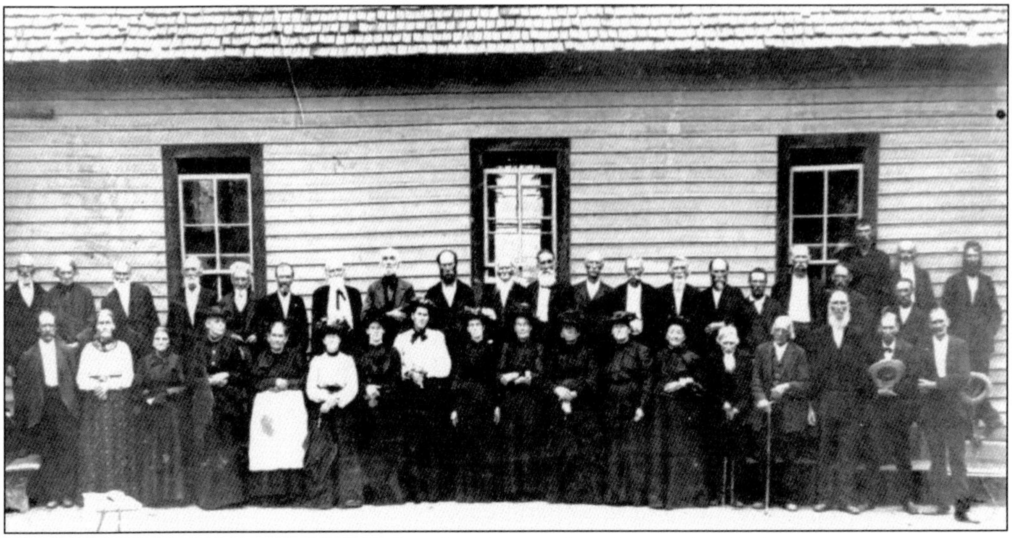

Baptist Churches. There were already a few Baptist churches in the Crabtree community in the late 1800s, but the upper Crabtree community decided to organize its own church and school near a large rock spring in 1884. Rock Springs Baptist Church burned in 1890, so a new building was constructed in 1893. It was moved down the hill in 1947 to install electricity. Since then, there have been further renovations. In the 1903 photograph above, members of the congregation and guests celebrated "Old Folks Day" to honor those who were 60 years old and older. Below, Baptist churches would hold baptismal ceremonies outdoors at local ponds or lakes. In this photograph taken in the early 1950s, the Crabtree Baptist Church congregation holds a baptism on Joe Palmer's farm in the Rush Fork section of Crabtree. (Both courtesy of Clarine Best.)

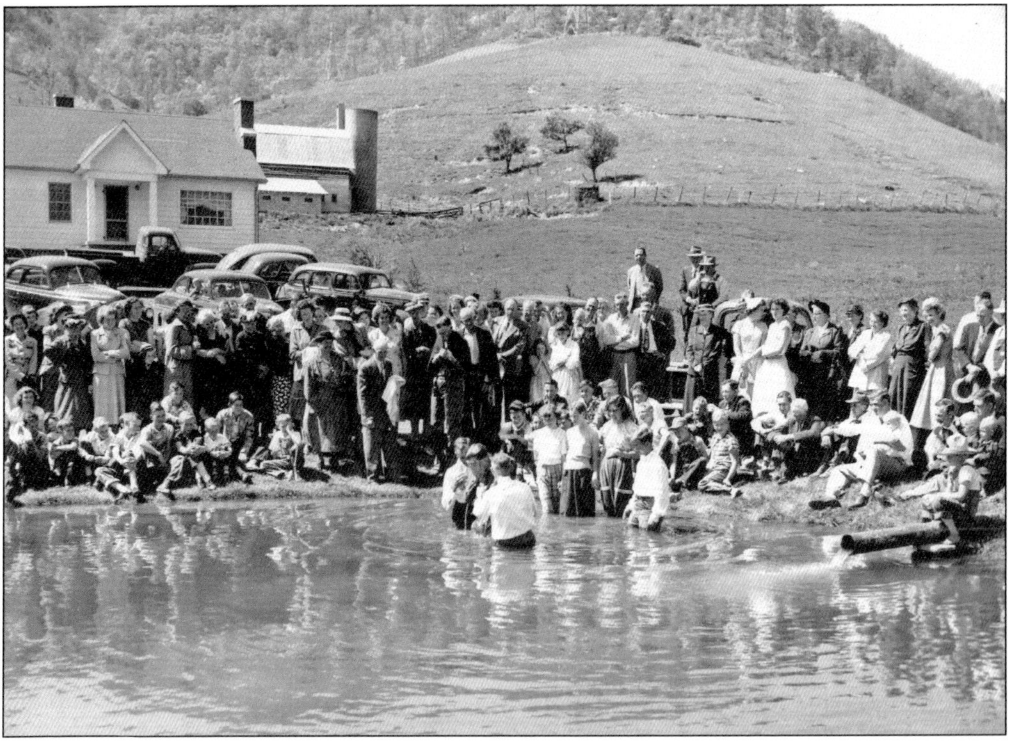

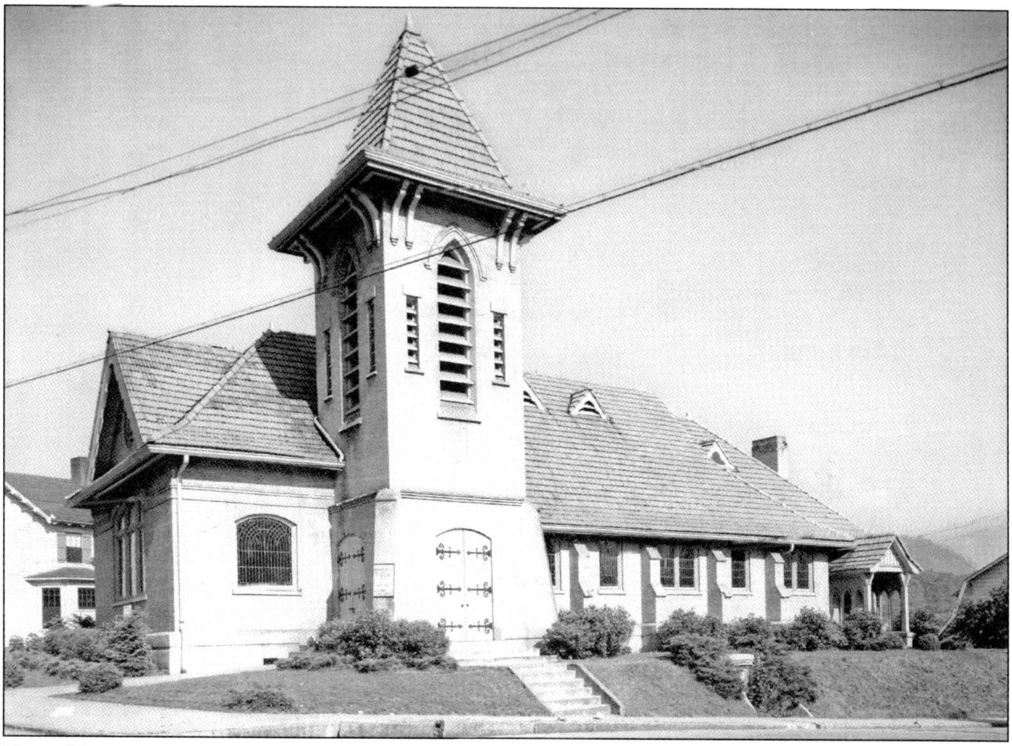

First Presbyterian Church of Waynesville. Organized in 1875 with help from a Charlotte evangelist, this church began with just eight members. After several years of meeting once a month in the Methodist church on Green Hill (now Green Hill Cemetery), the congregation decided to build a new church. R. G. A. Love provided the corner lot on Main and Walnut Streets. (Photograph by Elliot Lyman Fisher; courtesy of the *Mountaineer*.)

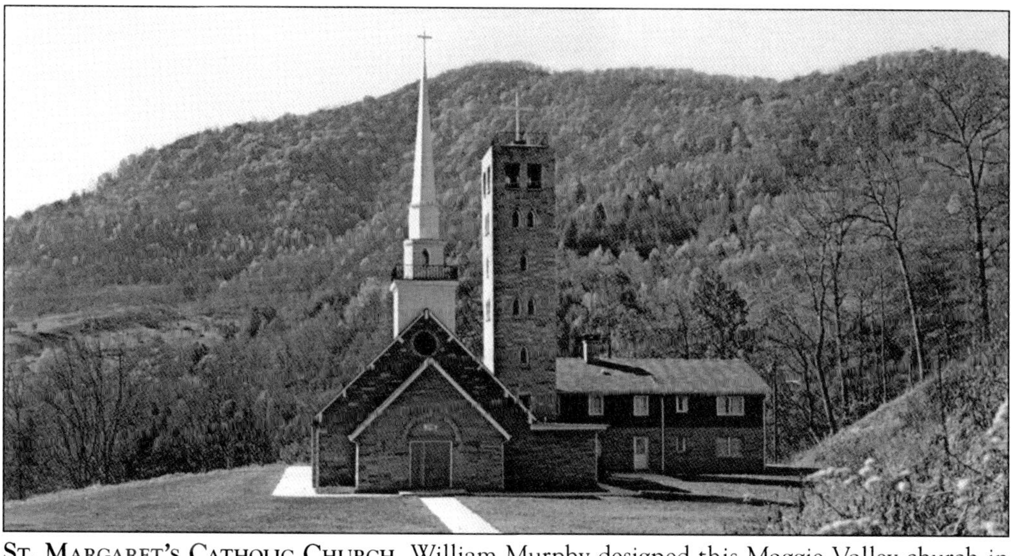

St. Margaret's Catholic Church. William Murphy designed this Maggie Valley church in 1967, naming it in honor of his mother, a devout Catholic. The congregation grew, and three and a half years later, Murphy, at the age of 80, became an ordained priest, serving in St. Margaret's until well into his 90s. (Courtesy of the *Mountaineer*.)

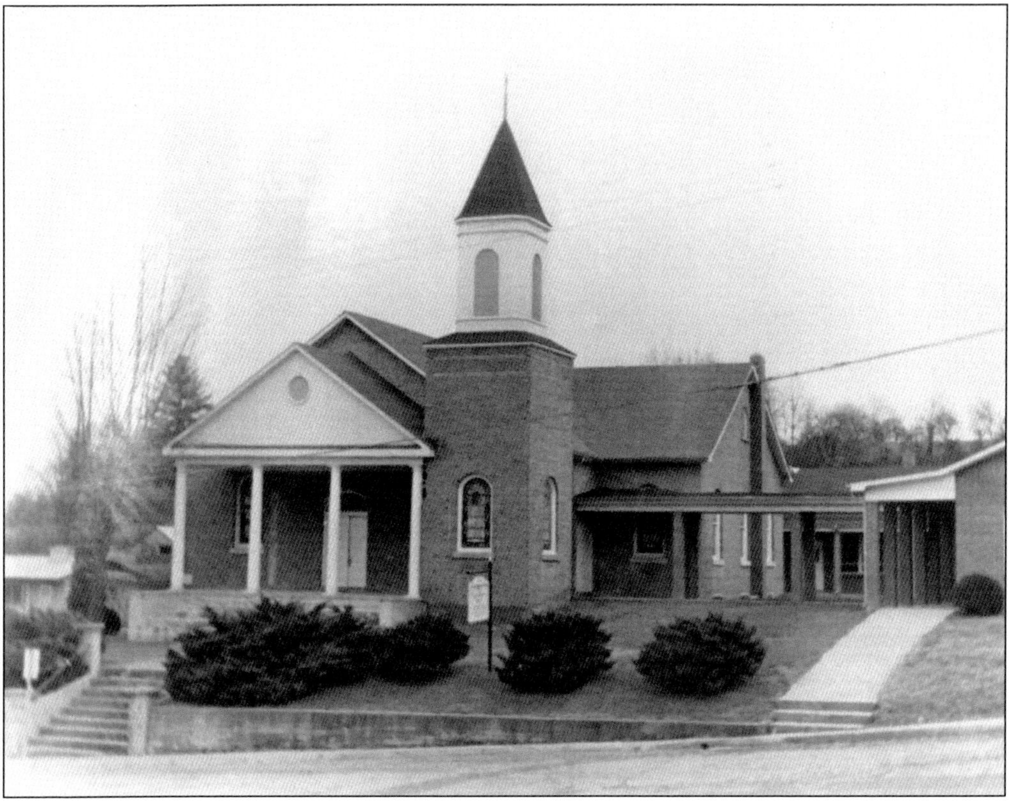

First Baptist Church of Clyde. This church started the Haywood Institute, a distinguished boarding school that prepared young men and women for college. Located across the street from the church, the institute operated from 1893 to 1927 and could accommodate about 200 students, who studied history, science, math, English, Latin, music, and home economics. The main dormitories have been torn down, but the brick building offices still stand along Charles Street. (Courtesy of the Town of Clyde.)

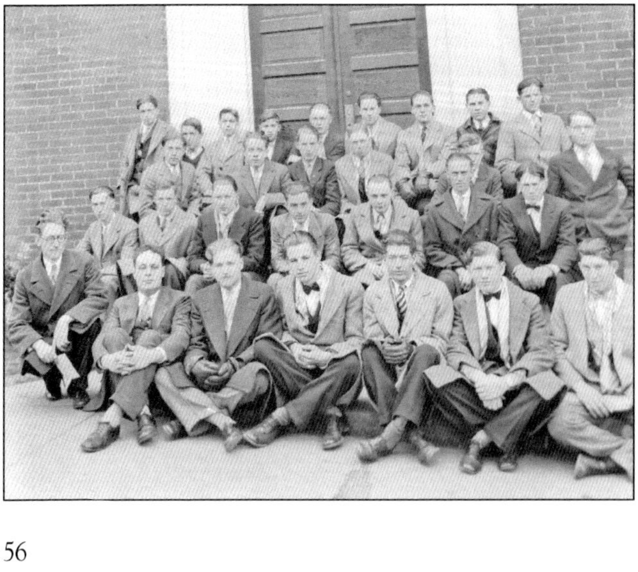

Sunday School. Members of the adult Sunday school Barraca Class gather on the steps of First Baptist Church of Canton in 1929. The word "Barraca" comes from the Hebrew word for "blessing." It was a popular program among Baptist churches throughout the Southeast. This church's predecessor, Locust Old Fields Church, was Haywood's earliest church. Its cemetery rests at the top of Academy Street across from the present-day Canton public library. (Courtesy of Canton Historical Museum.)

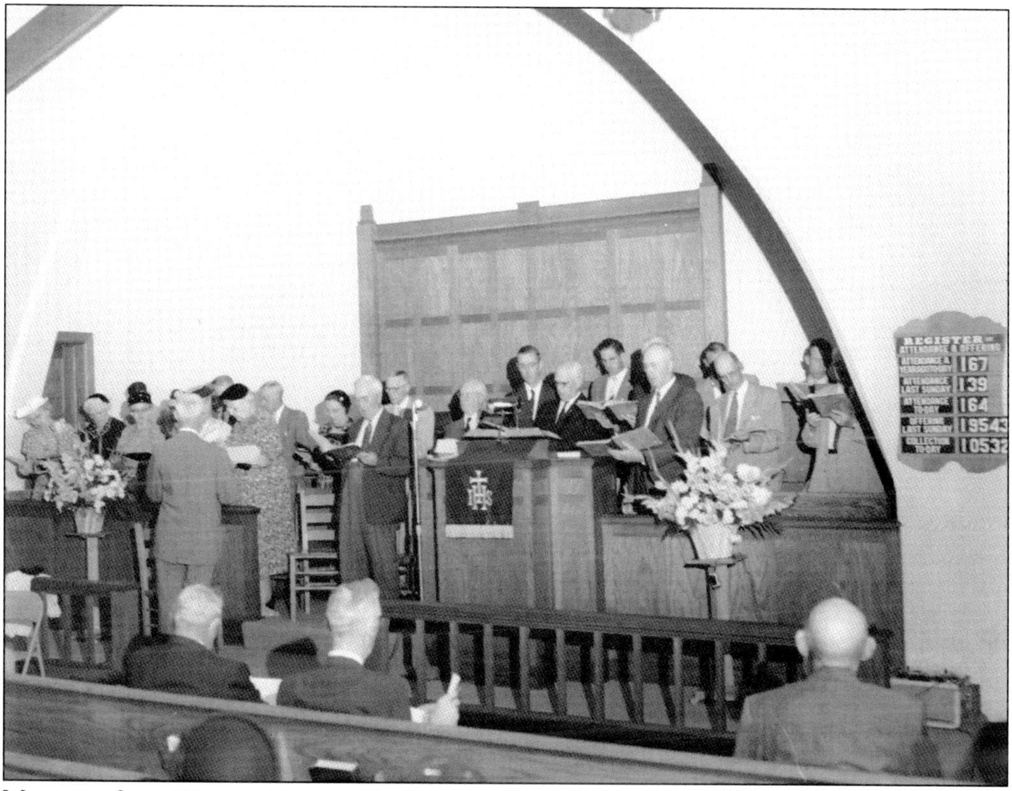

Morning Star United Methodist Church. First organized in 1825 as a Lutheran church by Germans settlers who came to the Dutch Cove community, Morning Star's congregation later converted to Methodism in 1866. The church is known for its shape-note singing choir. Members read specially shaped "do-re-mi" notes in their sheet music as a way of learning how to harmonize with congregational hymns. (Courtesy of Canton Historical Museum.)

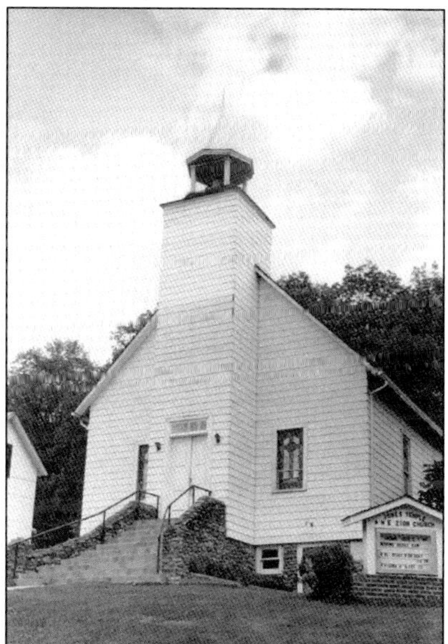

Jones Temple AME Zion Church. This church, originally built in 1855, stood atop Green Hill but was moved to its present location on Pigeon Street, where it became a predominantly African American church. Green Hill is now a cemetery, one of the largest in the county. The Jones Temple building continues as the oldest church structure in the county. (Courtesy of the *Mountaineer.*)

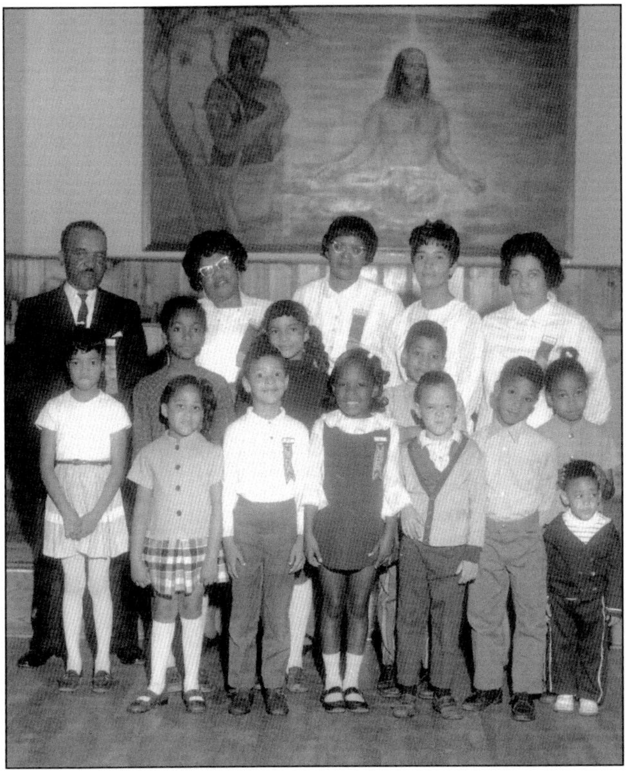

Congregation. This *c.* 1970 photograph includes members of the Pleasant Grove Missionary Baptist Church in Canton, a predominantly African American church founded in 1911. Services were held twice a month until 1967, when the church gained a full-time minister. (Courtesy of Canton Historical Museum.)

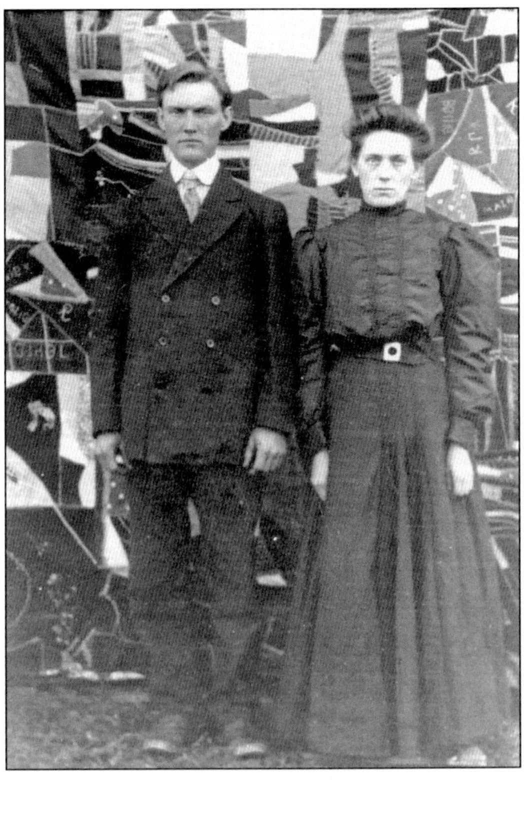

Crabtree Couple. Forest Ferguson (left) and his wife, Ada Kirkpatrick Ferguson (right), were both born in the same year (1880) and both died in the same year (1965). Forest was a farmer and a self-taught preacher in Baptist churches for 40 years. Ada was also active in local churches, serving as a song leader, Sunday school superintendent, and youth program organizer. Note the crazy quilt pattern used as a backdrop. (Courtesy of Clarine Best.)

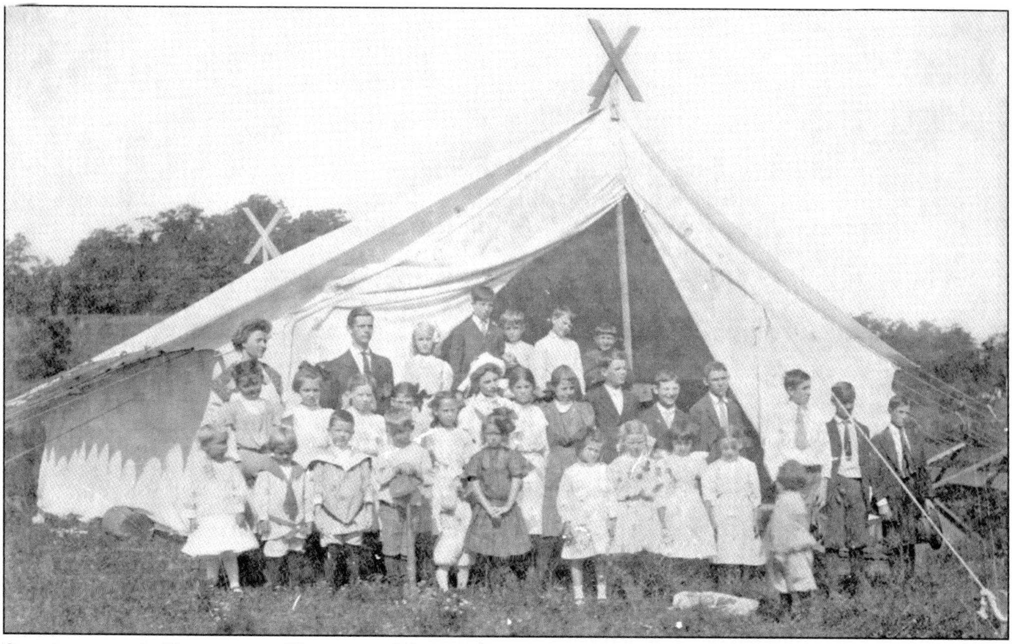

St. Andrew's Episcopal Church. The Holy Innocents Mission School formed in Fiberville in 1906 to provide public schooling and Sunday worship for the families of the Champion Fibre Company. It was called "Holy Innocents" because most of those served were children. On July 22, 1923, the Episcopal church held its first service at its current location on Academy Street. The church's stonework came from nearby Sunburst. Wooden pews, the altar, and trusses were built by workers at the Suncrest lumber mill in Sunburst. (Courtesy of St. Andrew's Episcopal Church.)

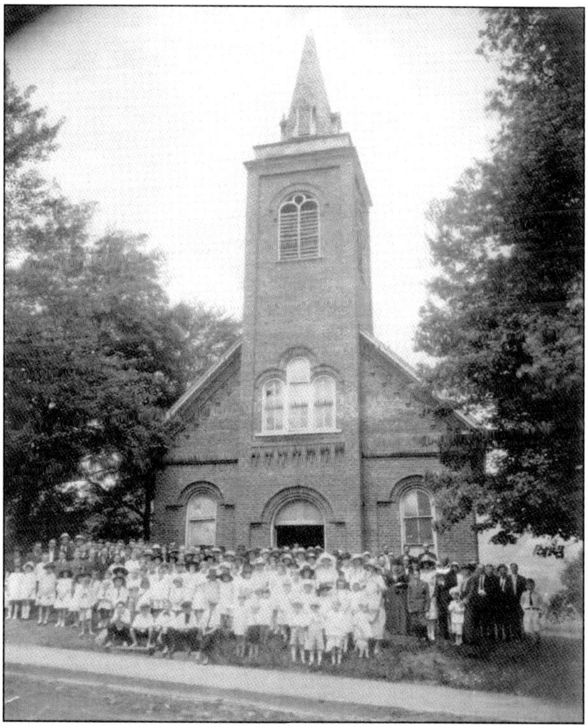

Church Growth. First United Methodist Church of Waynesville dates back to 1831, when it began atop Green Hill. The church later moved to its present site on Haywood Street, where construction of this brick structure began in the spring of 1881 and was completed in August 1884. As the congregation grew, this building was torn down in 1922 so that a newer, bigger church could take its place in 1924. (Courtesy of First United Methodist Church of Waynesville.)

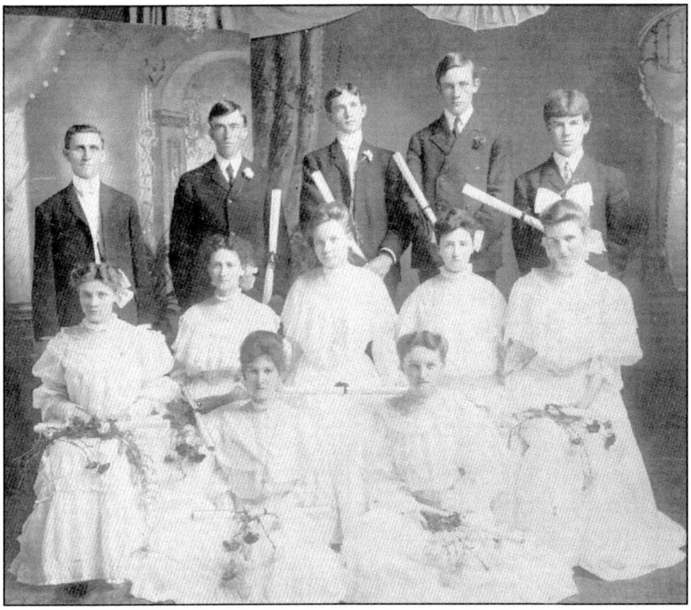

Waynesville High School. The graduating class of 1905 included, from left to right, (first row) Josie Hyatt and Lillie Satterthwaite; (second row) Clarine Lee, Sadie Miller, Bessie Sloan, Nellie Davis, and Amelia F. MacFayden; (third row) Prof. W. C. Allen, Millard Clark, Hiram Kirkpatrick, Charles Adams, and Lloyd Baker. Allen later became superintendent of Haywood County Schools and was a well-respected Haywood County author of local history. (Courtesy of Henry Foy.)

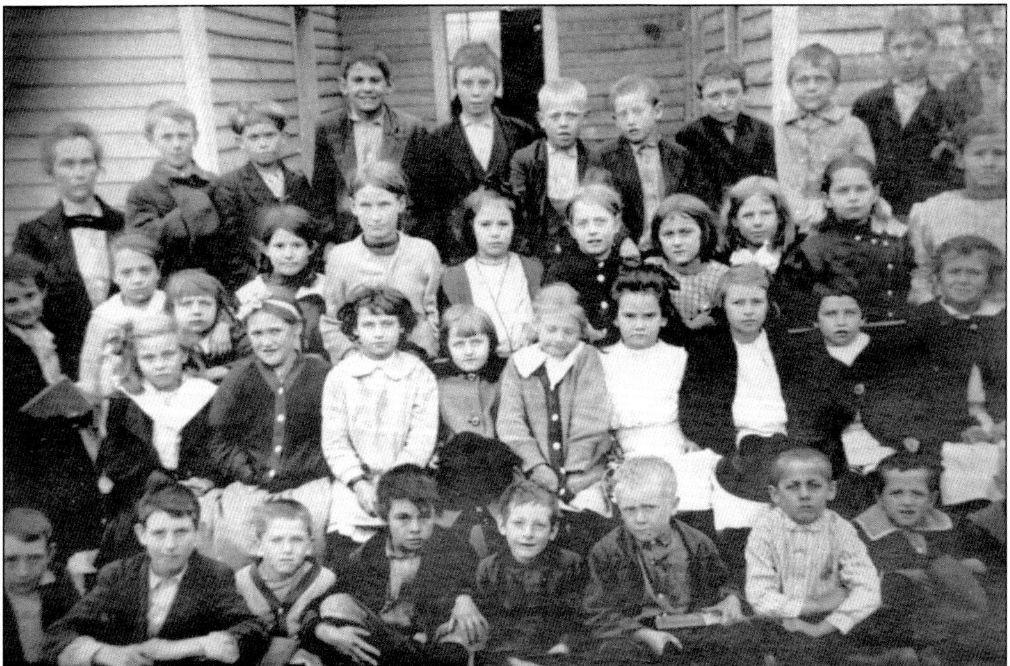

Clyde School. First and second graders gather for this 1912 class photograph. Mrs. Moss, their teacher, stands on the far left, third row. This would have been before the days of kindergarten, which had not yet been instituted in North Carolina's public schools. In the first row, second from right, is Amos Medford, later a Clyde alderman and historian. (Courtesy of the Town of Clyde.)

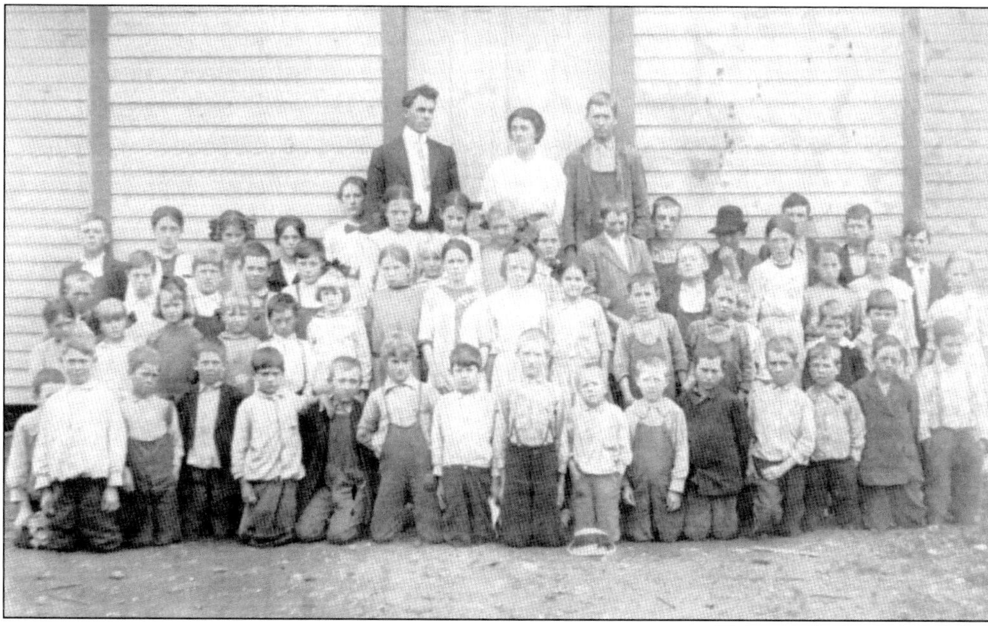

ALLENS CREEK SCHOOL. Dr. Nick Medford and his sister Myrtle Medford served as teachers for this school, located on the west side of Waynesville. Class sizes were quite large when compared to modern public schools. One or two teachers may have had an entire school to operate, with a variety of ages and abilities. (Courtesy of Bruce Briggs.)

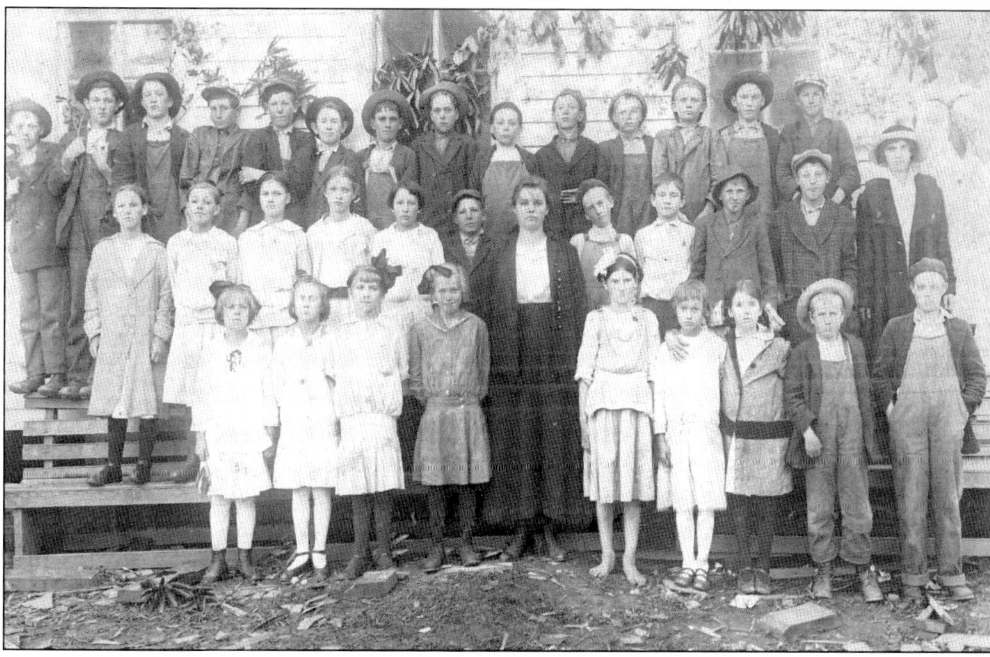

JONATHAN CREEK SCHOOL. This 1917 class photograph includes teacher Glee Clark Queen, center. Queen, the youngest of 14 children, was born and raised in the White Oak community. She boarded with the Hugh Sloan family in Waynesville while attending high school and graduated valedictorian of her class. After extensive schooling in college, she went on to teach and served as the county's welfare director from 1939 to 1963. (Courtesy of Betty Ferguson.)

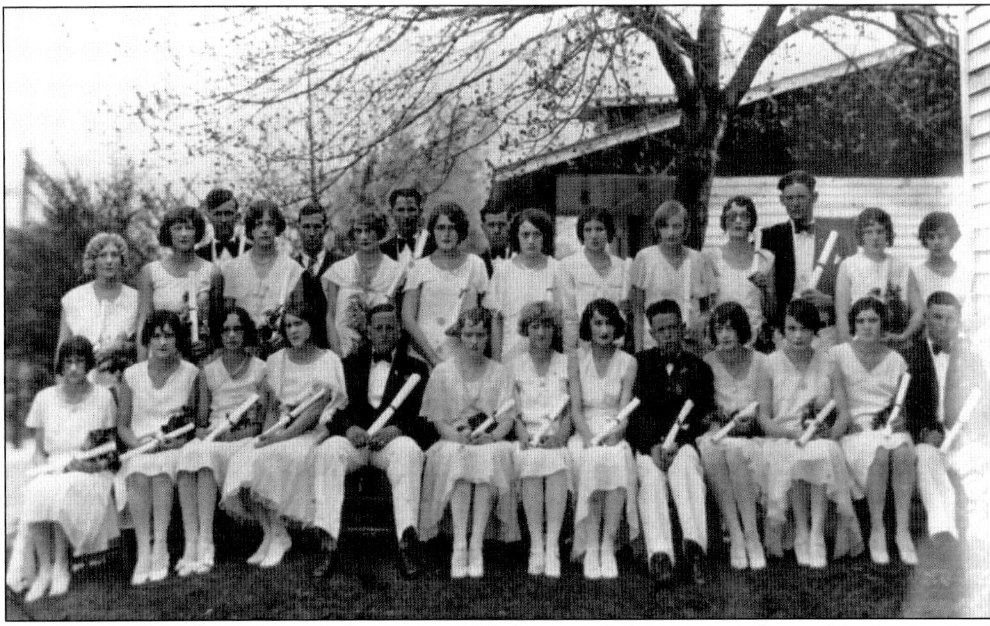

CLYDE HIGH SCHOOL. In 1918, the town of Clyde erected the county's first public high school along the Pigeon River where the present-day Central Haywood High School now stands. Clyde residents voted for a special tax to pay for a two-story brick building, which initially had 12 classrooms and an auditorium. Students came from Clyde and the neighboring Crabtree and Fines Creek communities. Due to increased enrollment, the auditorium was subdivided into classrooms. Pictured here is the graduating class of 1930. (Courtesy of Clyde Town Hall.)

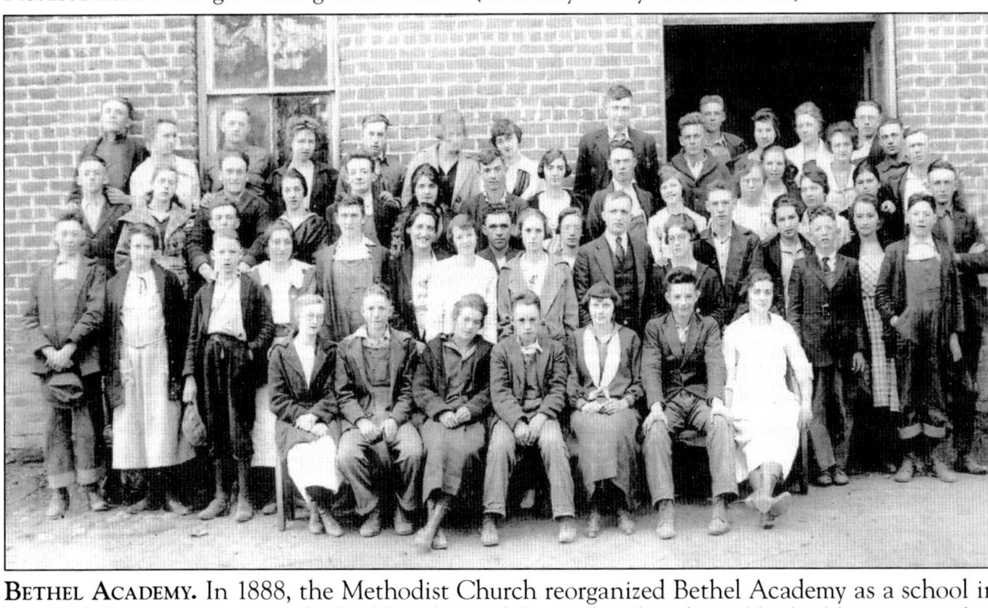

BETHEL ACADEMY. In 1888, the Methodist Church reorganized Bethel Academy as a school in the Bethel community, but the building burned the night after the public had been invited to view its completion. It was rebuilt using a new wooden frame on brick walls. By 1921, the county consolidated schools in Bethel, Garden Creek, and Cruso, giving free bus transportation to the Bethel High School. This photograph, taken in 1922, includes students on the grounds where Bethel Middle School now stands. (Courtesy of Doris Cathey.)

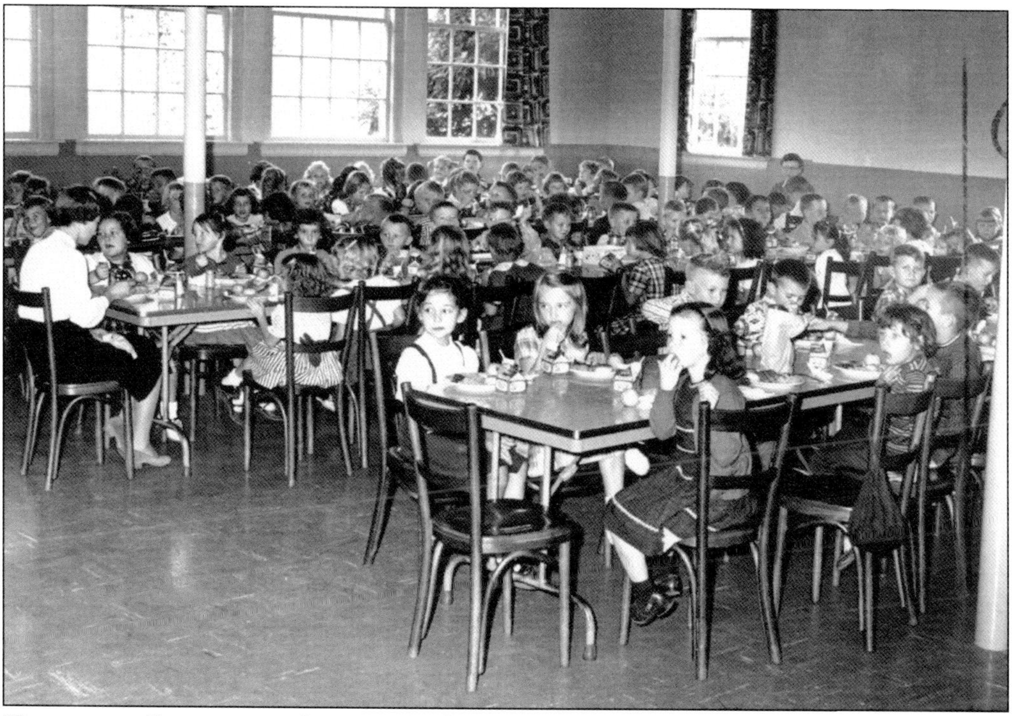

Hazelwood Elementary School. Students and teachers share a lunch in the Hazelwood Elementary School cafeteria after it had been remodeled in 1958. In 1923, a brick building with 10 classrooms opened on Virginia Avenue. Over the next few decades, several more buildings were added as enrollment grew. The aging school eventually closed in 2000, and a new Hazelwood Elementary opened in another location. The old Hazelwood school was renovated and reopened as the Folkmoot Friendship Center, the headquarters for the international Folkmoot festival. (Courtesy of the *Mountaineer*.)

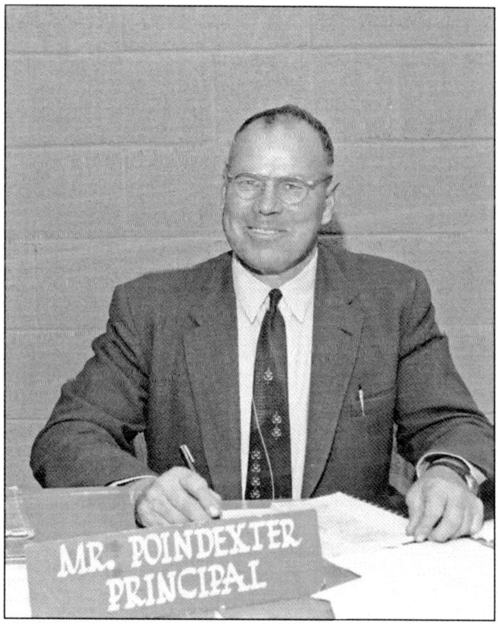

C. C. Poindexter. A well-known basketball and football coach at Canton and Bethel High Schools, Poindexter was also principal at Bethel High School before the county established two main high schools on either side of the county. His teams often proved to be tough opponents. (Courtesy of Canton Historical Museum.)

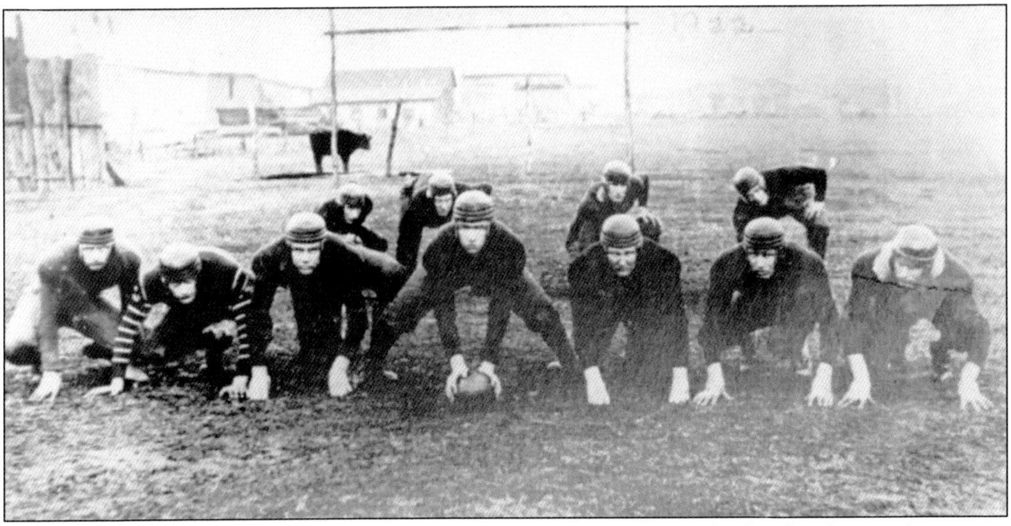

Canton Football. Canton has long been a sports powerhouse. Its high school teams have won state championships in football, wrestling, and basketball. Note the cow in the background of the above pigskin team photograph from 1922. Below, legendary Canton head football coach Boyd Allen, standing center at right, meets with his team in the locker room along with assistant Cliff Brookshire (left) back when Canton High School was located where Canton Middle School is today. In the late 1960s, when the county consolidated school districts and built two main high schools—Pisgah and Tuscola—a big cross-county rivalry began. Football games between the two schools continue to draw thousands. During one such contest, coach Allen had a heart attack and died at the game while coaching from the sideline. (Both courtesy of Canton Historical Museum.)

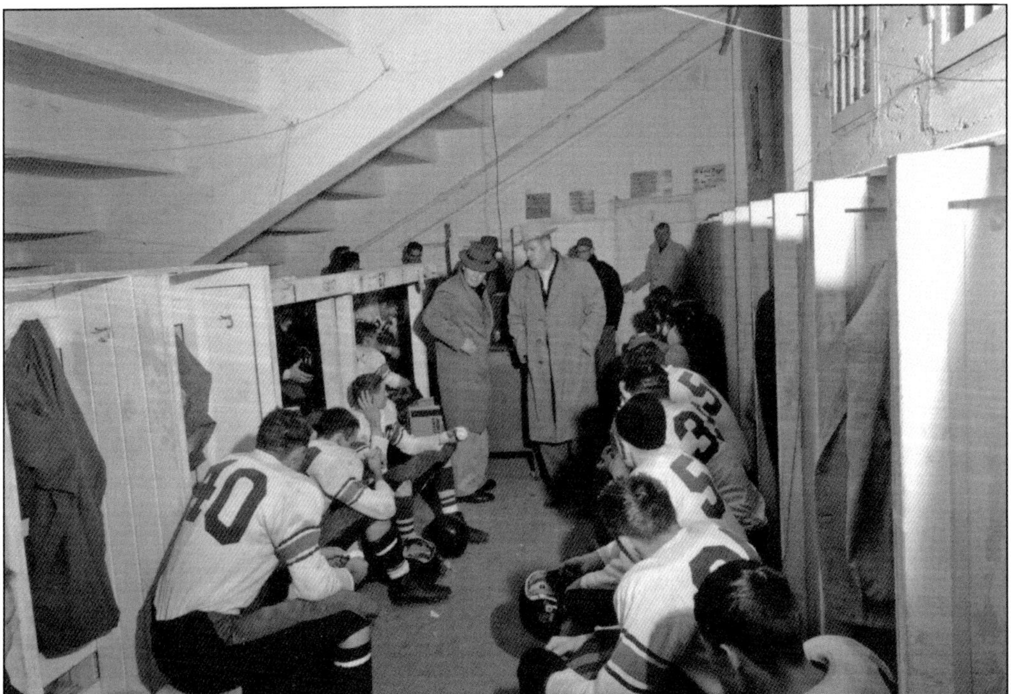

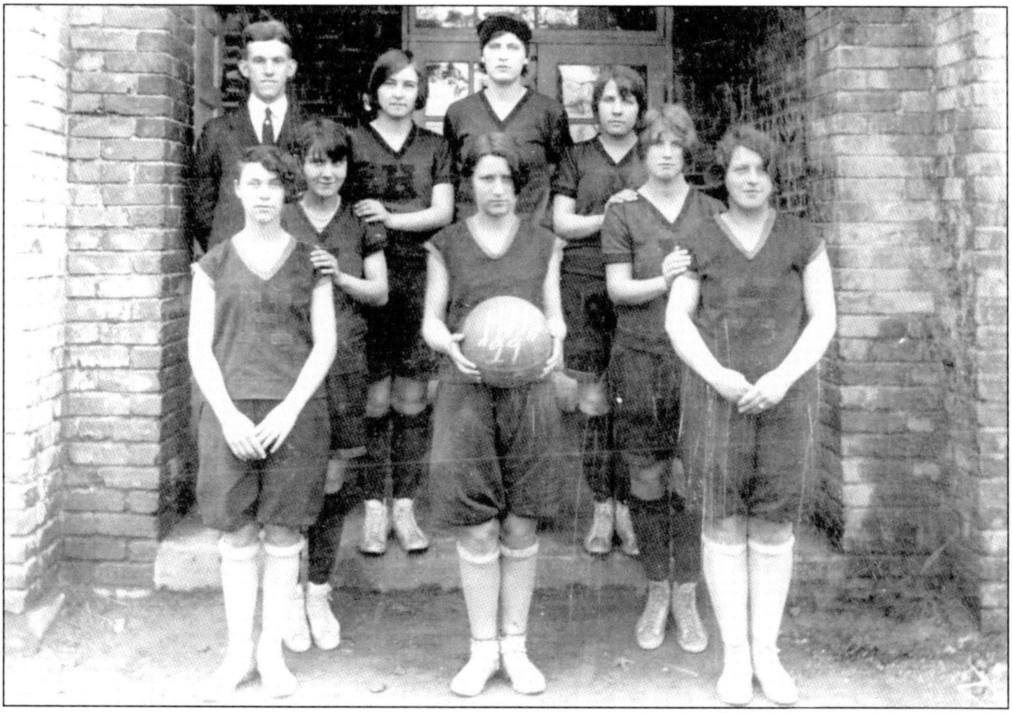

Basketball Team. In the early 1900s, local schools produced sports teams in basketball, baseball, and football. Long before the days of Title IX programs that allowed girls the same rights as boys to take part in sports, basketball was one of the few sports in which girls could participate. This team from 1929 represented Waynesville High School. (Courtesy of Clarine Best.)

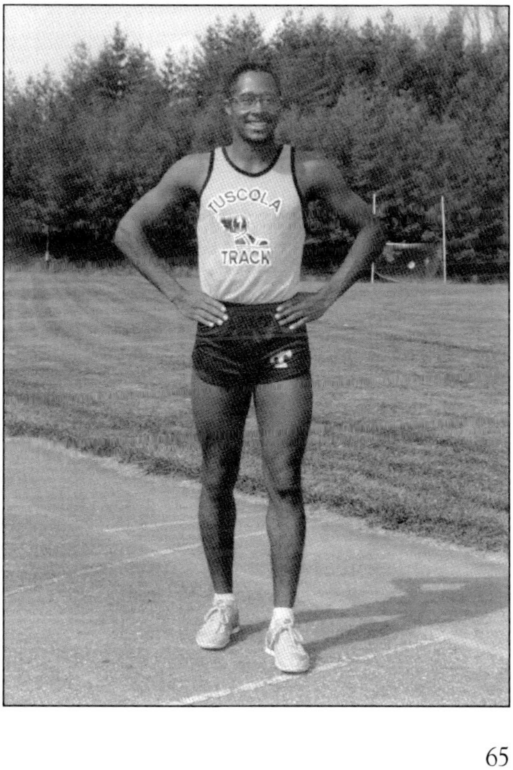

Tuscola Track Star. One of the most decorated athletes Haywood County has ever produced, James Martin was a two-time state champion in the triple jump and a two-time National High School All-American in track 1985–1986. At Tuscola High School, he set records in the triple jump, long jump, 100-meter dash, and sprint relays and garnered a staggering 185 first-place finishes. (Courtesy of Tuscola High School.)

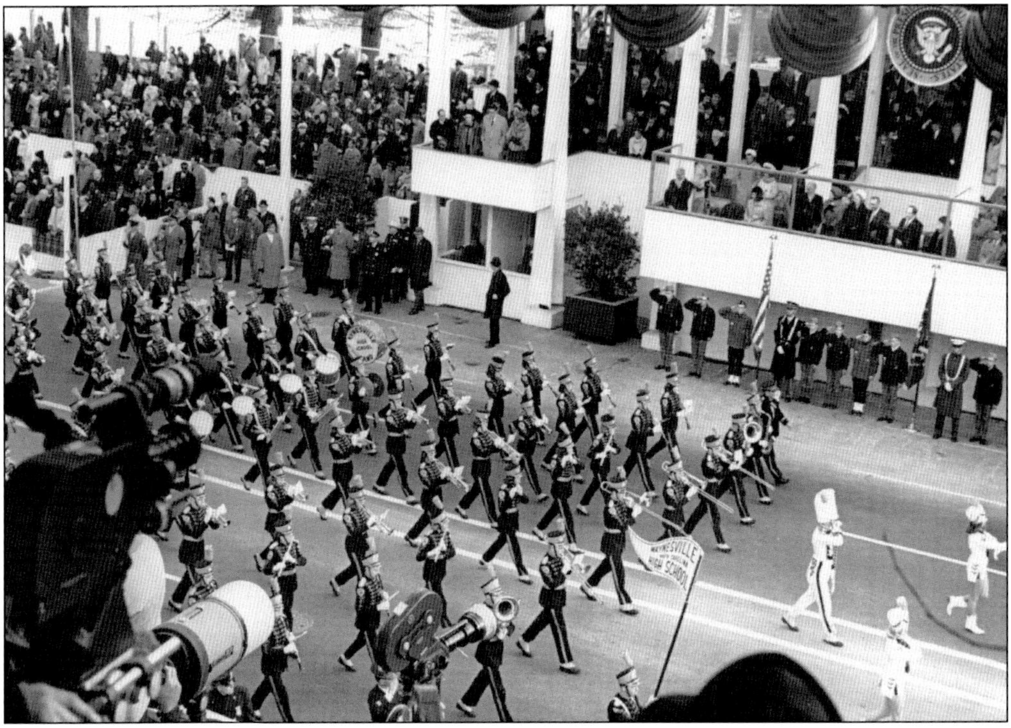

INAUGURAL PARADE. In 1965, the Waynesville High School marching band, under the leadership of band director Jim Crocker, marched and performed in the parade for the inauguration of Pres. Lyndon Johnson. Looking on from behind the glass-paned observation boxes in the first row are President Johnson and his wife, Lady Bird Johnson, (fourth and fifth from right) as well as former First Lady Jacqueline Kennedy (in the black hat, standing by herself three seats to the left). (Courtesy of Jimmy Crocker.)

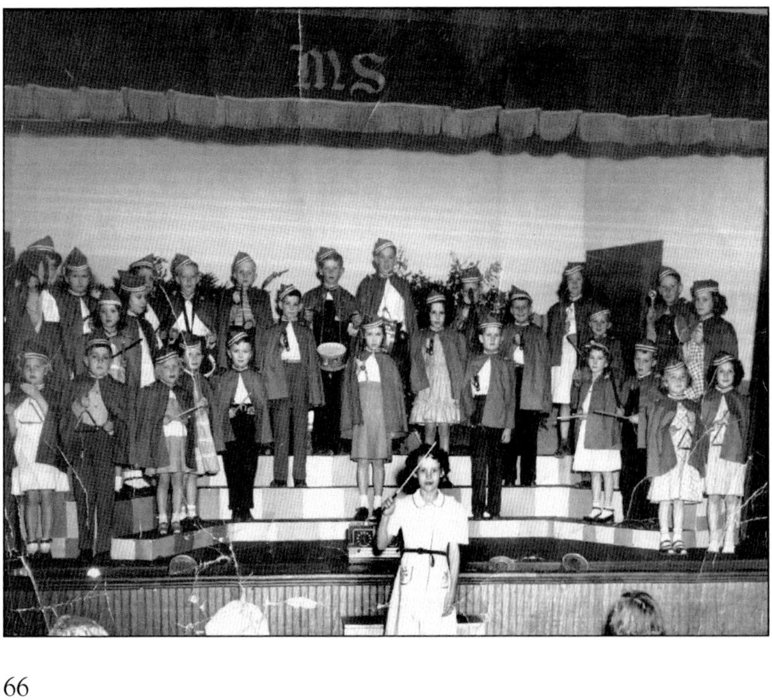

RHYTHM BAND MUSIC RECITAL. Elementary school students from the former Maggie Valley School (the old rock building, now Maggie Valley Town Hall and library) presented music recitals for parents and guests. Estelle Hyde Setzer Allison was their music teacher. (Courtesy of Betty Ferguson.)

Five

DOWNTOWN

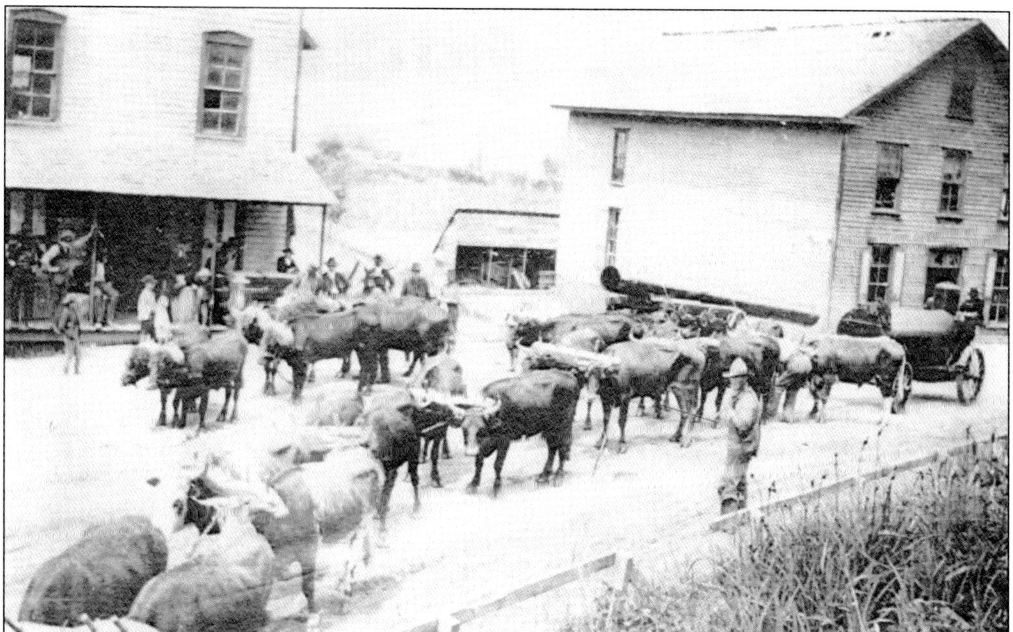

CANTON'S MAIN STREET. In the early days of Canton, a team of oxen coming down Main Street was certainly a noteworthy occasion. In this photograph from the 1890s, oxen pull a portable sawmill through town. (Courtesy of Canton Historical Museum.)

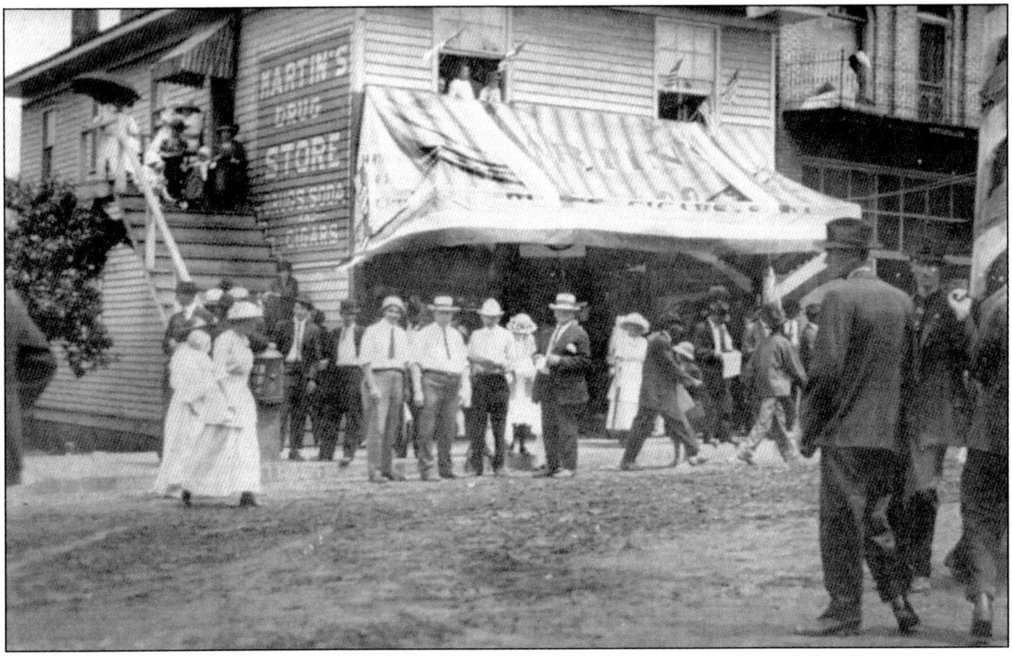

MARTIN'S DRUG STORE. When Dr. Walter S. Martin came to Canton in 1910, he opened this drugstore on Park Street, offering prescription drugs, medicines, candy, assorted household items, and a popular soda fountain. This photograph, taken on Independence Day 1910, shows the building before it was torn down around 1917 and rebuilt as a brick, two-story commercial structure. Martin rented out space to various businesses, including a jewelry shop, insurance office, barbershop, and restaurant. (Courtesy of Canton Historical Museum.)

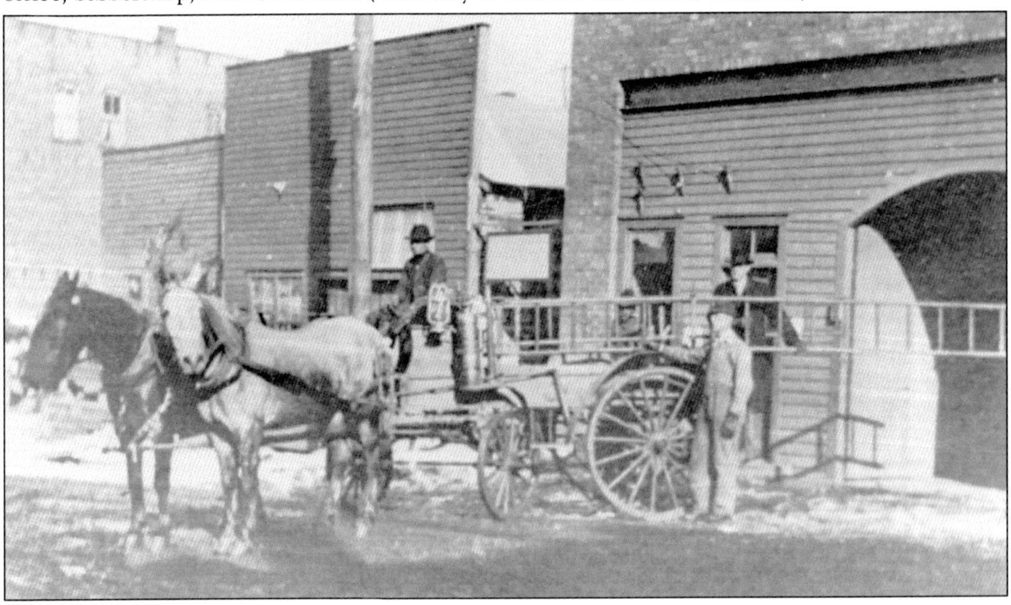

CANTON FIRE DEPARTMENT. In 1909, the town of Canton established its first fire station at 155 Main Street. By 1930, the department moved to a new site on 27 Church Street, where it upgraded to include a motorized LaFrance fire truck and boosted its membership to 20 volunteer firefighters under the leadership of fire chief C. L. Westmoreland. (Courtesy of Canton Historical Museum.)

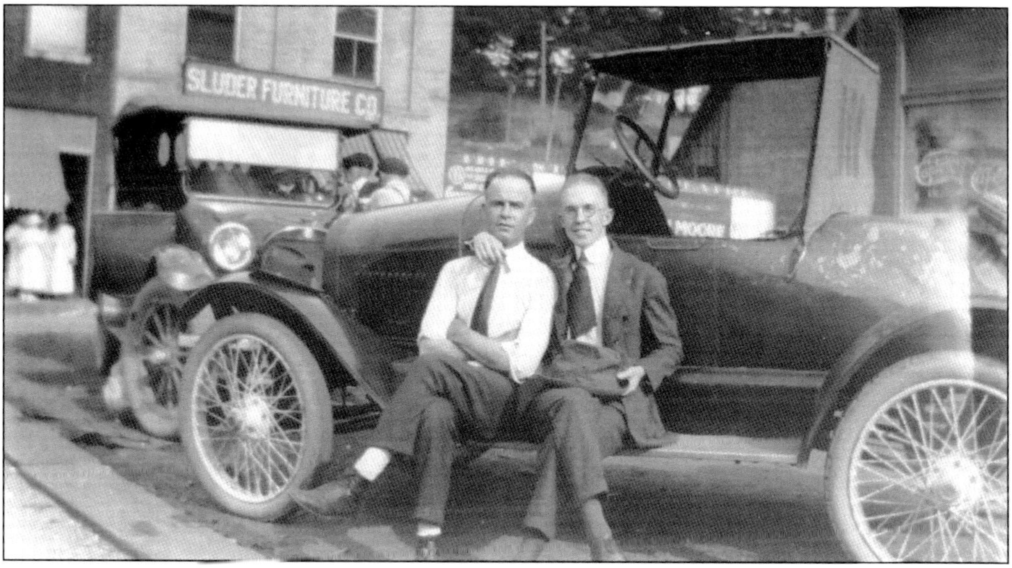

EARLY CANTON BUSINESSES. Clyde Freel (left), a founding partner in Canton's Sluder Furniture Company, and Dr. Carey Wells Sr. (right), a dentist, share a friendly embrace in the 1922 photograph above. In the background is the Sluder Furniture building, which began in 1915. Among its products were kitchen cabinets and steel oven ranges. The photograph below of Canton's Main Street (around 1905) could have been for a Fourth of July parade. The Hampton house appears on a hill in the upper left. Its owner, W. J. Hampton, came to Haywood County in 1873 and moved his family into the house about 1880. He expanded the size of the structure substantially. After his death in 1928, his daughter kept the house another 30 years before it was sold, demolished, and rebuilt as a supermarket. (Both courtesy of Canton Historical Museum.)

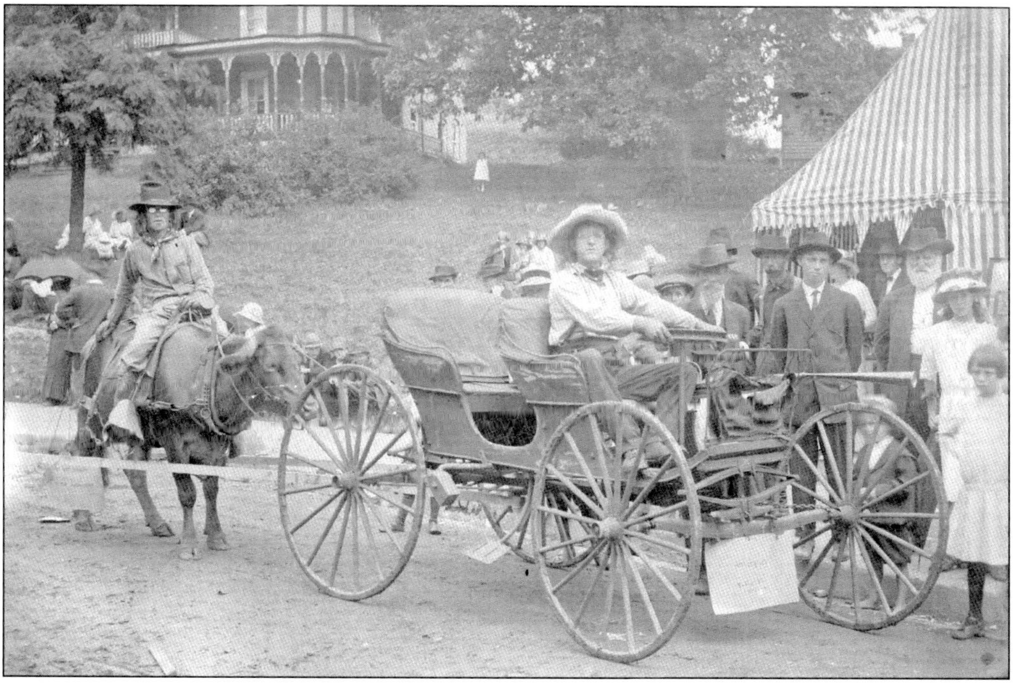

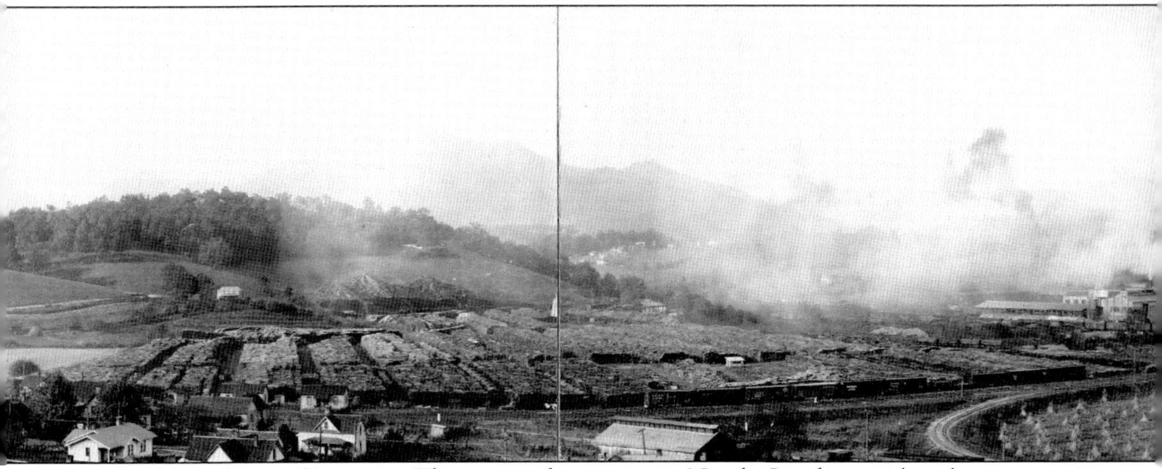

Champion Fibre Company. There were few towns in North Carolina with a downtown view like Canton had in the early 1900s. Note in the foreground the stalks of burley tobacco speared on sticks to look like rows of teepees. The scene illustrates the town's juxtaposed industries of agriculture and the paper mill. The huge mill not only proved to be a steady source of jobs. Under local leadership, the company maintained a strong local loyalty by painting and servicing its employees' homes, renting and financing their homes, donating to local charities and civic organizations, and establishing the town's wastewater treatment plant. Over the years, Champion played a major role in the economic and environmental landscape of the region. In addition to its property in Canton, Champion owned tens of thousands of acres of forestland in Western North Carolina to produce the wood pulp for the mill. In the 1930s, the company sold more

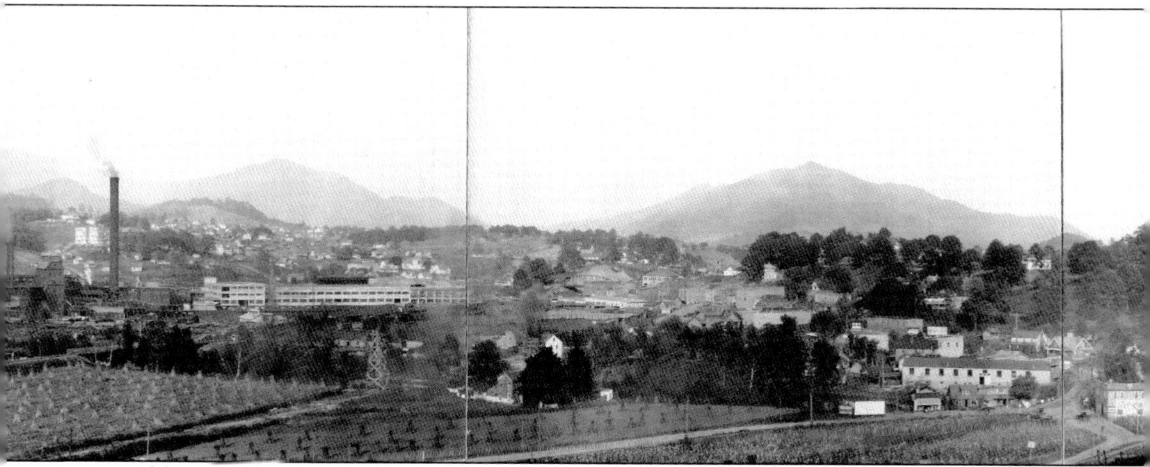

than 90,000 acres of its land holdings for $3 million to help create the Great Smoky Mountains National Park. While Champion maintained a sizeable workforce in Canton—employment at the mill peaked in 1959 with 3,338 workers—air and water pollution from the mill brought plenty of critics. Local residents refer to the lingering odor from the plant as "the smell of money." In the 1990s, a $300 million modernization process helped to cut down on the mill's pollution, though environmentalists continue to dispute the plant's detrimental impact on air quality. By the mid-1990s, Champion put the Canton mill up for sale. Employees organized to buy part of the stock in the mill in 1999 and renamed it Blue Ridge Paper Products. Then, in 2007, it was sold to a New Zealand–based corporation and was renamed once again as Evergreen Packaging, Inc. (Courtesy of Canton Historical Museum.)

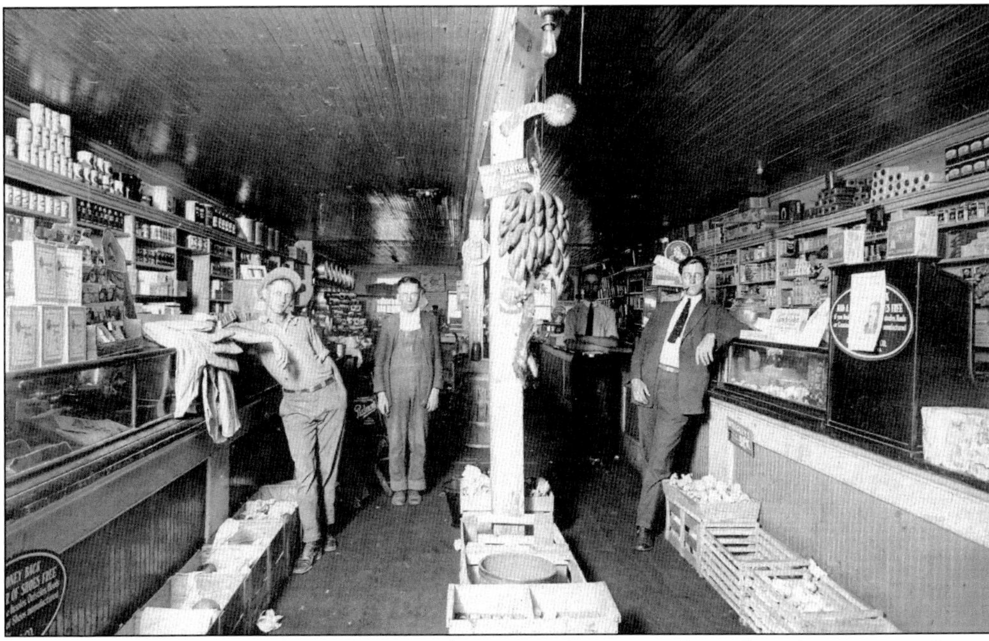

Haywood Restaurant. This eatery on Park Street in Canton in the early 1900s was one of many businesses that sprouted up after railroad lines came through the area and after a large paper mill brought an influx of families, salespeople, and entrepreneurs eager to find a new opportunity in a mountain town. (Courtesy of Canton Historical Museum.)

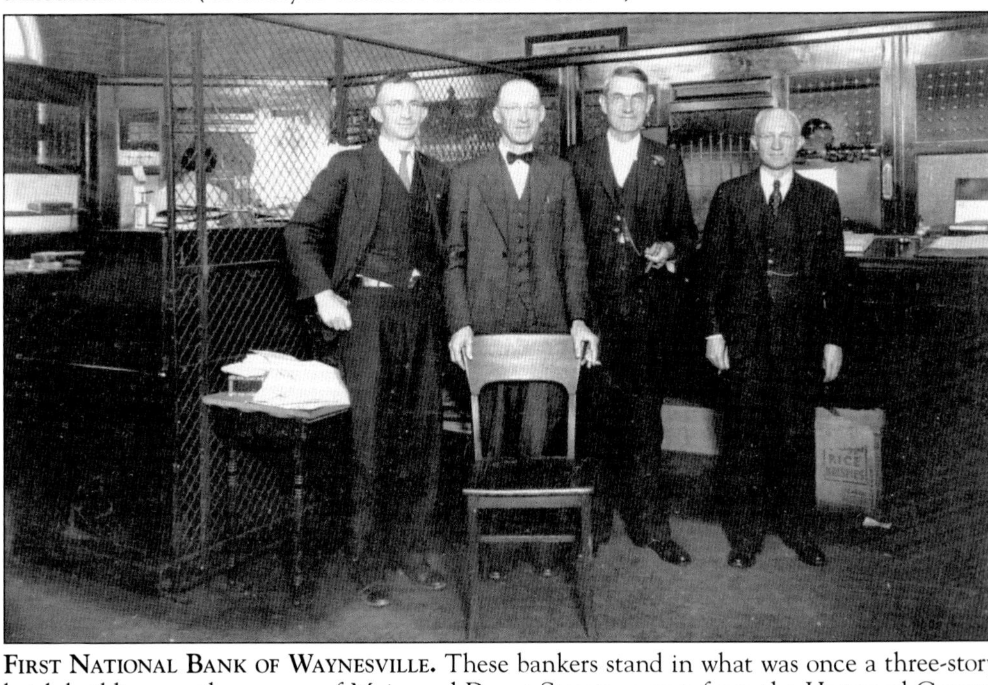

First National Bank of Waynesville. These bankers stand in what was once a three-story brick building on the corner of Main and Depot Streets, across from the Haywood County Courthouse. One of its presidents, Jonathan Woody, was a powerful businessman, county leader, and diligent community fund-raiser during World War II, drumming up support for numerous war bond campaigns. (Courtesy of the *Mountaineer.*)

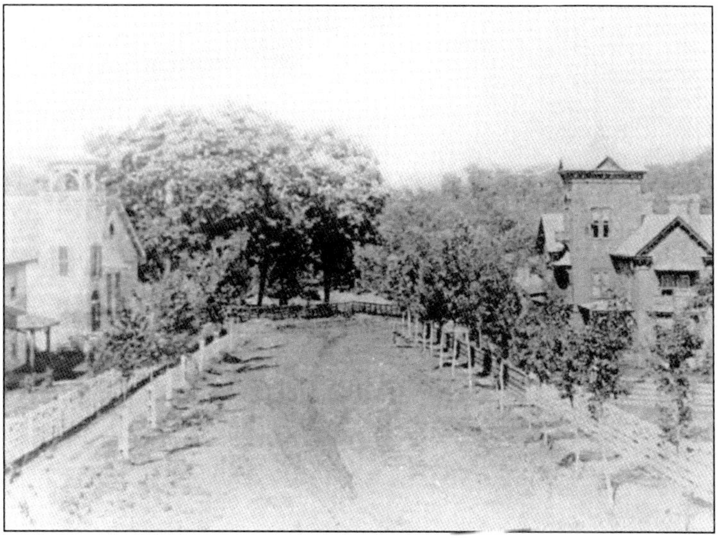

WAYNESVILLE'S MAIN STREET. This view looking north shows the W. L. Hardin home on the far left next to the First Presbyterian Church. On the opposite side of the dirt road was Alden Howell's home, which later became the site of the Gordon Hotel. Of these buildings, only the church remains. (Courtesy of Henry Foy.)

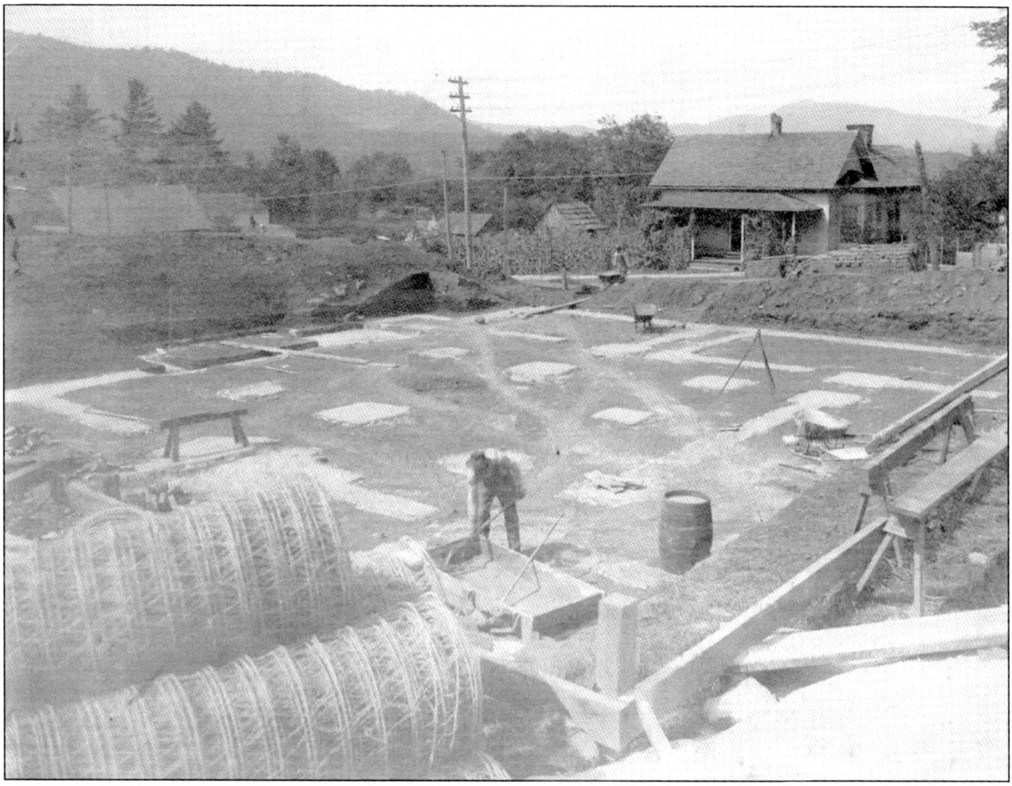

OLD WAYNESVILLE POST OFFICE. In this September 1916 photograph, work had just begun on a new Waynesville Post Office building on the corner of Main and Church Streets. The building, completed in the spring of 1917, would eventually become the Waynesville Town Hall. The house in the back right faces Church Street and is the present-day site for The Patio Bistro. (Courtesy of Henry Foy.)

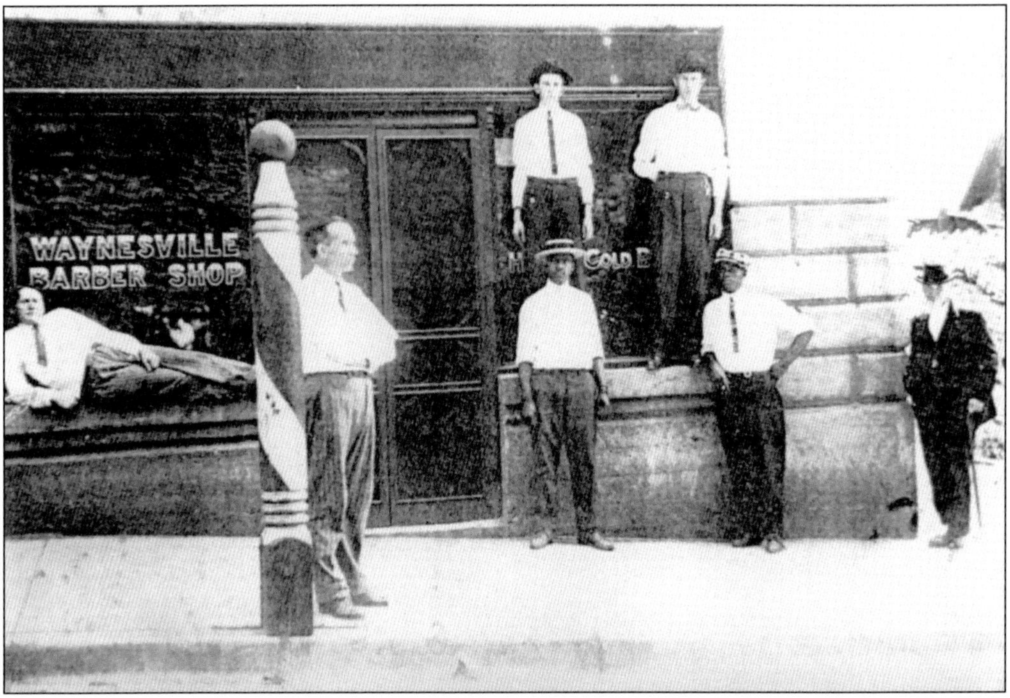

Waynesville Barbershop. Several barbershops operated in Waynesville in the early 1900s offering a warm shave and a fine haircut. Jack Welch, a slave, was thought to be the first African American barber in Waynesville. The red, white, and blue barber poles, prominently displayed outside barbershops, originated from the practice of bloodletting. Barbers would drain a sick person's blood and then treat the patient with long bandages that were wrapped around poles. (Courtesy of Henry Foy.)

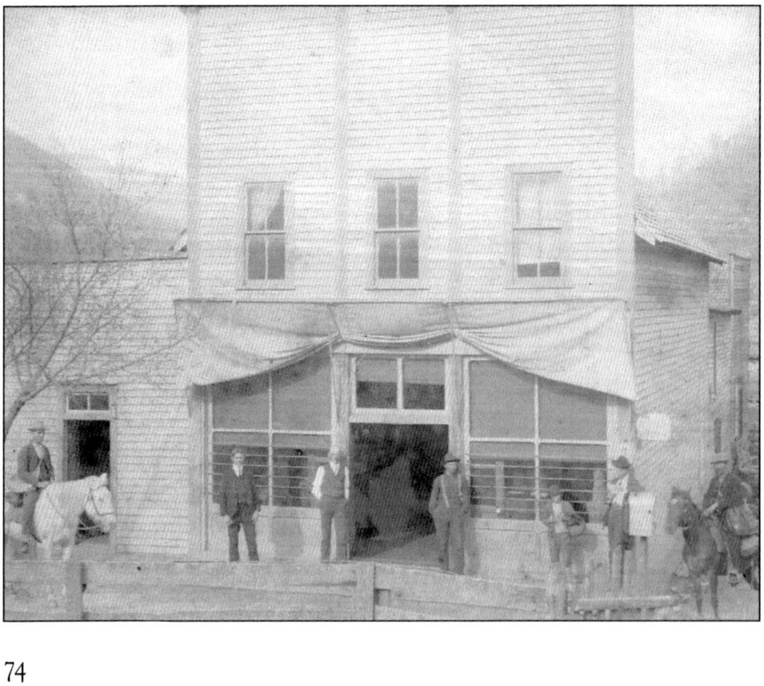

Lee and Mock General Store. A century before the days of Wal-Mart and box stores, the community general store, like this one on Waynesville's Main Street, sold dry goods, food, and supplies. Note the store's tall facade, which made the building stand out among others. (Courtesy of Henry Foy.)

DAVIS JEWELRY. John M. Davis opened a watch store in Waynesville after the Civil War, and his son, Jere Davis (left), took over the family tradition in 1900. Located on the corner of Main and Church Streets in the building where the present-day Kitchen Shop now stands, the upscale store sold gems, rings, necklaces, bracelets, watches, clocks, fountain pens, and silverware and also provided watch repair and engraving services. A 1916 advertisement proclaimed the store "kept the town of Waynesville on time." (Courtesy of Henry Foy.)

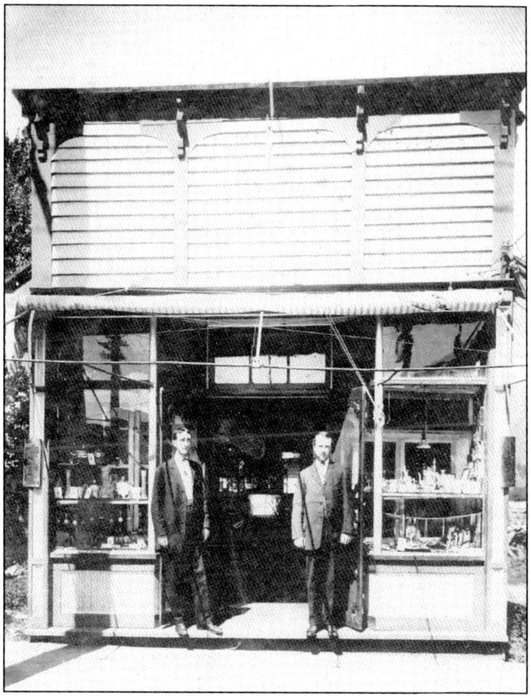

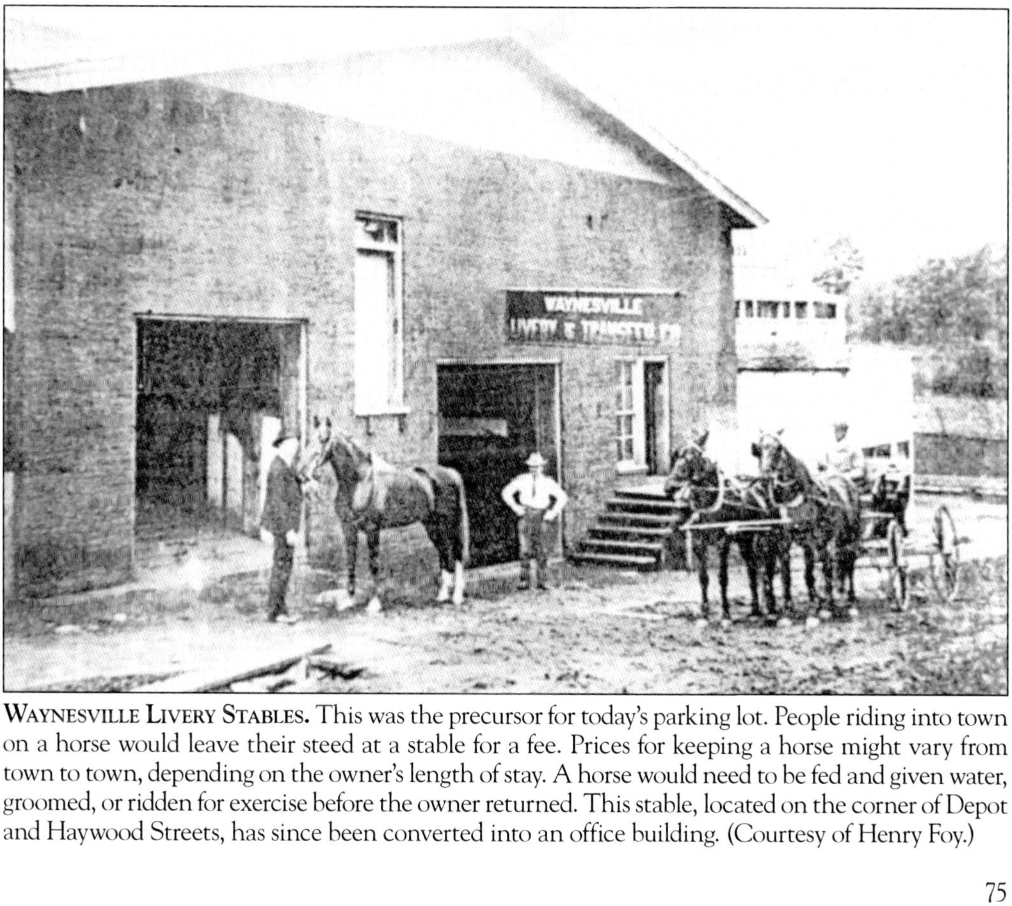

WAYNESVILLE LIVERY STABLES. This was the precursor for today's parking lot. People riding into town on a horse would leave their steed at a stable for a fee. Prices for keeping a horse might vary from town to town, depending on the owner's length of stay. A horse would need to be fed and given water, groomed, or ridden for exercise before the owner returned. This stable, located on the corner of Depot and Haywood Streets, has since been converted into an office building. (Courtesy of Henry Foy.)

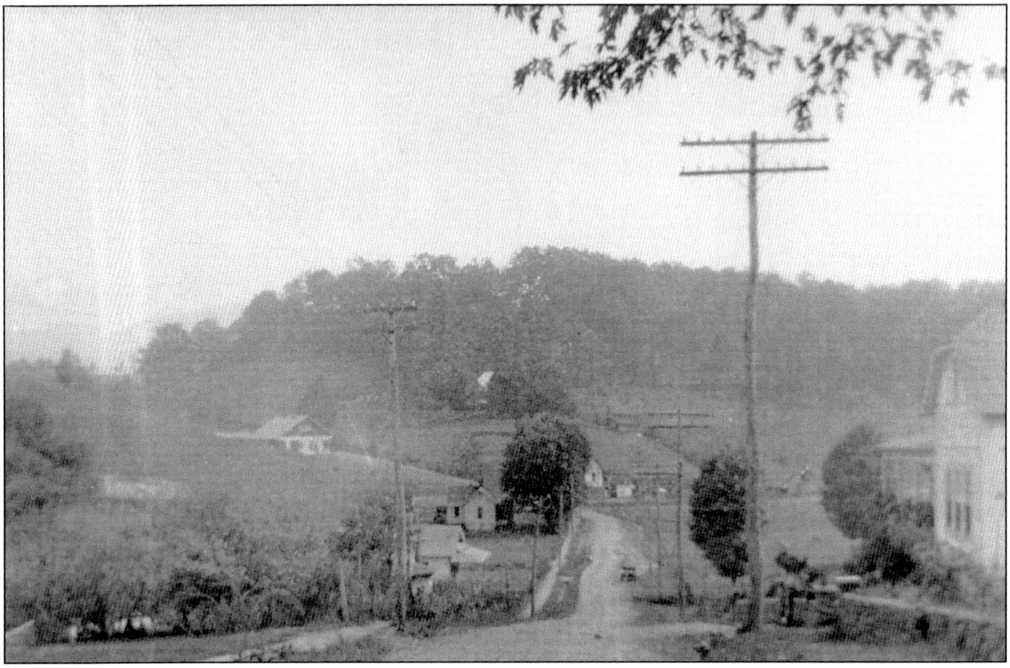

EAST STREET. In Waynesville's early years, the center of town was known as the Town Square, with the main intersection being Main Street running north and south and Cross Street running east and west. Cross Street was later renamed Church Street (running west from Main Street) and East Street (running east). This photograph from the early 1920s shows a view looking down East Street. (Courtesy of Henry Foy.)

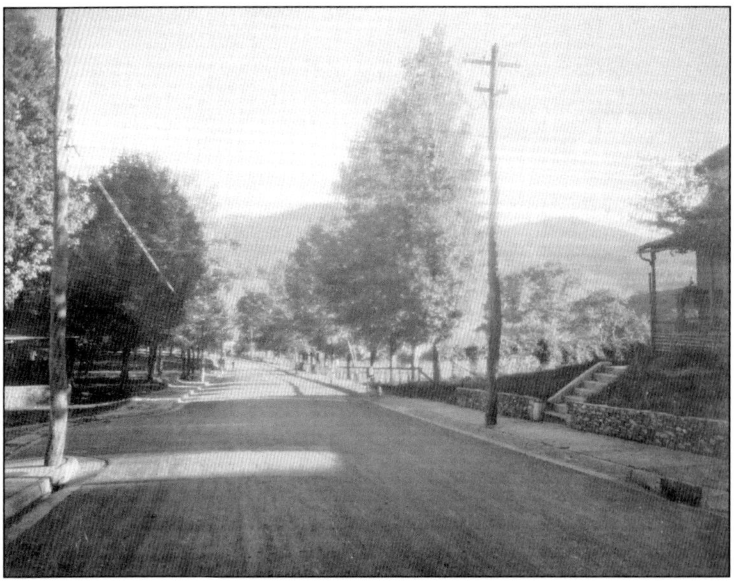

PIGEON STREET. This serene, tree-lined, dirt road in the 1920s ran east from South Main Street and later became U.S. 276, linking Waynesville to the Bethel community. Just down this street on the left was the county's first hospital, a building that no longer stands. (Courtesy of Henry Foy.)

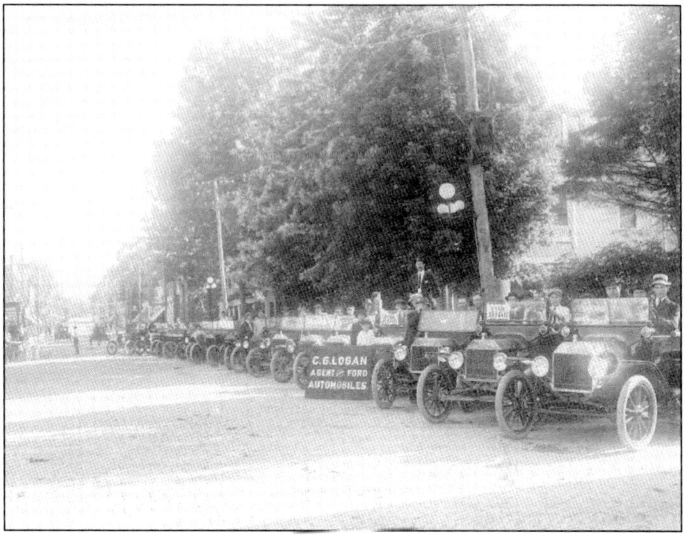

Ford Dealer. Curtis Logan ran Waynesville's first automobile dealership on Main Street in front of the present-day United Community Bank. This photograph, taken in 1914, shows the bricked street. For years, merchants and townspeople had pushed for improved street conditions, as inclement weather often created muddy holes that hampered vehicles traversing the street. (Courtesy of Henry Foy.)

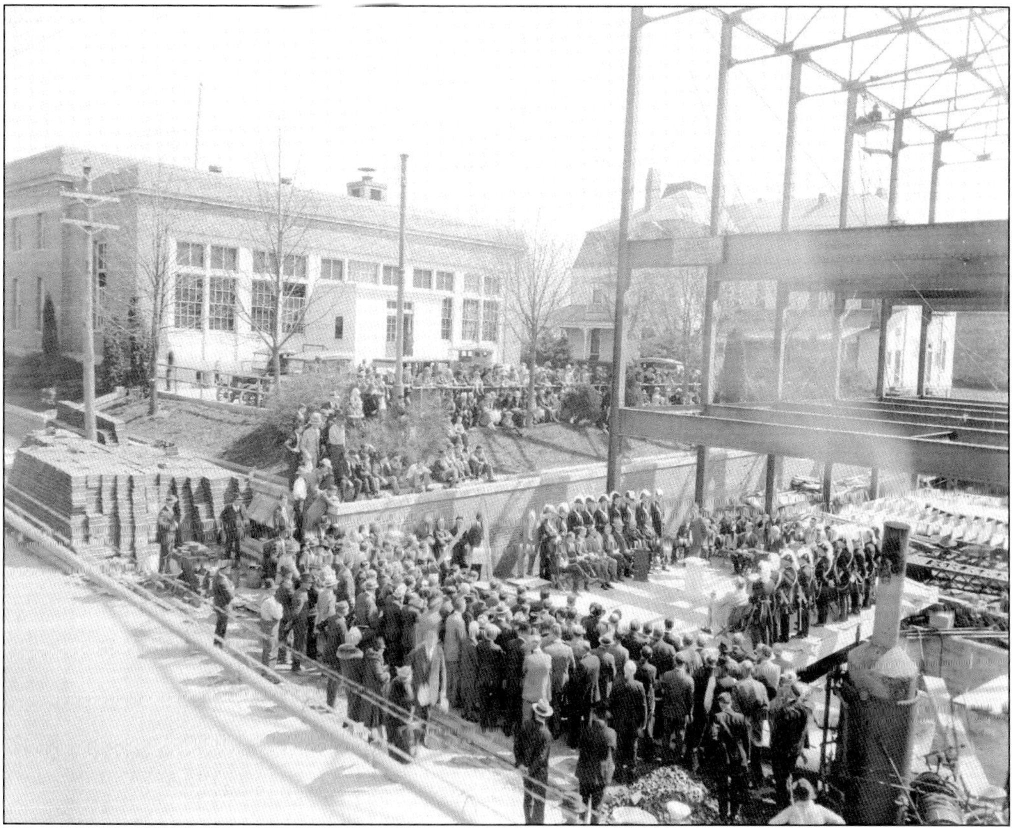

Masonic Temple. In 1927, Waynesville's Masons commissioned a four-story, neoclassical brick temple building on Church Street just before the stock market crash of 1929. A spacious, high-ceiling ballroom on the top floor went unused for years, but the bottom floors served as medical offices and once housed the Haywood County Arts Council. Recently renovated and under new ownership as the Gateway Club, the building features office space for business meetings, fine dining, and entertainment. (Courtesy of the Haywood County Public Library Digital Collection.)

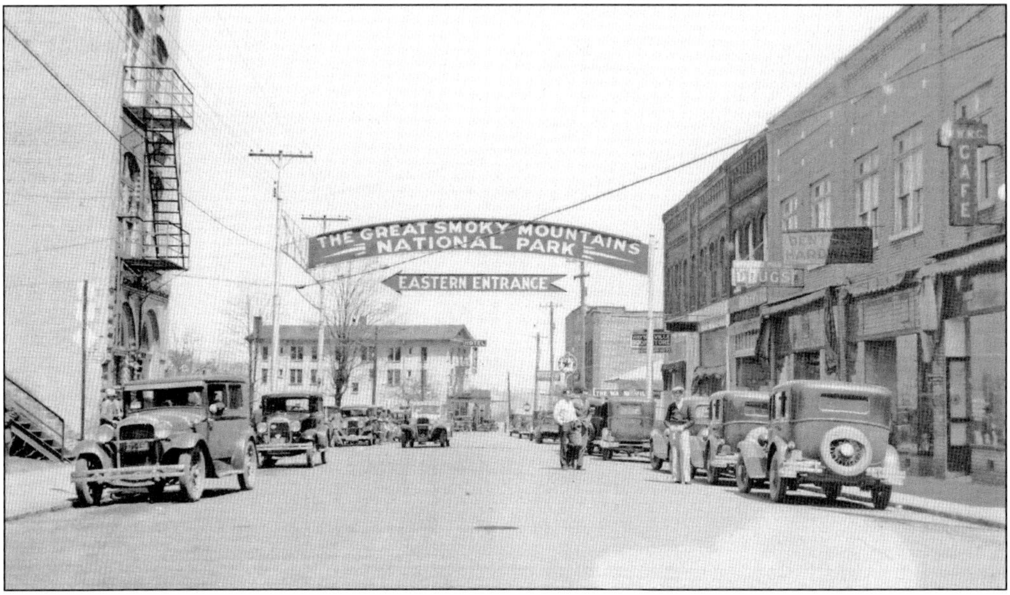

GATEWAY TO THE GREAT SMOKIES. The Great Smoky Mountains National Park officially opened in 1934, and in 1936, Pres. Franklin Delano Roosevelt was driven through downtown Waynesville when he came to speak at the park's dedication ceremony. The eastern entrance to the park was in Haywood County, so to help promote the tourist attraction, town officials had a sign erected across Main Street. It became a popular image for tourists. (Courtesy of Henry Foy.)

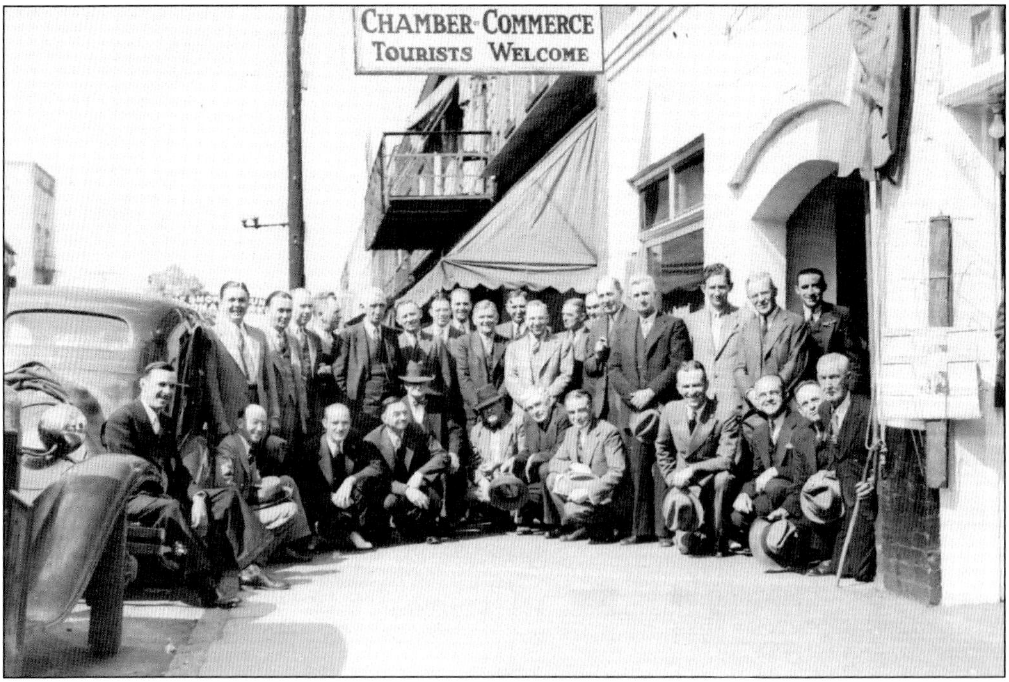

CHAMBER OF COMMERCE. Bullish on tourism and its influx of dollars to the local economy after the creation of the Great Smoky Mountains National Park, these sharp-dressed Waynesville businessmen of the 1930s met in front of what was once the American Fruit Stand on Main Street in Waynesville. (Courtesy of Henry Foy.)

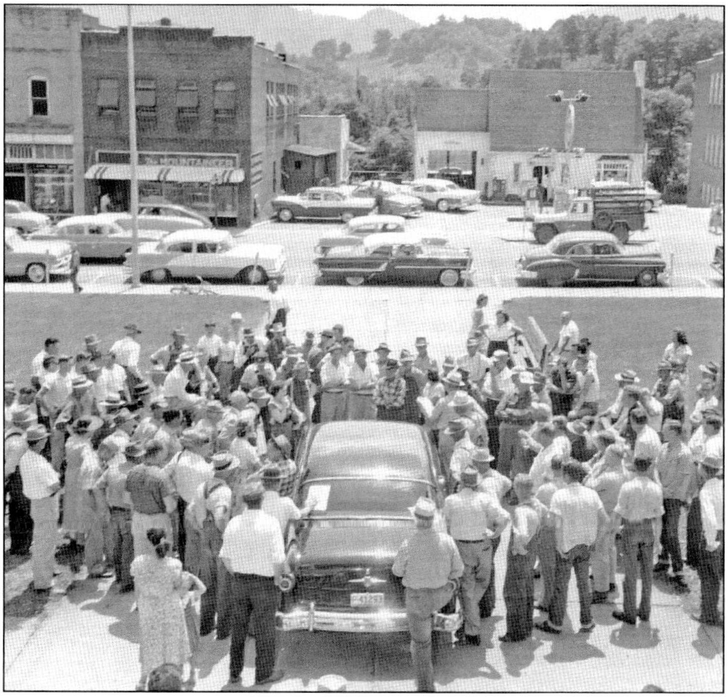

AUCTION. A crowd gathers on the Haywood County Courthouse lawn for a car auction. Across the street is the Pure Oil station, where motorists once bought gas for 25¢ a gallon. This property is now part of the *Mountaineer* newspaper office. To the left of the gas station is the *Mountaineer* building, and to the left of that was the Waynesville Hardware Store, owned by the Coffey sisters. (Courtesy of Henry Foy.)

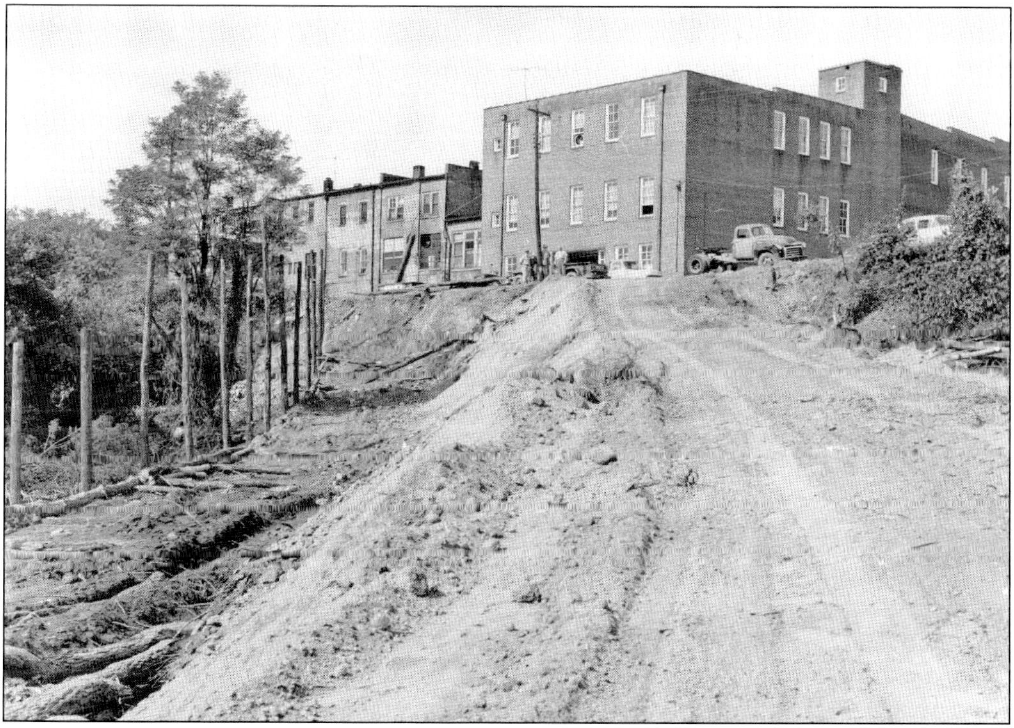

WALL STREET. In the fall of 1957, Waynesville expanded Wall Street to its present-day route as a parallel road on the east side of Main Street. This view faces the back side of the present-day *Mountaineer* newspaper parking lot in the upper right corner. The large building in the center was once Garrett Furniture Store. (Courtesy of Henry Foy.)

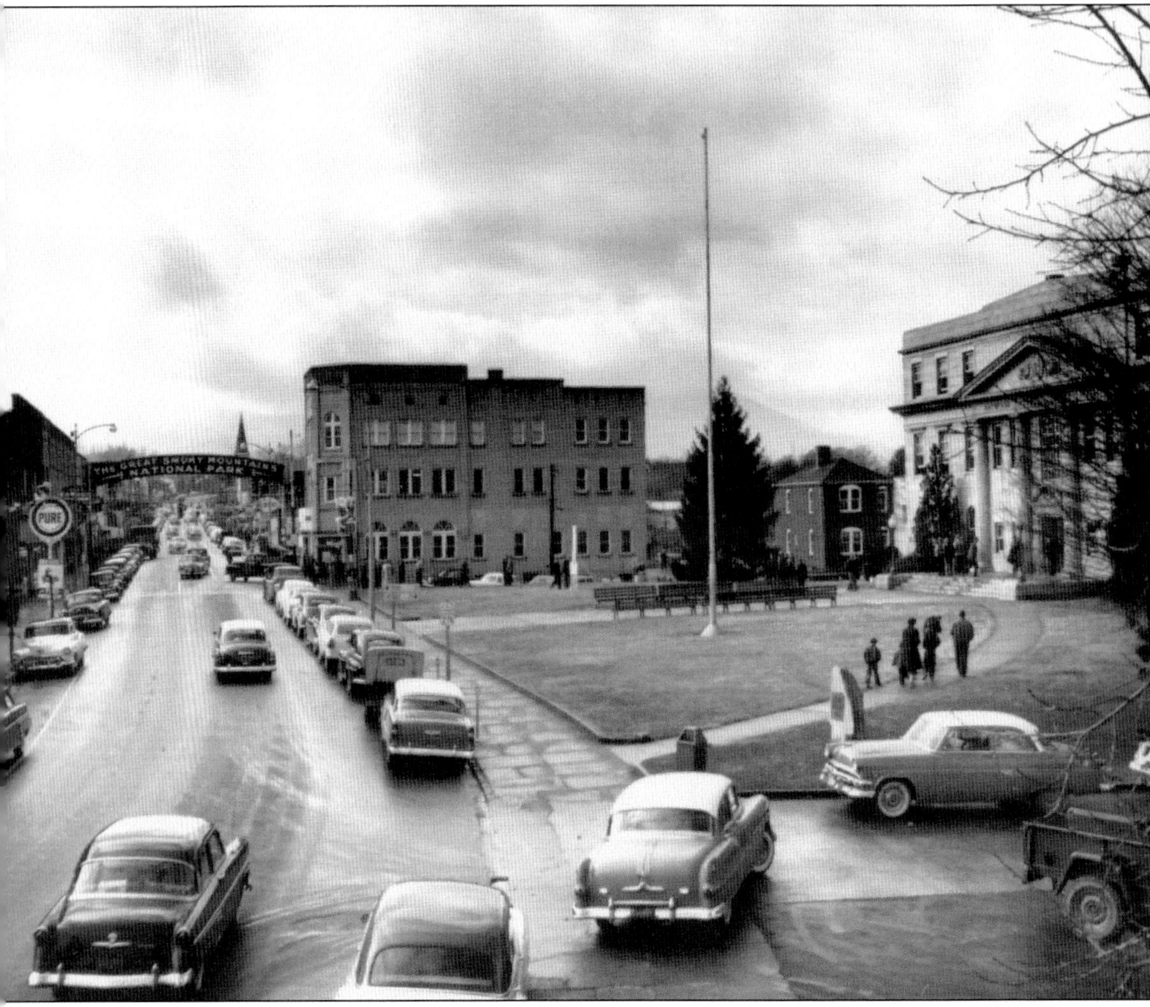

COURTHOUSE LAWN. It may be hard for some to imagine today, but the front of the county courthouse was once a wide-open space. Today tall maples and evergreens offer a peaceful shade to visitors and local residents who come for festivals, speeches, and special events hosted on the courthouse lawn. The first county courthouse opened in 1812 on the Town Square near the present-day site of the Waynesville Town Hall. A second courthouse was built on the corner of Main and East Streets. It lasted from 1831 to 1885. The next courthouse (1885–1932) was located on the corner of Main and Depot Streets. The present-day courthouse, pictured here in the 1950s, was erected in 1932. After a recent restoration process over several years, it was reopened in 2009. (Courtesy of Henry Foy.)

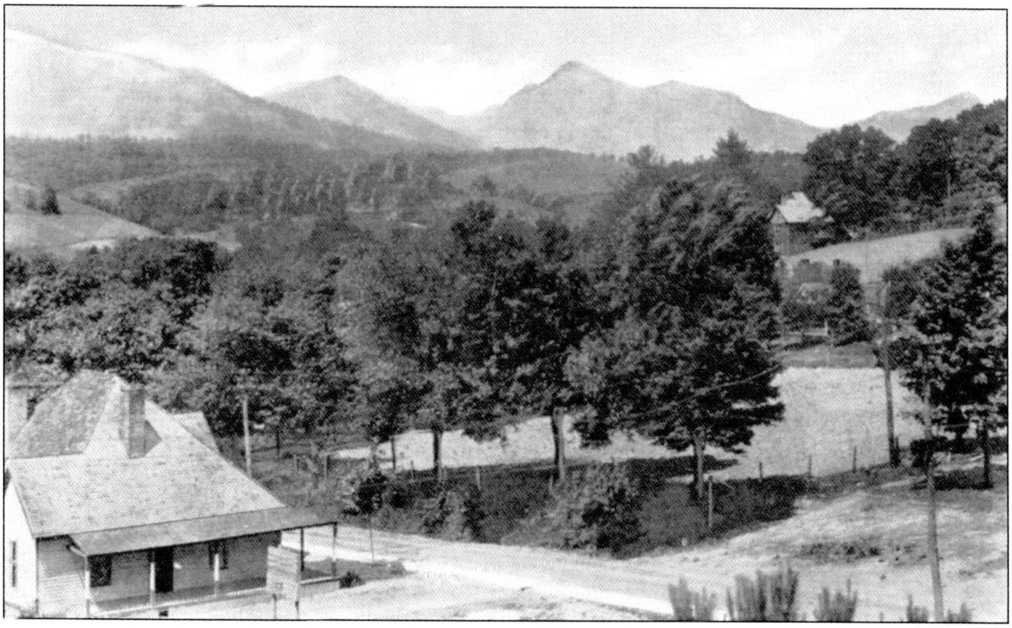

Downtown Clyde. Above, Clyde's Main Street, with its view of Buck Cove Mountain, was once little more than a dirt road lined with verdant trees and fields. Though its central district was not as developed as Canton or Waynesville, Clyde maintained a modest downtown over the years with stores like the one seen below. The woman second from left is Eve West Smathers, mother of Janice and Julian Smathers and wife of W. G. Smathers. (Both courtesy of the Town of Clyde.)

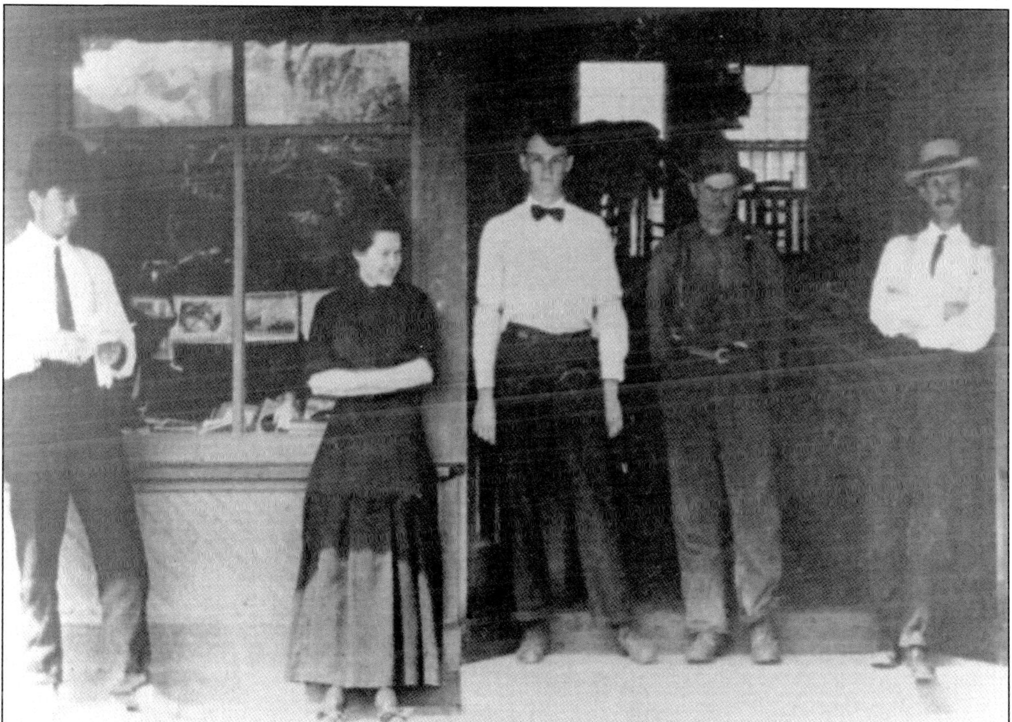

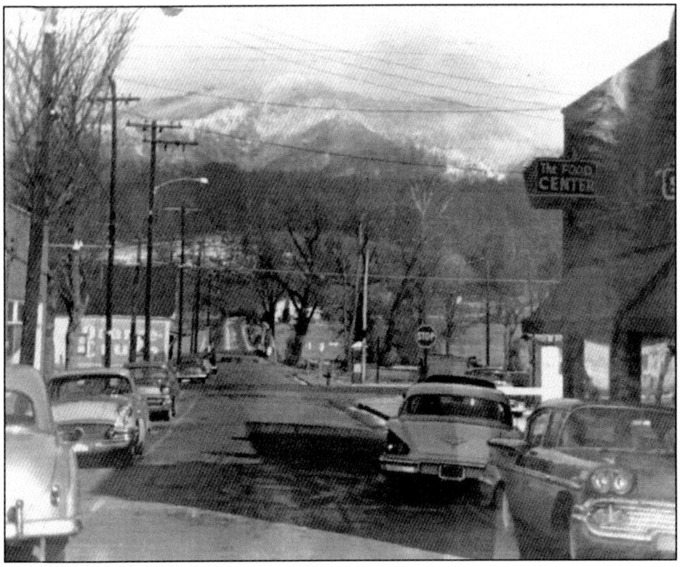

MODERN-DAY CLYDE. Trains arrived in Clyde in the early 1880s, and business steadily increased. In fact, Clyde got its name from a railroad executive. Nevertheless, it maintained a peaceful charm with surrounding mountains, as this view from the 1950s shows. (Courtesy of the Town of Clyde.)

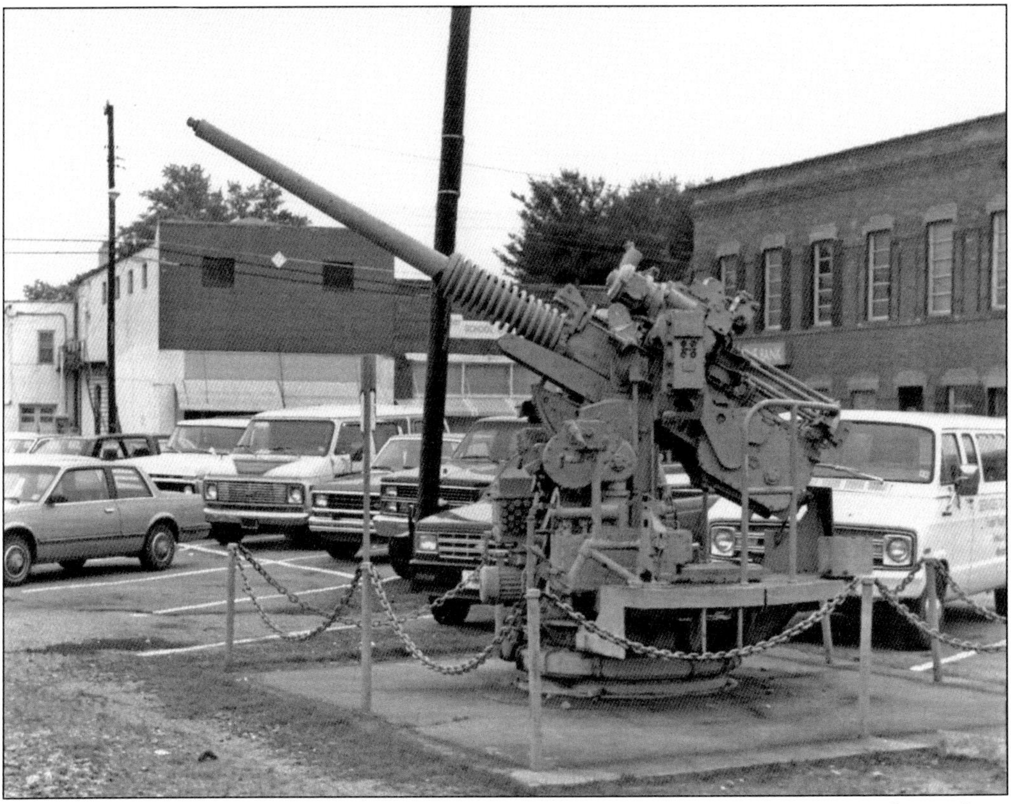

THE BIG GUN. One of the county's most notable landmarks, this 50-mm antiaircraft gun from Norfolk Naval Base was placed in the Clyde town square and dedicated on May 15, 1965, as a memorial to veterans who died in World War I, World War II, the Korean Conflict, and the Vietnam War. When people want to meet in downtown Clyde, they say, "Meet me at the Big Gun." Adding to the armed services theme is one of Clyde's most popular downtown businesses, Old Grouch's, a military surplus store. (Courtesy of the Town of Clyde.)

Six

BUSINESS AND INDUSTRY

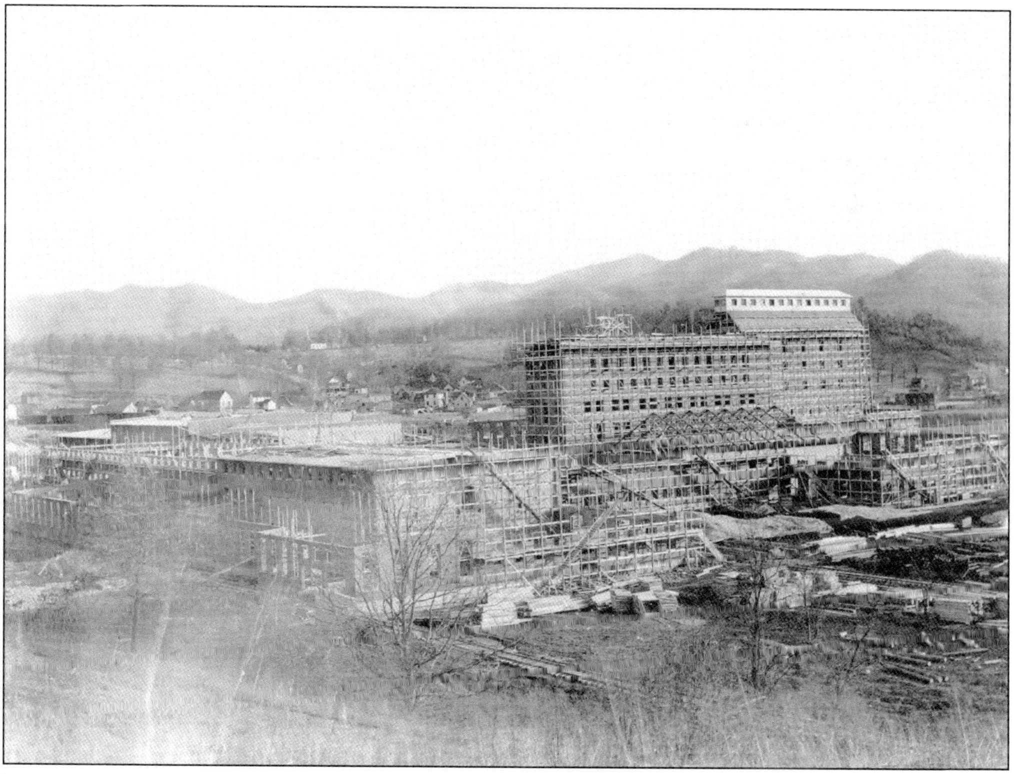

UNDER CONSTRUCTION. Peter G. Thomson, an industrialist from Ohio who established the Champion paper company in 1893, sought out new forests for his expanding industry. In Haywood County, he found plentiful timber and a site for a new paper mill. The mill's construction in Canton began in 1906 and was completed the following year, despite heavy rains that delayed work. (Courtesy of Canton Historical Museum.)

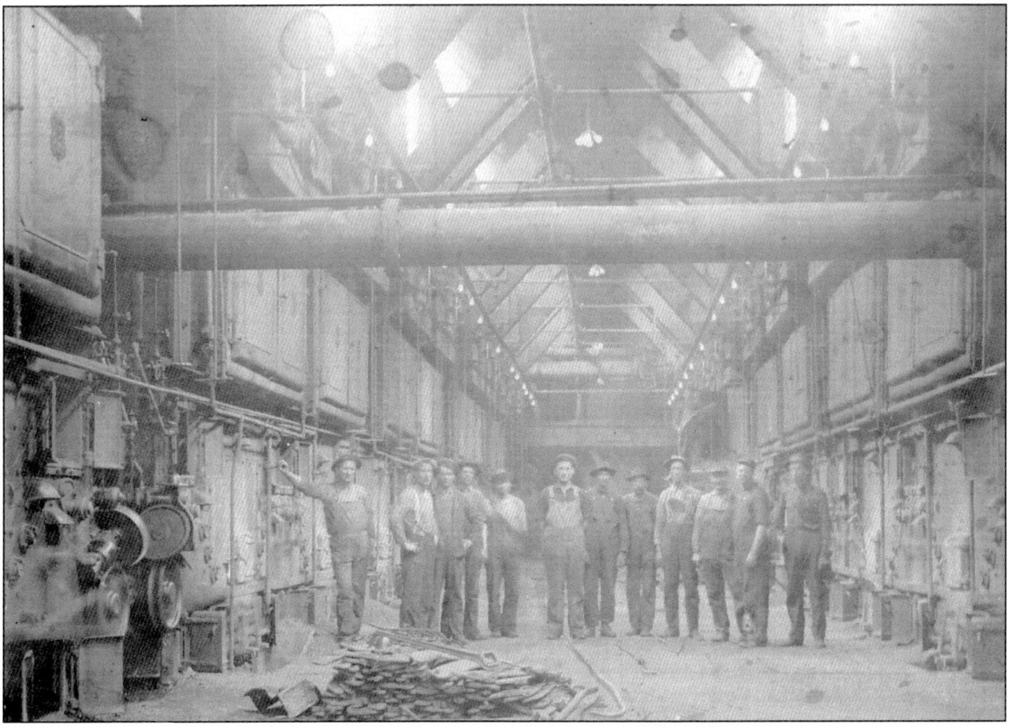

BOILER ROOM. One of the earliest known photographs taken inside the Champion Fibre Company (around 1908) is known for its ghost-like figure in the very center. The haunting image appears to show an extra worker tucked among the men. (Courtesy of Canton Historical Museum.)

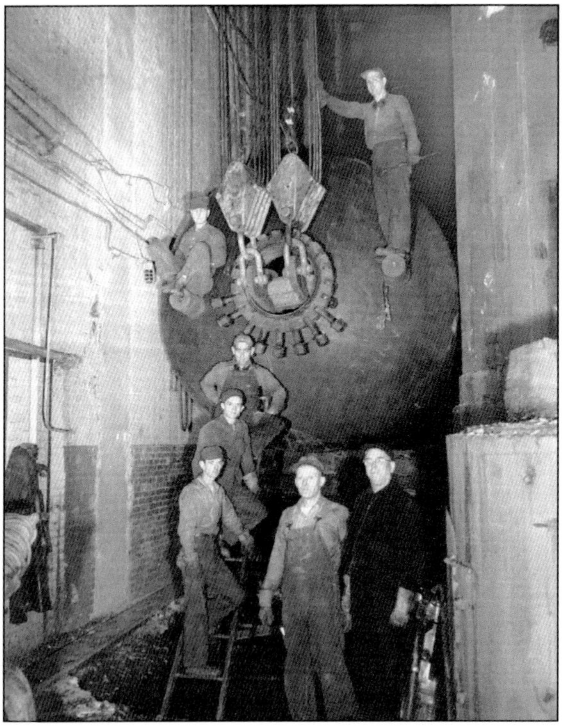

CHANGING THE DIGESTER. Like miners in the depths of a mine shaft, these Champion workers change out a digester in 1953. Wood chips were loaded into this steam-pressured vessel and injected with chemicals to break down the wood's cells into a pulp. The pulp was then fed into a series of tanks where it was washed and processed until it turned white and was ready for making paper. (Courtesy of Canton Historical Museum.)

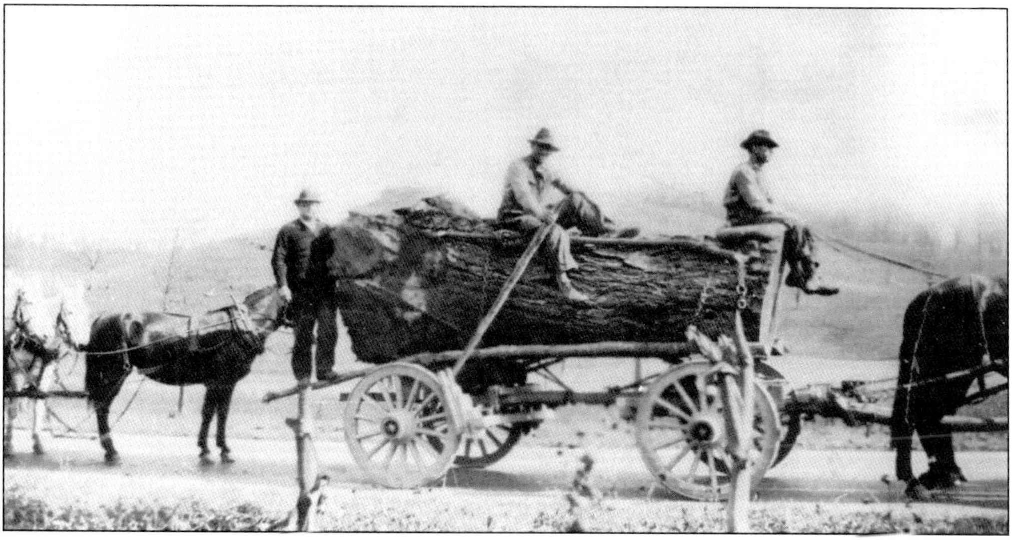

Horsepower. Iron Duff brothers Will, Horace, and Harley Bryson hauled this 10,000-pound log from Cataloochee to a nearby sawmill. Before the days of tractors and heavy-duty trucks, oxen, mules, and horses pulled these kinds of heavy loads. Will's mules could haul just about anything—and did in those days. (Courtesy of Clarine Best.)

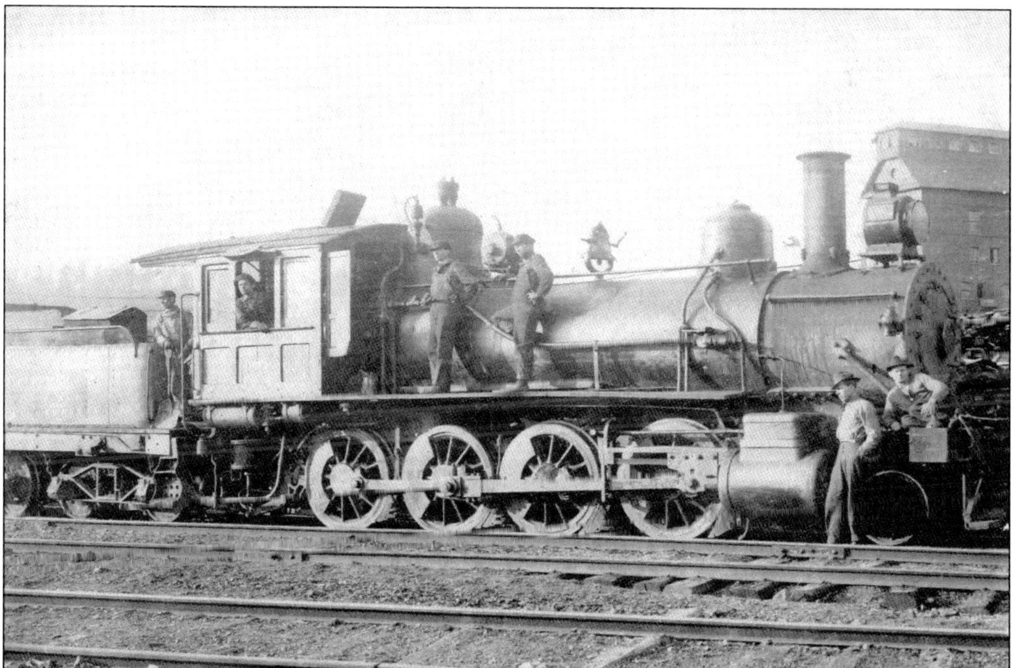

Steam Train. These trains carried logs and wood chips through the mill's vast campus and were a regular part of the town's economy through the mid-1900s. The train pictured here was one of the early trains that came through the mill. (Courtesy of Canton Historical Museum.)

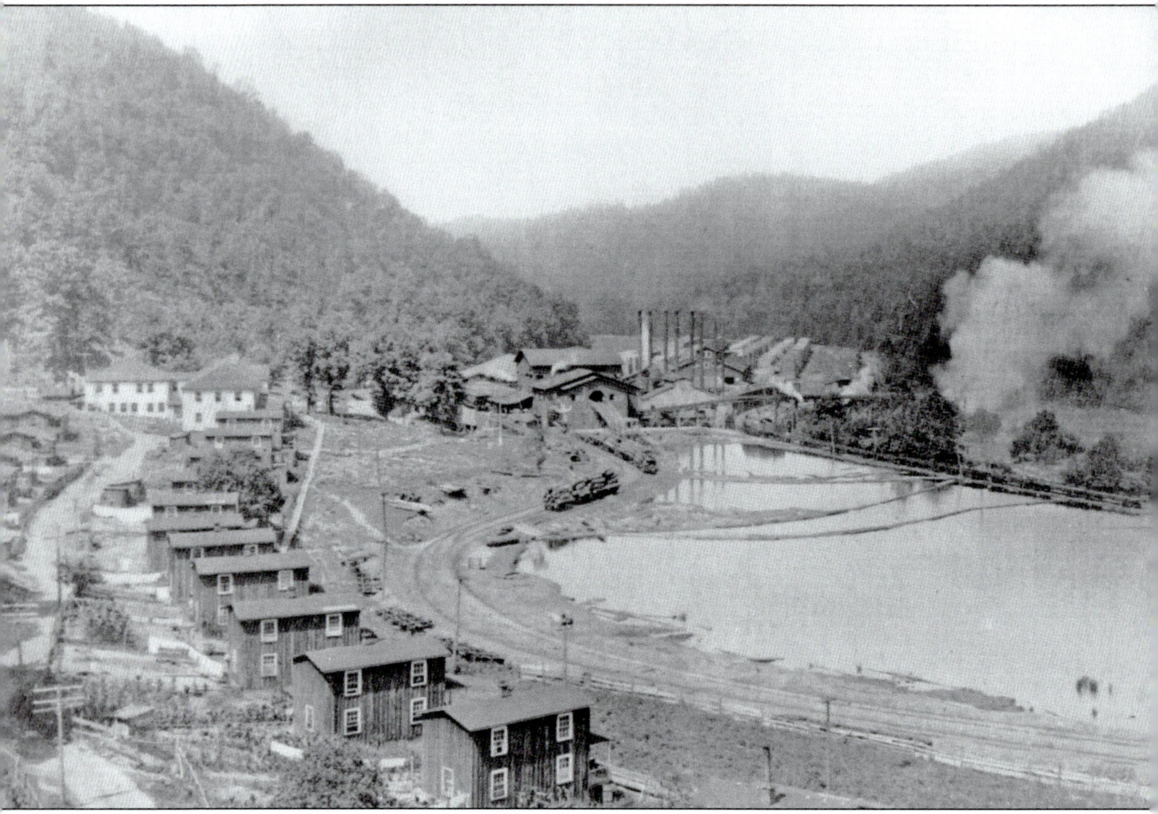

SUNBURST. The Sunburst logging camp was located at the bottom of what is now Lake Logan. During the late 1890s and early 1900s, it was a bustling town. The daily operation required many to take on specialized jobs that earned nicknames. "Lobby hogs" served meals and cleaned the dining hall. "Grab jacks" drove grabbing instruments into the logs so they could be pulled. "Swampers" carved out skid trails for horses and oxen to haul the logs away. Champion's paper mill contracted with Sunburst to access timber. As new tracts of spruce were discovered, a second Sunburst opened several miles north of the first site. By the late 1920s, much of the best timber had been harvested, and a huge wildfire in 1925 scorched the mountainsides around Sunburst, including its sawmill. Under financial distress, Sunburst teamed up with Champion and renamed itself Suncrest Lumber Company before moving to Waynesville. During an extended dry season, Champion built a reservoir at Sunburst to ensure itself a source of water for plant operations. The dam flooded the original Sunburst site and created Lake Logan. (Courtesy of Canton Historical Museum.)

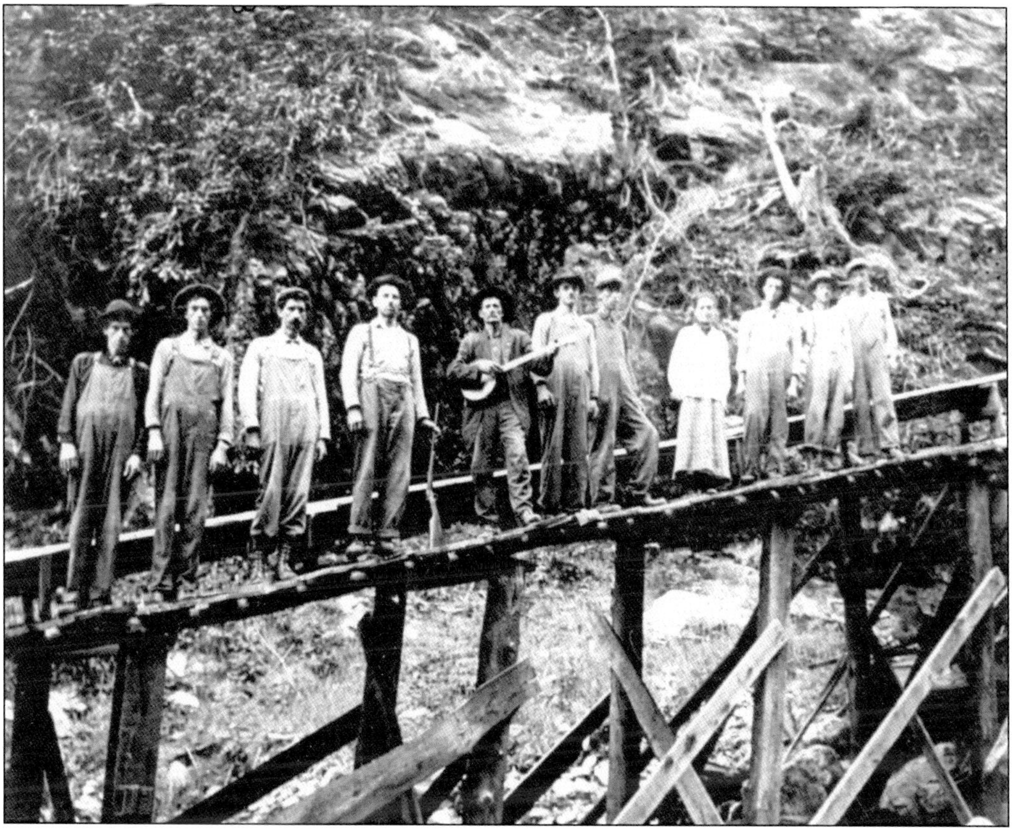

LOGGING. As timber was cut in logging camps like this one, above, in the White Oak community, log slides or water channels were built to carry logs downstream or loaded onto sloped, V-shaped tracks called flumes. The logs were then taken to lumber mills like the one below, which operated on Betsy's Gap Road in Fines Creek in the early 1900s. Thomas McCracken's sawmill cut logs into planks and board wood that could be used for building and furniture construction. (Both courtesy of Clarine Best.)

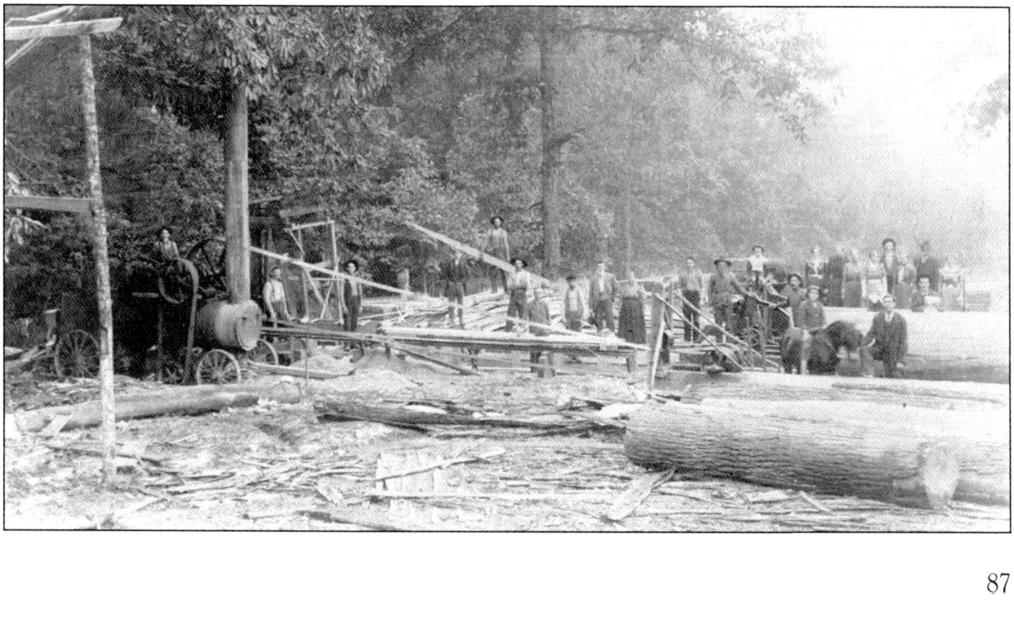

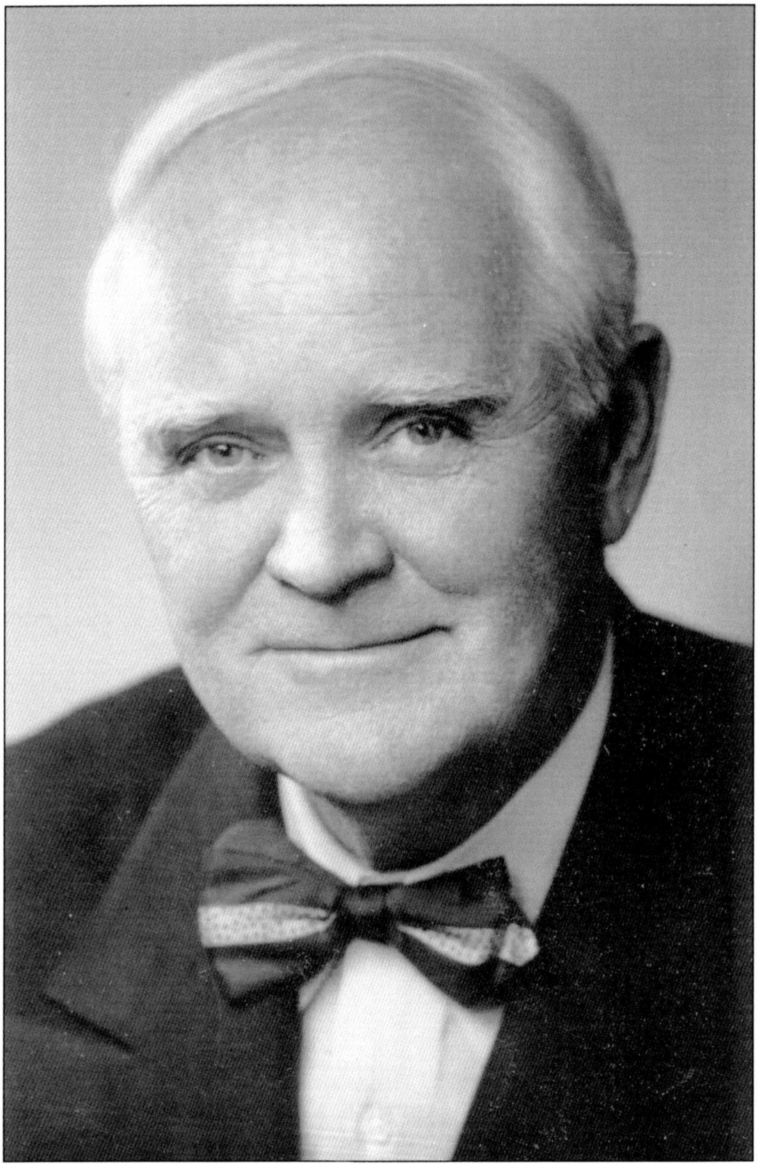

Reuben Robertson. A well-loved company president who was the face of Champion for decades, this Cincinnati-born Yale graduate started his career as a lawyer. Through his work, he met and later married Hope Thomson, the daughter of Champion's founder, Peter G. Thomson. Robertson oversaw construction of the Canton mill and negotiated land sales with the federal government in the creation of the Great Smoky Mountains National Park. He gradually climbed the corporate ladder to become president and chairman of the board of Champion Paper and Fibre Company. Robertson helped promote forest conservation and had two trees planted for every one the Canton mill cut down. He was also very active in the community and won distinguished awards for his service. He was instrumental in starting the YMCA in Canton and donated land for the Canton public library. A professorship at North Carolina State University, a dorm at Western Carolina University, and a scholarship were named in his honor. His family's legacy lives on with Haywood County place names like Camp Hope, named after his wife, and Lake Logan, named after one of his sons. (Courtesy of Canton Historical Museum.)

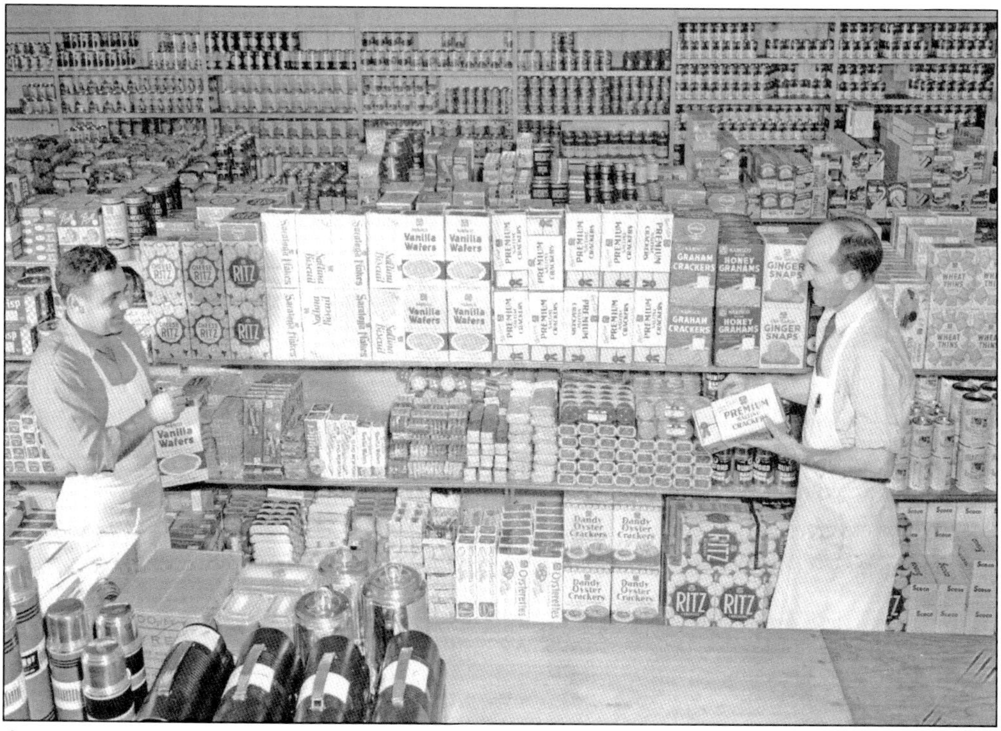

Champion Company Store. Before the 1950s, the Champion paper mill in Canton had its own supermarket, above, which offered fresh produce from local farmers, as well as dry goods and a soda fountain. Customers would come with a list or phone in their requests, and a clerk would gather all the items and send them to the customer's home through a fleet of delivery trucks, below. Eventually, the store expanded to include a second story and two side wings. Before World War II, employees could use company scrip or "doogaloo" in lieu of cash. As a Christmas present from the company, employees received a dividend for two weeks' worth of groceries each December. In 1959, Champion tore down the store along with the YMCA building to make room for a mill expansion. (Both courtesy of Canton Historical Museum.)

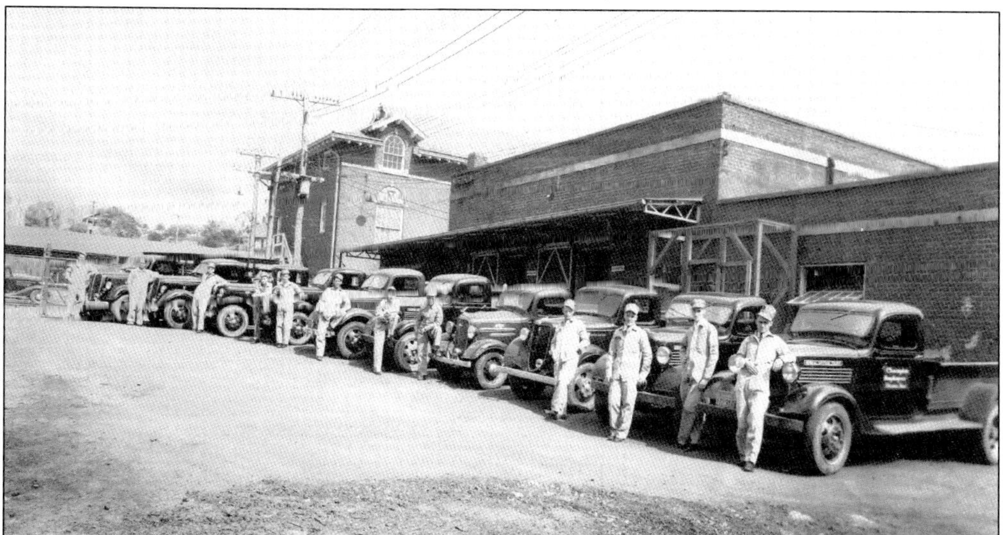

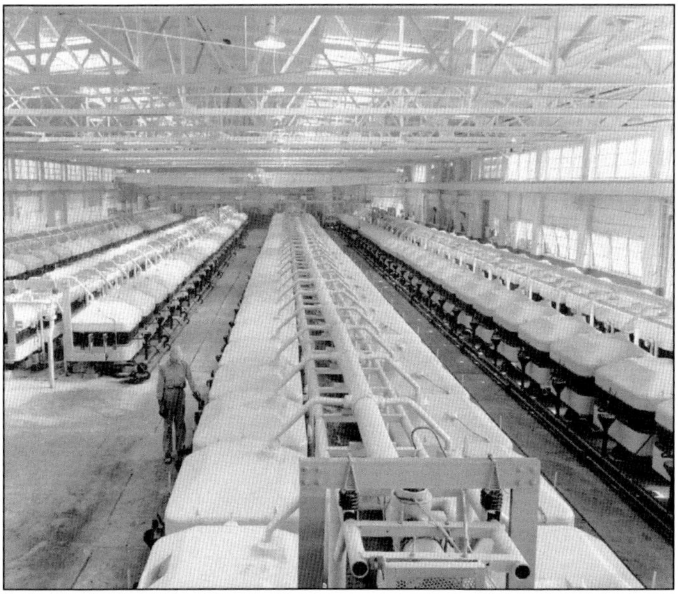

Chemical Factory. By the mid-1900s, the Champion mill had the largest tannic acid plant in the world, producing more than 500 barrels of liquid chestnut extract a day. It also produced its own caustics and bleaches. In this cell room, an electric current was fed through saltwater to produce a caustic used for breaking down wood chips. Another by-product was a bleach called SO-HY, which Champion sold and shipped by truck and train to cotton companies in the Southeast. (Courtesy of Canton Historical Museum.)

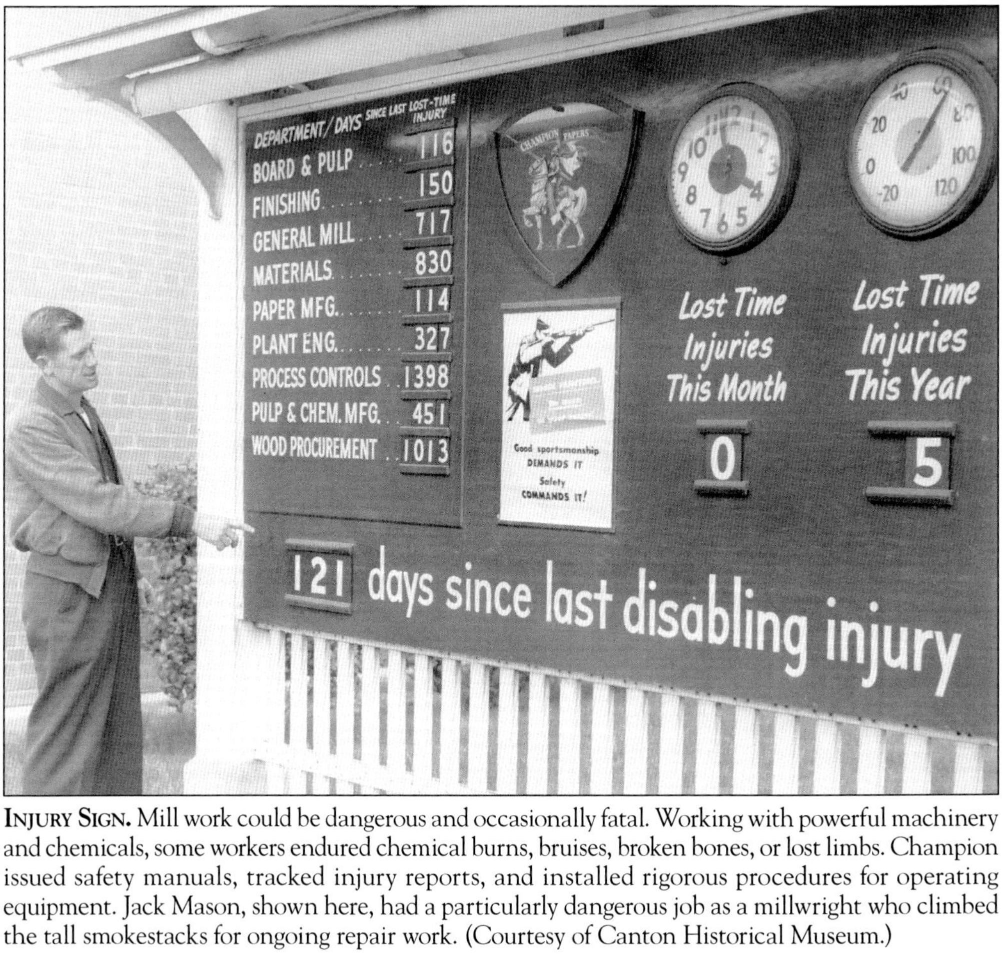

Injury Sign. Mill work could be dangerous and occasionally fatal. Working with powerful machinery and chemicals, some workers endured chemical burns, bruises, broken bones, or lost limbs. Champion issued safety manuals, tracked injury reports, and installed rigorous procedures for operating equipment. Jack Mason, shown here, had a particularly dangerous job as a millwright who climbed the tall smokestacks for ongoing repair work. (Courtesy of Canton Historical Museum.)

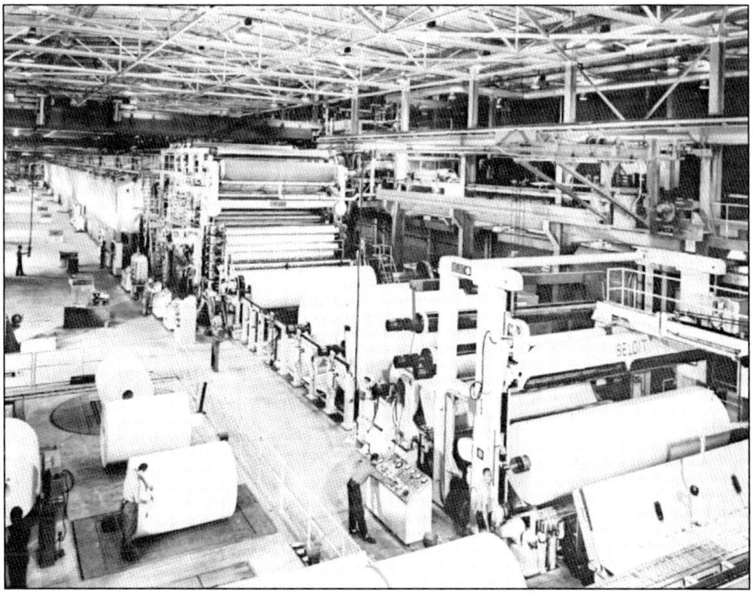

Machine No. 19. As Champion continued to grow, this massive, multimillion-dollar machine started operating in 1965. It could produce enough paperboard to make a pint milk carton for every man, woman, and child in the United States. At that time, the mill's No. 20 machine could produce a mile of paper 20 feet wide every three minutes. (Courtesy of Canton Historical Museum.)

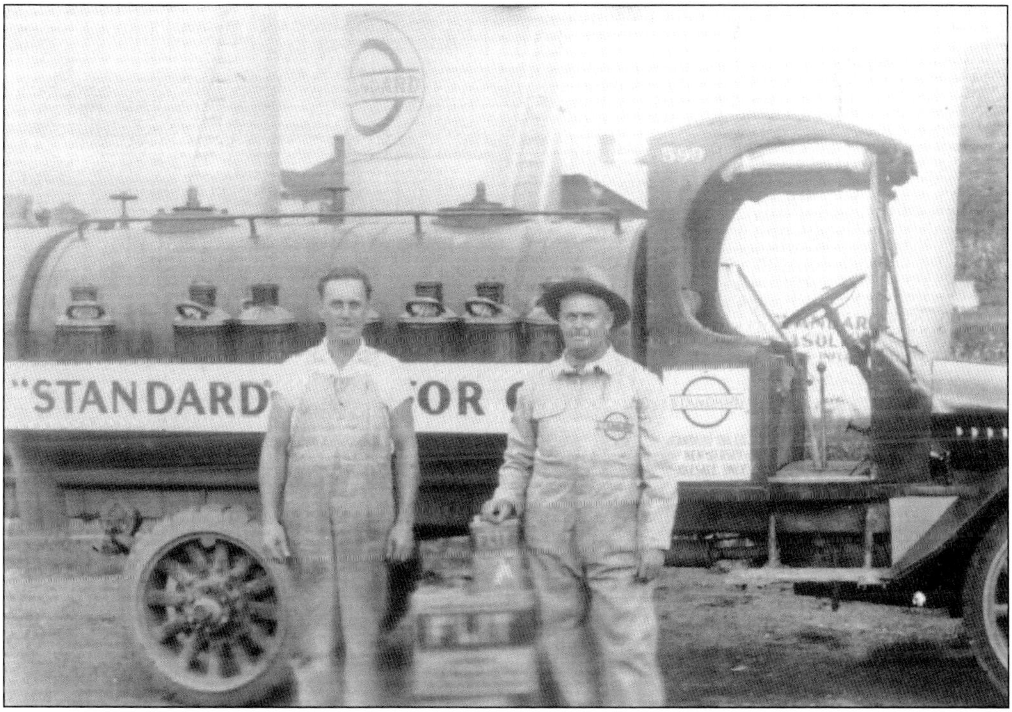

Oil Delivery. This Standard Oil truck was the first motorized oil truck of its kind in Canton, delivering kerosene and lamp oil to local homes and businesses starting in the early 1920s. Standing in front of the truck are, from left to right, Matkey Smathers and F. W. Woody. (Courtesy of Canton Historical Museum.)

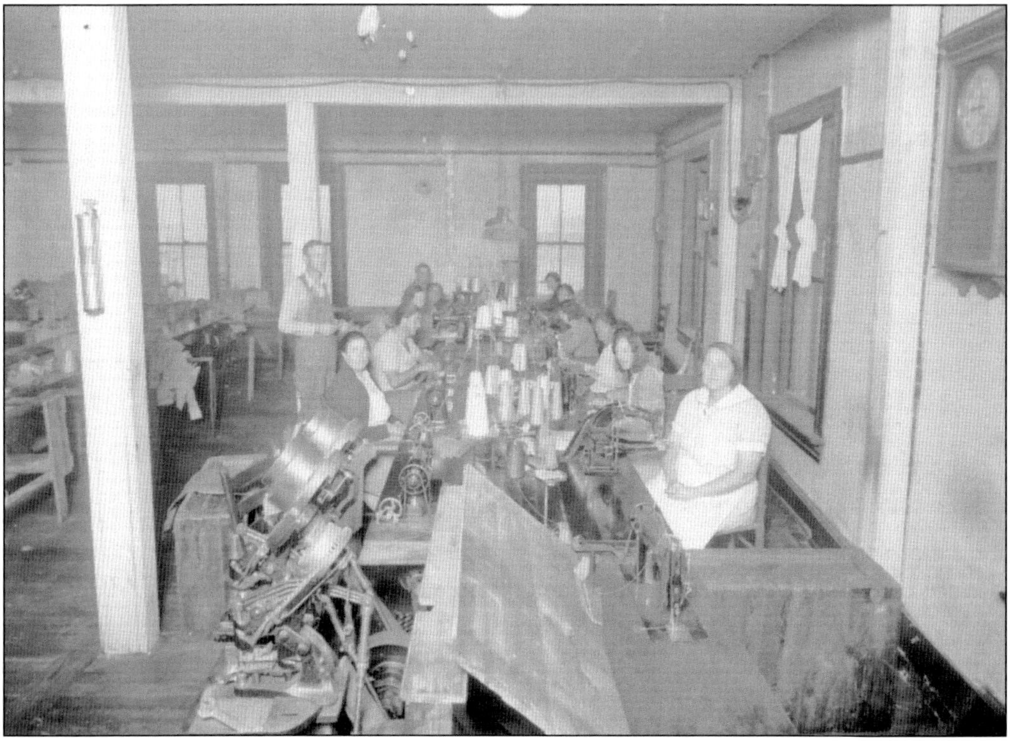

OVERALLS FACTORY. This lesser-known business in Canton, pictured about 1932, once produced overalls in a factory located on Bridge Street in the building where the old Canton Library once stood. It is not clear whether the business was sold or absorbed by a larger company. (Courtesy of Canton Historical Museum.)

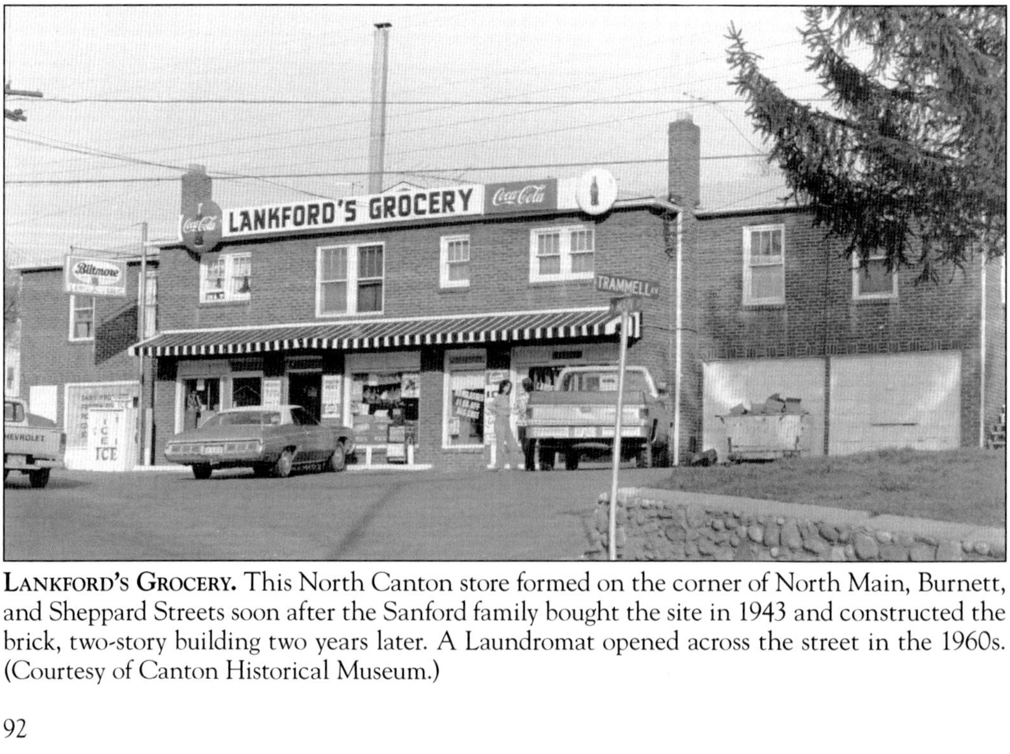

LANKFORD'S GROCERY. This North Canton store formed on the corner of North Main, Burnett, and Sheppard Streets soon after the Sanford family bought the site in 1943 and constructed the brick, two-story building two years later. A Laundromat opened across the street in the 1960s. (Courtesy of Canton Historical Museum.)

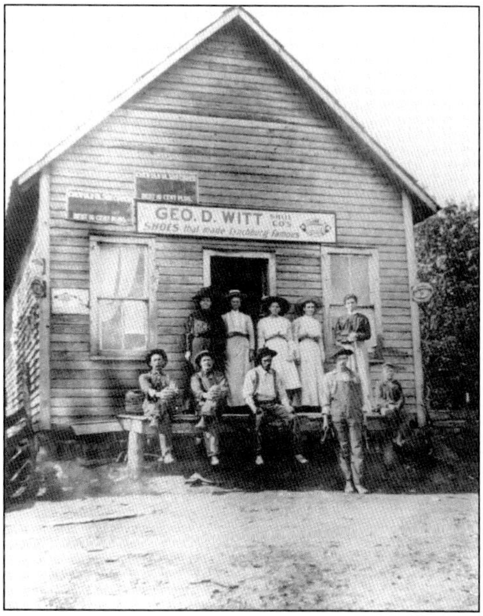

IRON DUFF STORE. John Burnette Medford in the Frog Level community of Iron Duff—not to be confused with Waynesville's Frog Level district—owned and operated this general store. The reference to frogs was probably due to the fact that it was a low-lying area near a river or stream that appeared level with frogs, especially after floods. (Courtesy of Clarine Best.)

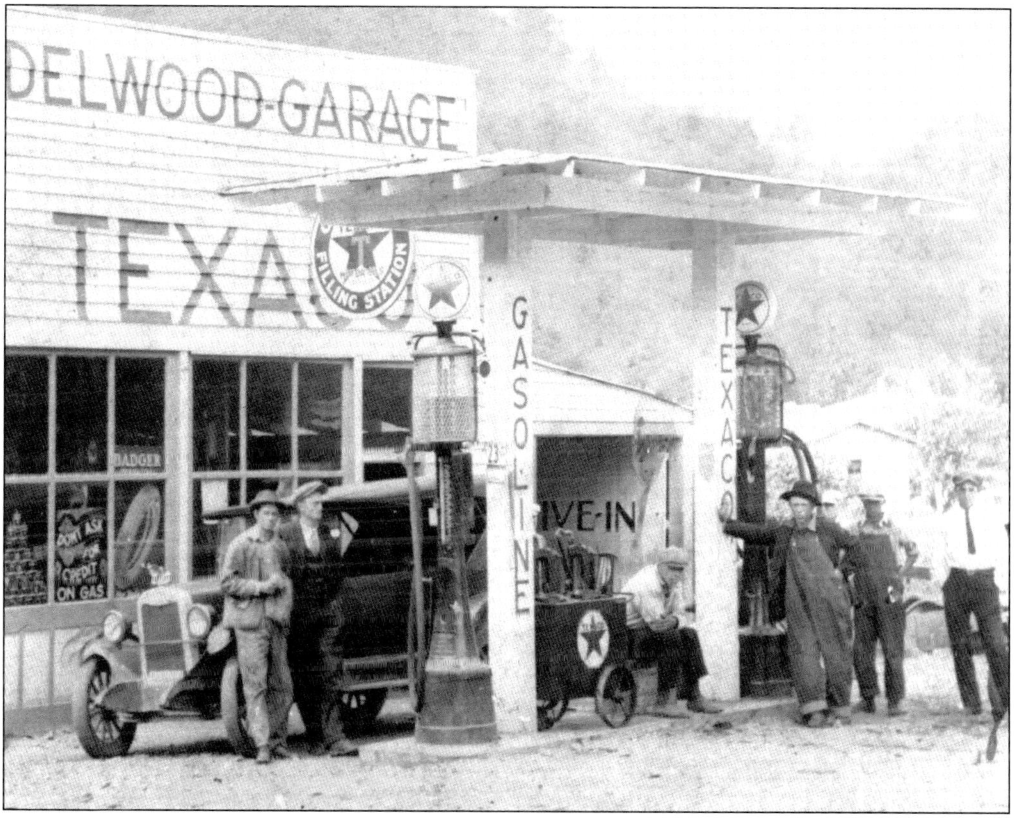

DELLWOOD GARAGE. This Texaco filling station in the Dellwood community was located about where the Maggie Valley Conference Center is today. Pictured from left to right are Lee Setzer, Vincent Russell, Bear Parker, Thurman Moody, Lee Evans (in back), an unidentified man, and Paul Hyde in the 1920s. (Courtesy of Betty Ferguson.)

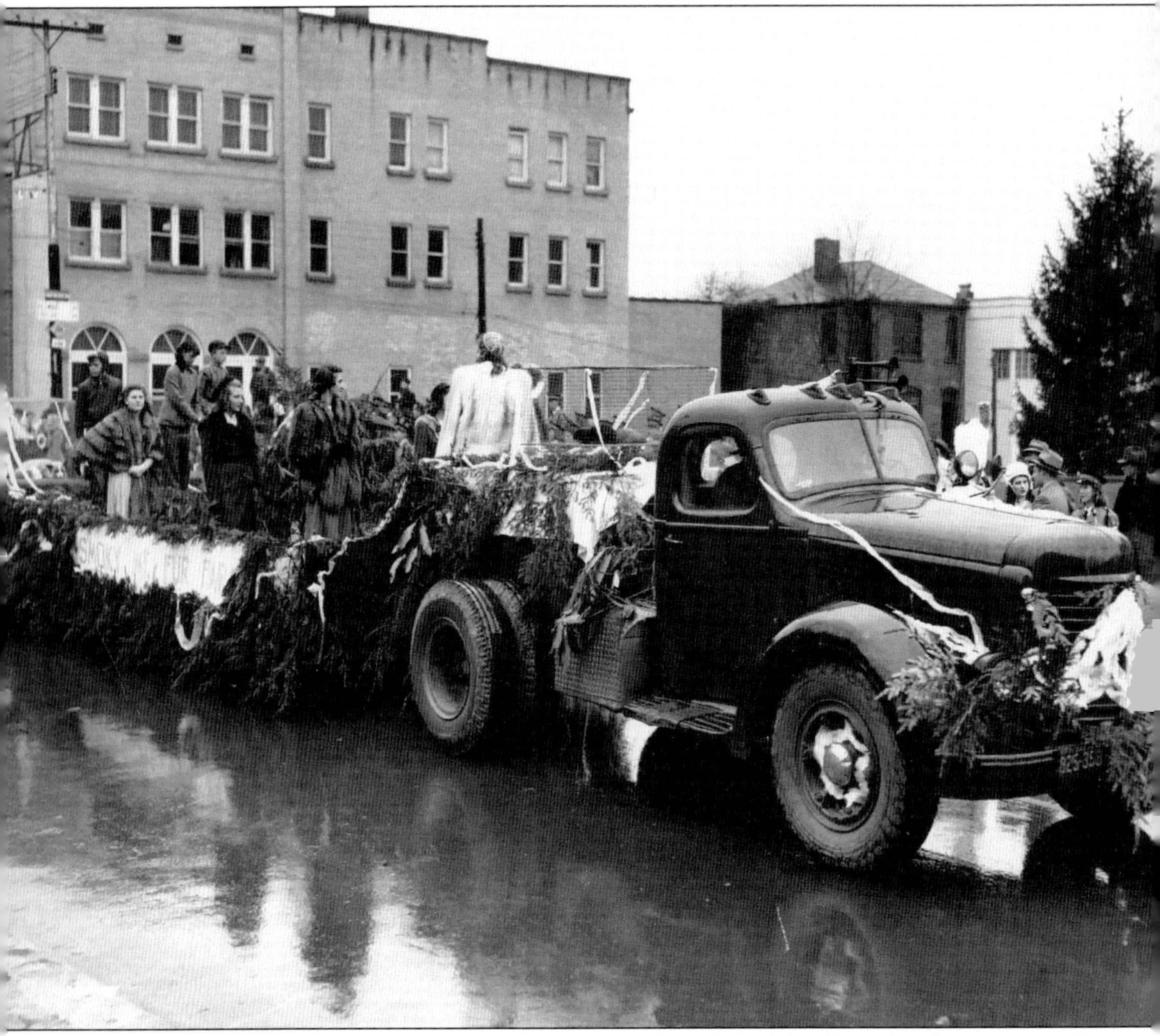

Fur Farm. The Smoky Mountain Fur Farm raised mink and fox for pelts that were used as decorative scarves, as seen in this photograph from a 1950s Waynesville Christmas parade float. Ned Moody got the idea for the fur farm after a trip to Canada and subsequent trips north to learn more about the fur and pelt industry. The operation was on Moody Farm, located in the vicinity of the present-day Maggie Valley Country Club. Hundreds of mink and foxes were raised in cages and fed ground beef mixed with milling and fortified vitamins. After they were killed, their furs were removed and kept in coolers until Moody found the right market to sell them. The business flourished during the 1940s and 1950s. (Courtesy of Betty Ferguson.)

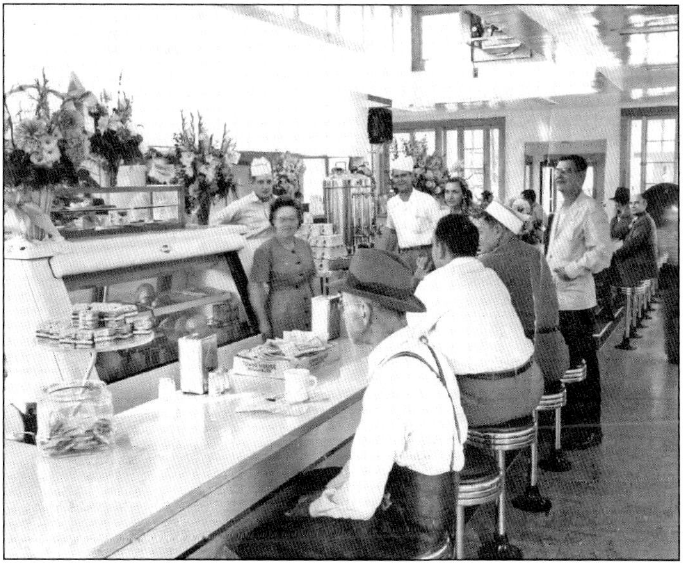

CHARLIE'S PLACE. As a popular Waynesville restaurant from the 1930s through the 1970s, Charlie's featured hot dogs, hamburgers, and a friendly atmosphere for generations of customers. Its owner, Charlie Woodard (pictured behind the counter in a white hat, center right), constructed a larger building in 1948 next to the old one. Charlie became so famous that he represented North Carolina and the region on a business mission through seven European countries in 1966. (Courtesy of the *Mountaineer.*)

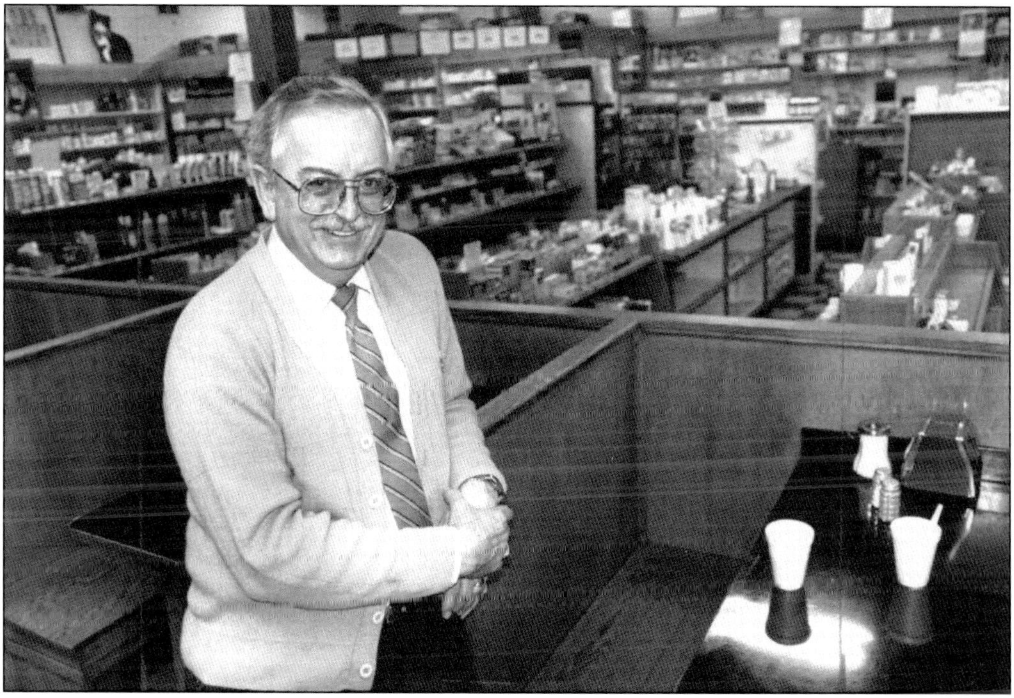

HAZELWOOD PHARMACY. Duke James, owner of the Hazelwood Pharmacy, served at this downtown Hazelwood institution over five decades, starting in 1958 when he began as an apprentice. Before the days of drugstore chains and big box stores, the independently owned pharmacy offered personal service to loyal customers and was a regular stop for factory workers on a lunch break and teenagers spending money on jukebox tunes, a milk shake, or a comic book. (Photograph by Kirk Wilson; courtesy of the *Mountaineer.*)

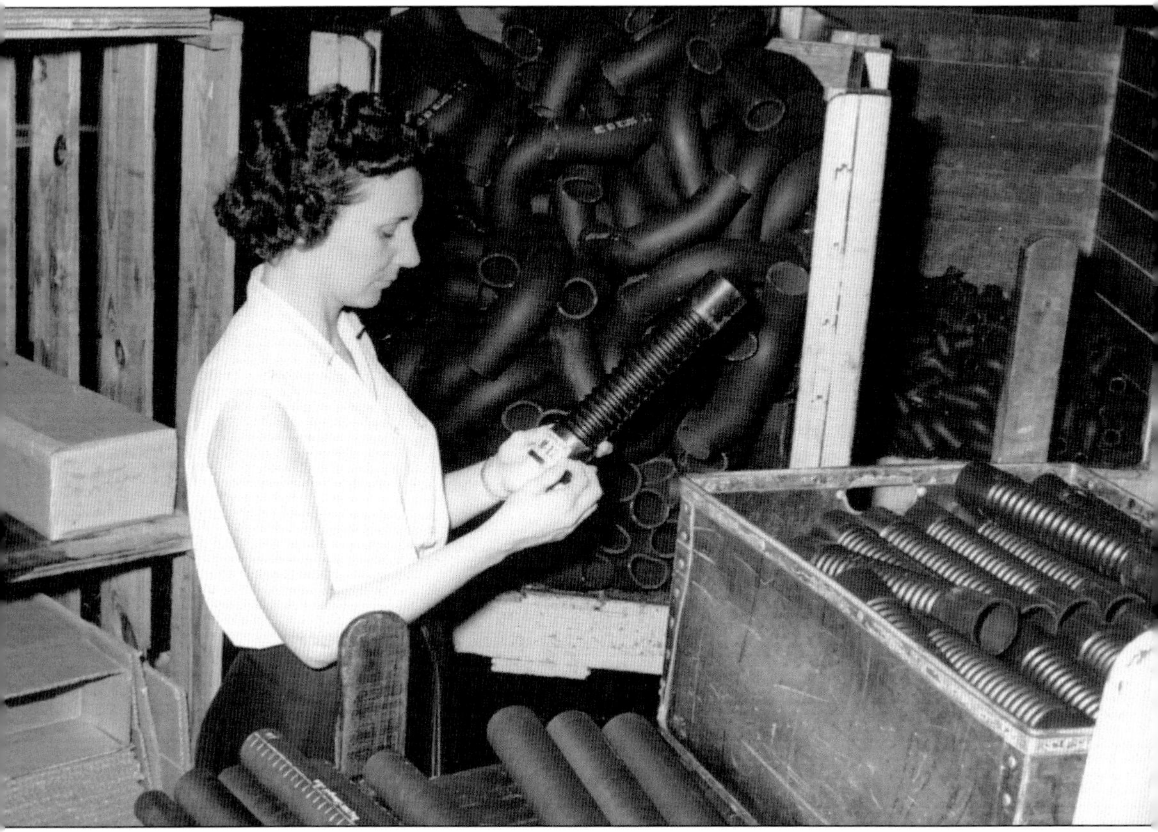

DAYCO. The Dayton Rubber Manufacturing Company opened in Hazelwood in 1941 just three months before the bombing of Pearl Harbor pulled the United States into World War II. During the war, the factory pumped out war materials such as oxygen hose masks, pontoons, and life rafts for the military. After the war, the company manufactured timing belts, fan belts, and automotive plastics. Employment rose to about 1,000, making it one of the largest employers in the county. But its parent company decided to close the plant in the 1990s. Its sprawling buildings stood vacant for about a decade until they were razed to build a shopping center. (Courtesy of the *Mountaineer*.)

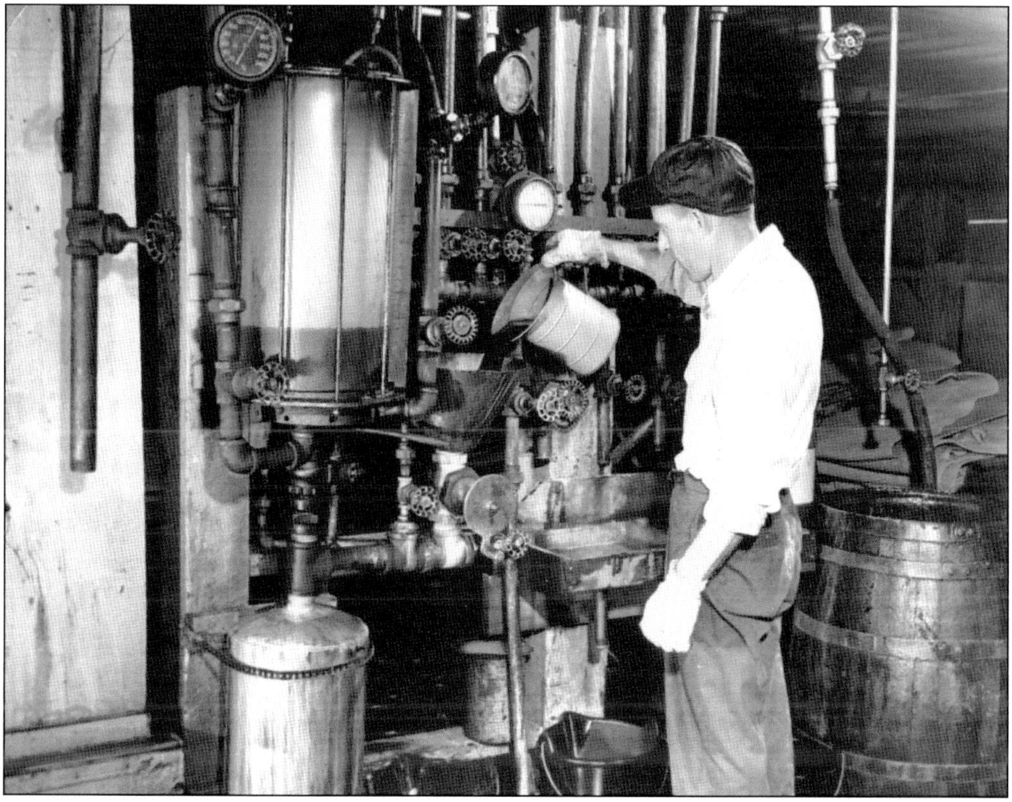

A. C. Lawrence Leather Company. This tannery was one of Haywood County's first major industrial businesses when it opened in 1896. First known as the Junaluska Tannery, then later as the England Walton Company, many local residents would recall its A. C. Lawrence Leather name. The tannery used chestnut, oak, and hemlock bark to tan animal hides. With its initial success, A. C. Lawrence inspired other industries to set up shop in Hazelwood, and the community grew into a bustling industrial town with furniture, lumber, and textile plants within just a few miles' radius. The tannery closed in 1986. In these 1955 photographs, Grady Davis (above) works in the scrub room while France Wright (below) flattens a piece of leather. (Both courtesy of the *Mountaineer*.)

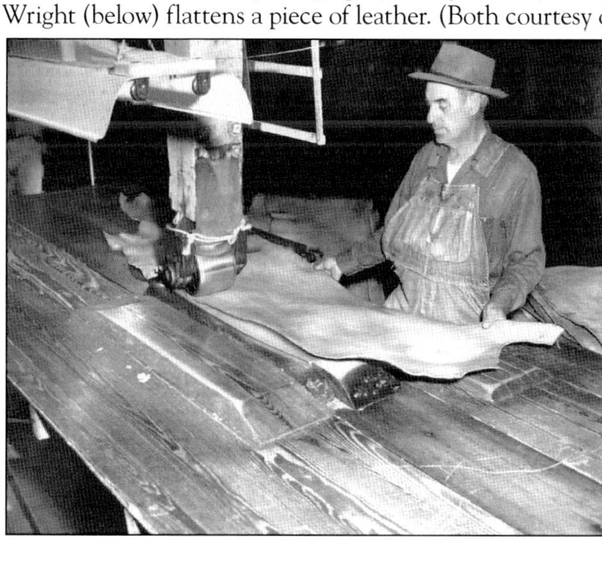

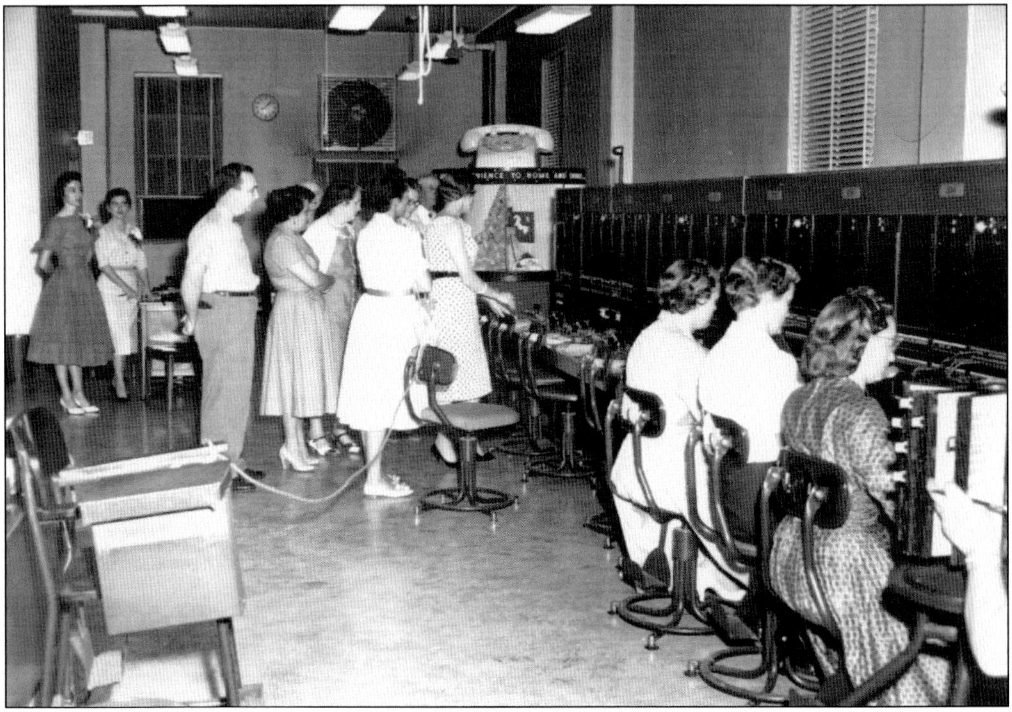

WAYNESVILLE SWITCHBOARD. When the Southern Bell Telephone Company in Waynesville held an open house on Monday, May 11, 1959, visitors were able to go behind the scenes to see how their calls were routed. Operators manually connected calls by inserting phone plugs into an appropriate jack. A switch on the cord circuit allowed the operator to talk to the customer, and a light above each jack lit up when the telephone receiver was in use. Note the giant telephone in the back of the room. (Courtesy of the *Mountaineer*.)

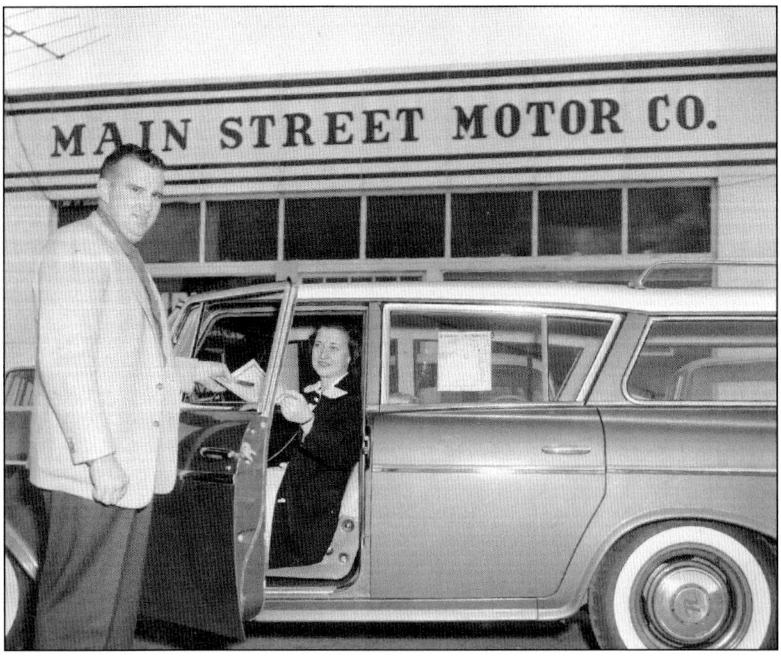

THE PRICE IS RIGHT. This lucky customer won a new car from the popular television game show in 1960. Car dealer J. R. Caldwell hands over the title of the station wagon to Mrs. Goss at the Main Street Motor Company in Waynesville. The Goss family lived in Bryson City. They won two cars on the game show. (Courtesy of Henry Foy.)

Seven

Tourism

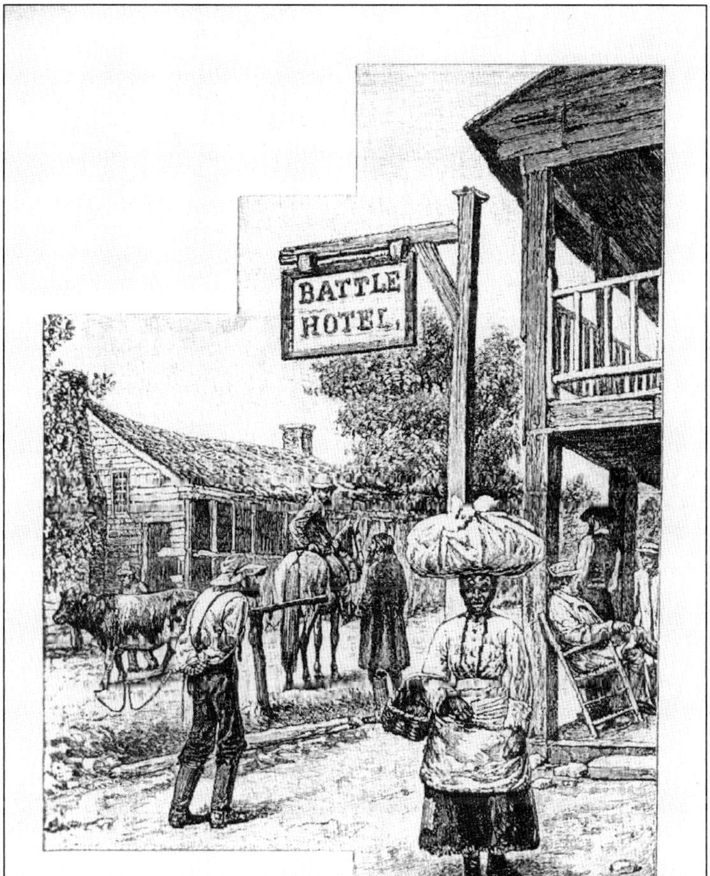

BATTLE HOTEL. This illustration by A. P. Frost, the artist for the famous Uncle Remus books, appeared in the nationally distributed *Harper's Weekly* magazine in 1880. At the time, its owner advertised rates of $1 per night and $20 to $30 a month. Holliman Battle opened the inn around 1810 as Waynesville's first tavern. It was later enlarged to two stories with front porches. This was the site on May 7, 1865, where local Confederate forces surrendered to Union troops at the close of the Civil War. (Courtesy of Henry Foy.)

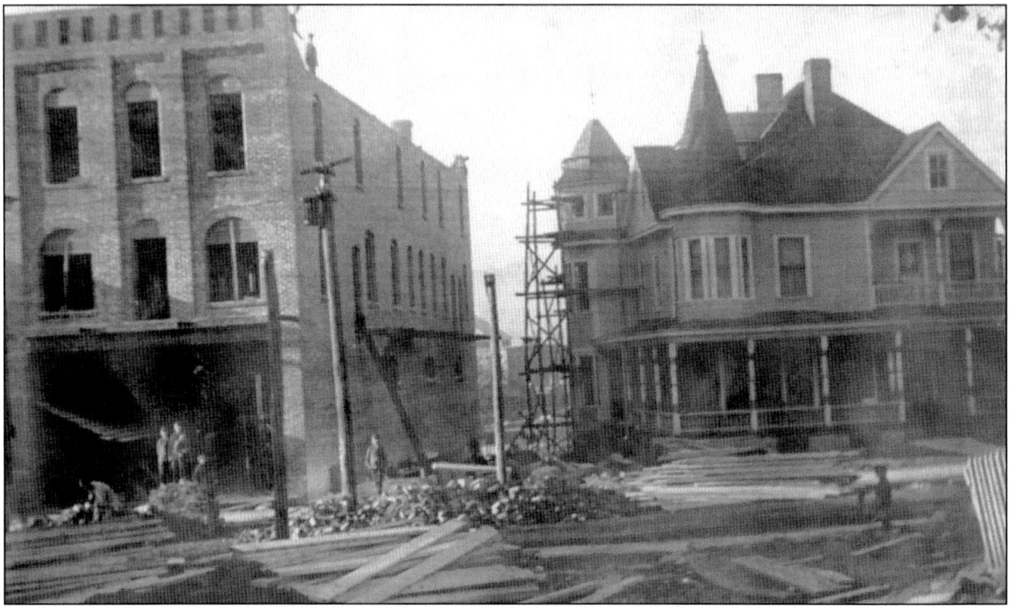

Imperial Hotel. Advertised in 1916 as "one of the state's best two dollar hotels," this downtown Canton inn, right, offered quality rooms for tourists, drummers (salesmen), and mill executives. E. M. Geir and his wife—both from New York City—founded the hotel after coming to Canton in 1911. The inn included about 40 rooms, spacious verandahs and hallways, and bountiful meals. Still standing today, it has been recently renovated by Canton mayor Pat Smathers. (Courtesy of Canton Historical Museum.)

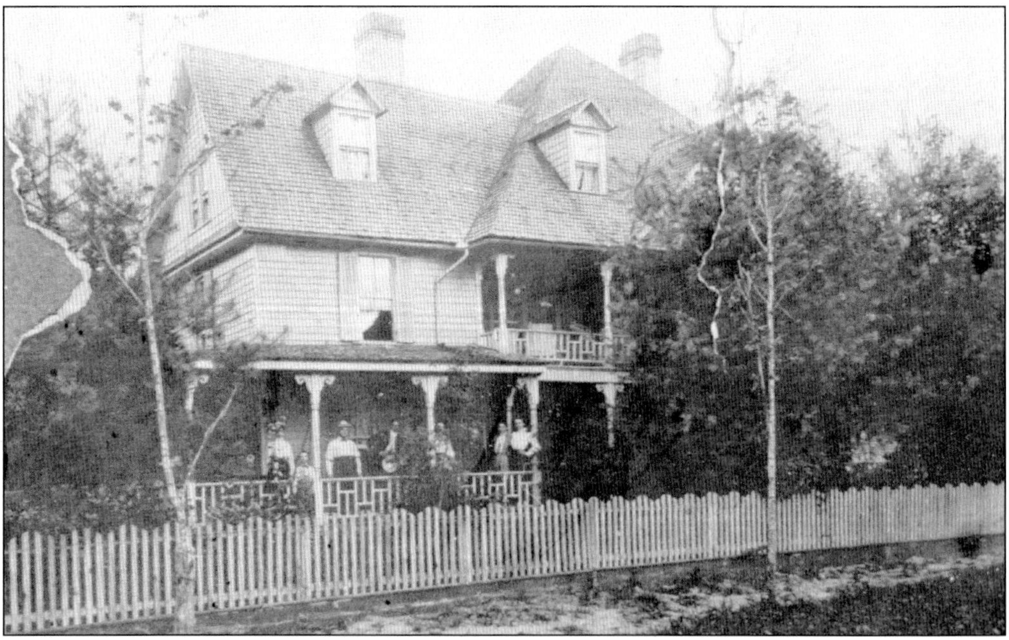

Spears Inn. Clyde once had eight boardinghouses and inns, including the Spears Inn (above), located on the corner lot of Main Street and U.S. 19/23 across from the present-day town hall, and the Drummer's Inn, torn down in the 1940s to make room for the highway. The Yankee Hipps Inn later became the site for a girls' camp. (Courtesy of Clyde Town Hall.)

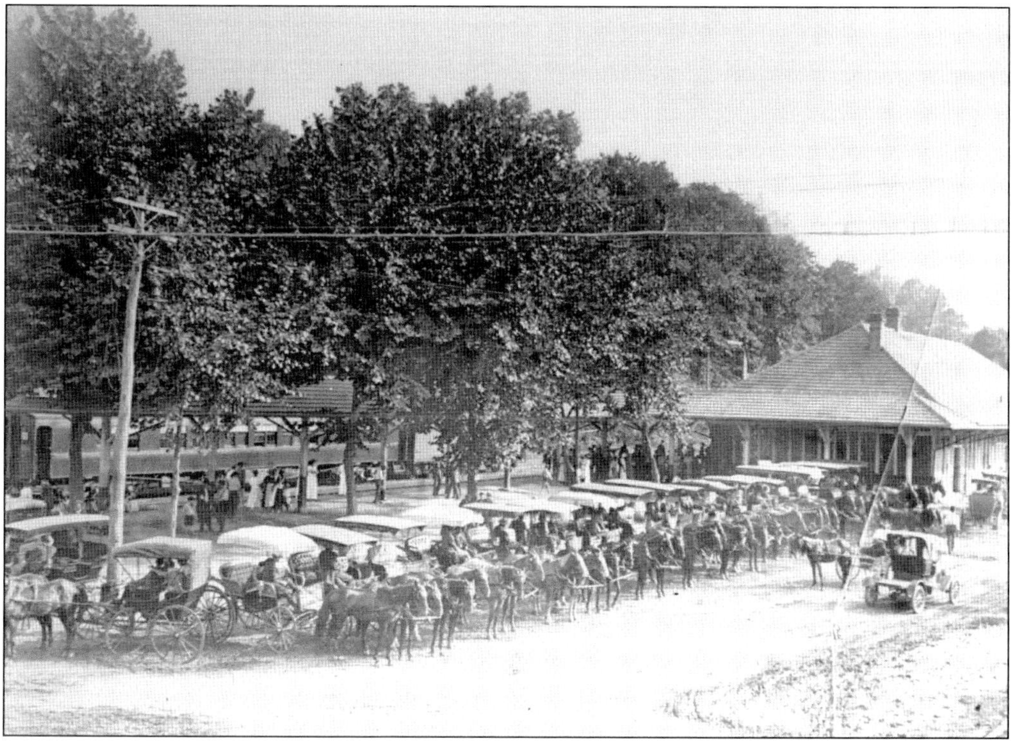

WAYNESVILLE DEPOT. Once the epicenter of Waynesville, this train depot, located across the street from the present-day Open Door Soup Kitchen, welcomed an annual influx of summer tourists from Southern states as temperatures rose and families traveled to cooler climes. (Courtesy of Henry Foy.)

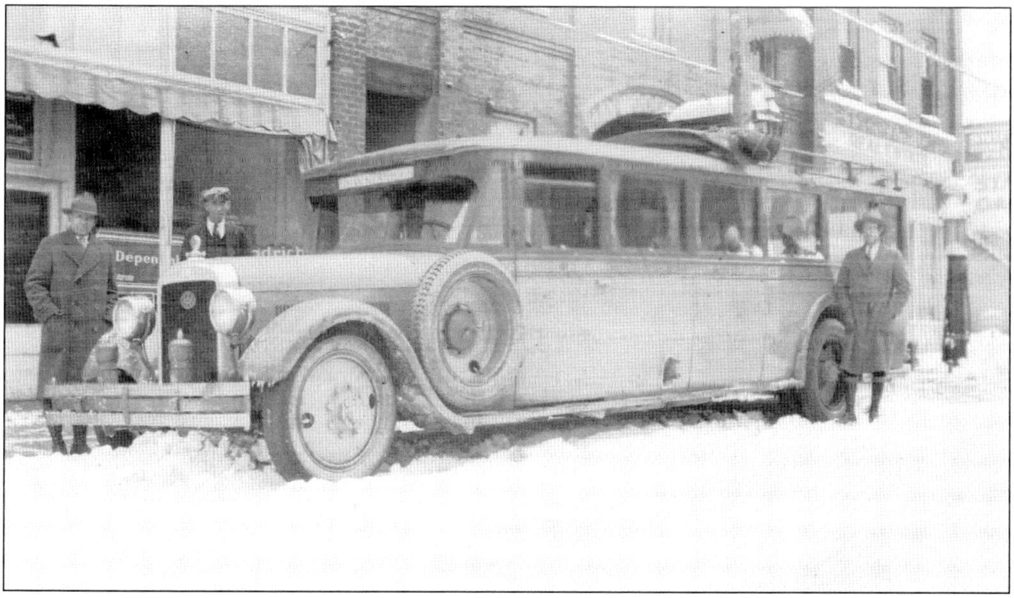

BUS SERVICE. For groups of tourists in need of transportation, these stretch buses operated in Waynesville and carried a dozen people comfortably. The Independent Coach Line even ran during winter weather, as this late-1920s photograph attests. (Courtesy of Henry Foy.)

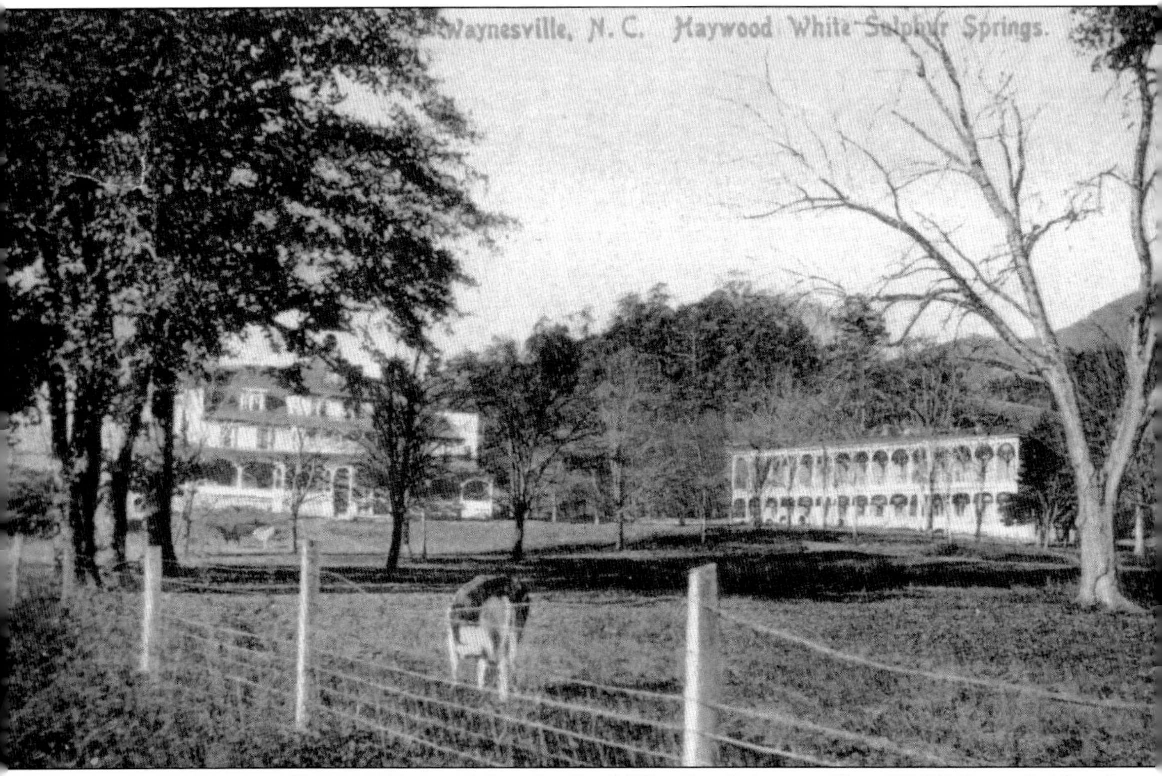

WHITE SULPHUR SPRINGS HOTEL. After the Civil War, Confederate officer W. W. Stringfield and his wife, Maria Love, operated what became one of Haywood's most storied hotels. Gen. Stonewall Jackson's widow stayed here, as did a honeymooning Woodrow Wilson. Groups met at this site to found the North Carolina Education Association and the first North Carolina chapter of the Daughters of the American Revolution. Once thought to be the site of a Native American mound and a Cherokee village, the grounds were reputed to have healing waters. The Love family who owned the property supposedly had a slave who discovered the sulfur spring and was granted his freedom. The hotel was completely destroyed by fire in 1892 and later rebuilt to include an annex for dances and grand parties. In 1918, the government leased the hotel, converting it into a military hospital. After the patients were relocated to a hospital near Asheville, the old luster of the hotel faded. It was eventually torn down. All that remains is the hotel's springhouse, which stands about 100 yards south of where the hotel once stood. (Courtesy of Betsy Ferguson.)

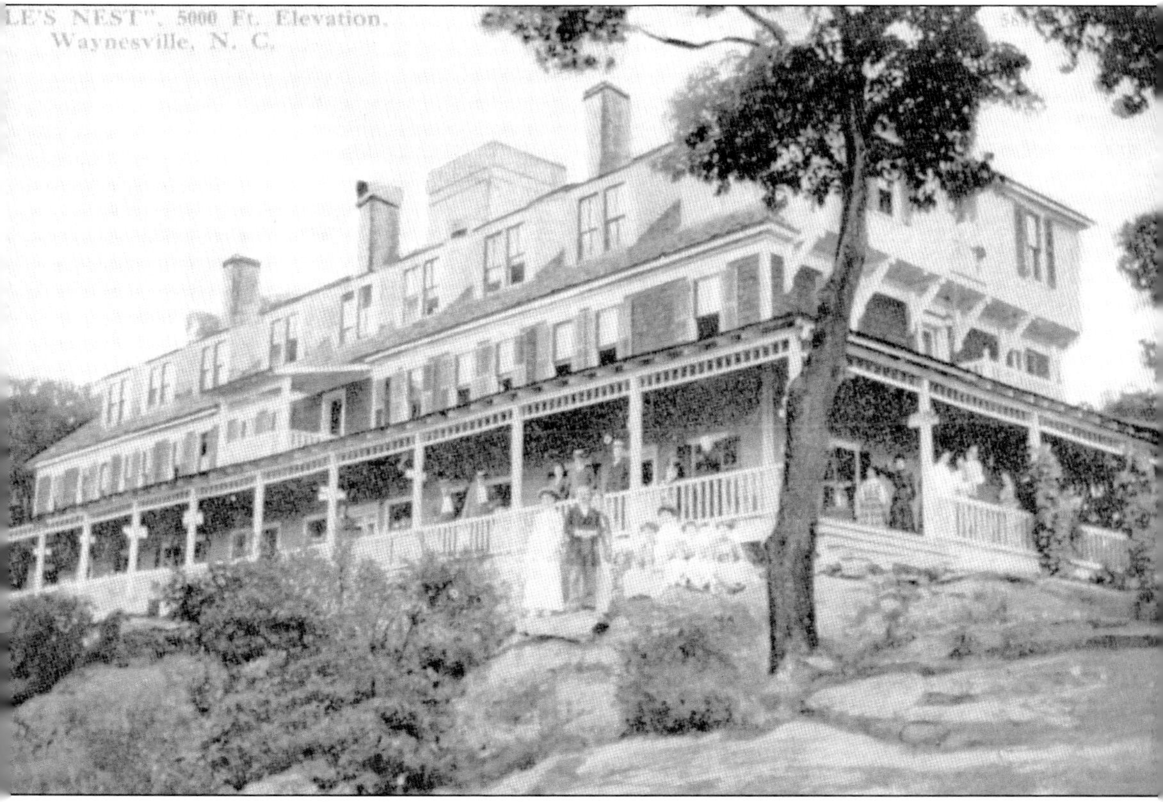

Eagle's Nest Hotel. Built at the summit of Junaluska Mountain overlooking Hazelwood, this impressive inn offered some of the best mountain views in the region. Owner S. C. Satterthwaite promoted the hotel's cool, clean air and fresh water as a remedy for those suffering from respiratory illnesses. Designed in the late Victorian model, the three-story hotel included 50 rooms, a wraparound porch, stone fireplaces, an observation tower, and a grand lobby with windows that looked over a majestic valley below. Guests enjoyed dances, card games, lavish dinners, and long hikes around the mountainsides. But the hotel's cozy perch, far from the cares of the world, also proved to be its downfall. Before the summer season in 1918, a brilliant fire erupted and fire crews could not make it up the mountain in time to save it. Neighbors and inn staff could only watch the destruction. The hotel was never rebuilt, but the mountain has since been renamed Eagles Nest. (Courtesy of Bruce Briggs.)

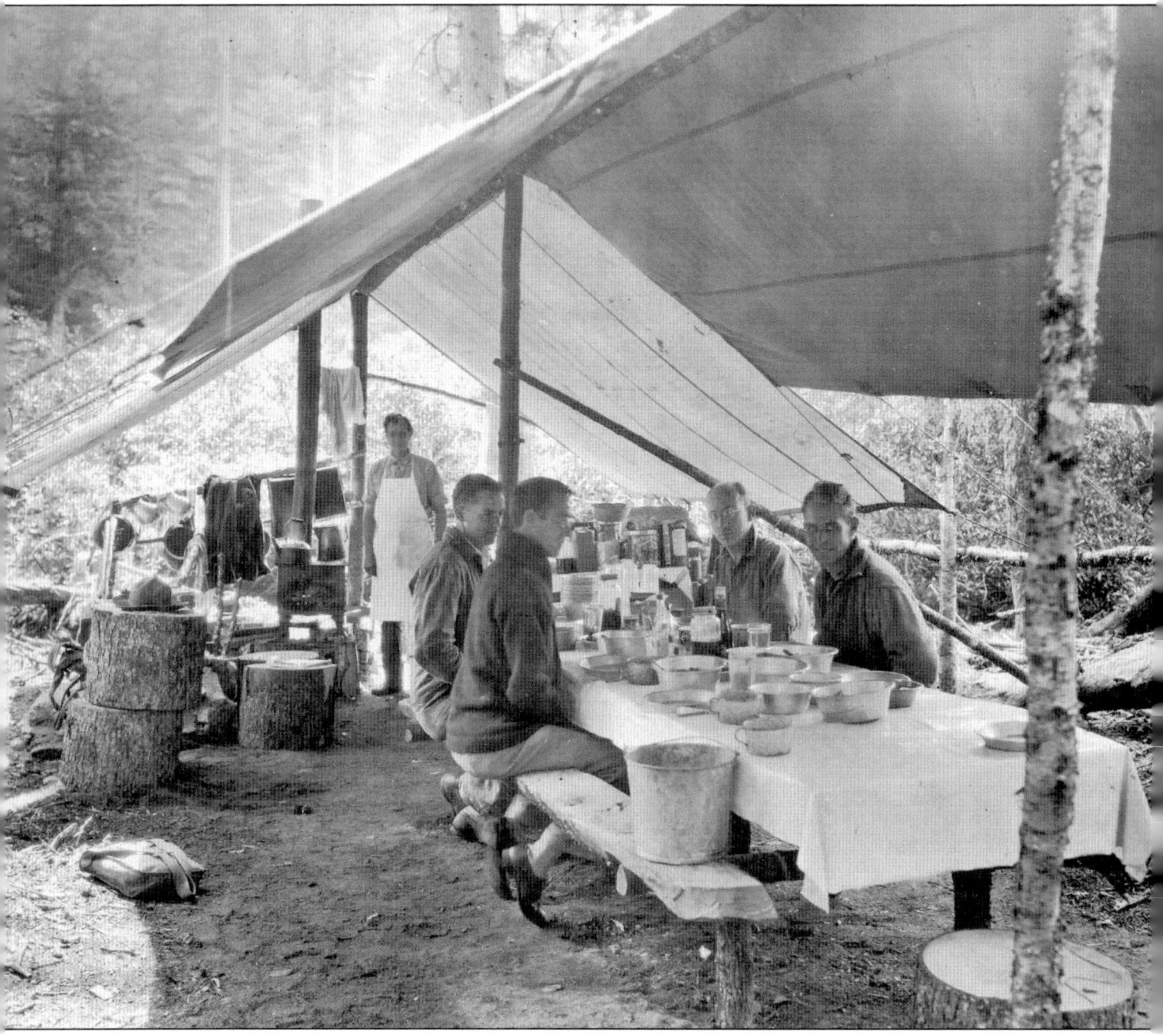

Three Forks. In 1929, Tom Alexander was working as an appraiser setting the value of timber lands in Western North Carolina when the stock market crashed. His employer went broke, so in lieu of a paycheck, Alexander accepted a collection of the company's camping equipment at Three Forks, a timber-cruisers' camp in a remote basin at the foot of the Great Smoky Mountains. Tom and his wife, Judy, started up a tourist camping business, providing hiking and fishing in this picturesque setting that included waterfalls, towering trees, rocky stream beds, and abundant wildflowers. Guests would hike in with supplies, pitch tents, explore the wilderness, and feast on fresh catches of speckled and rainbow trout served by cook Avery Gouge, standing. (Photograph by George Masa; courtesy of Cataloochee Ranch.)

Cataloochee Ski Area. During the 1940s, a local foreman, Larry Caldwell, fashioned skis for the Alexander family by taking thin strips of scrap lumber, boiling them in water, bending up the tips, and fastening harness straps to shoes that were fixed onto the skis. They would use golf clubs for ski poles and without any lessons plunged down the mountainside. In 1961, shortly before Christmas, Tom Alexander opened a modest ski area on a little hill behind his ranch house. In 1968, he relocated the ski area to its present location with multiple slopes, a snow-making machine, a ski lift, and a new lodge. (Courtesy of the *Mountaineer.*)

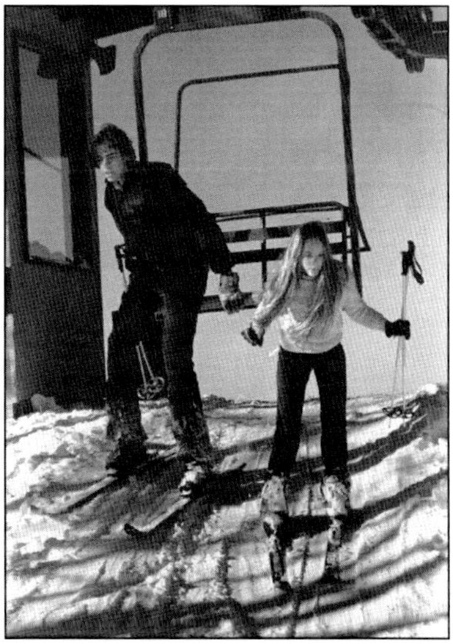

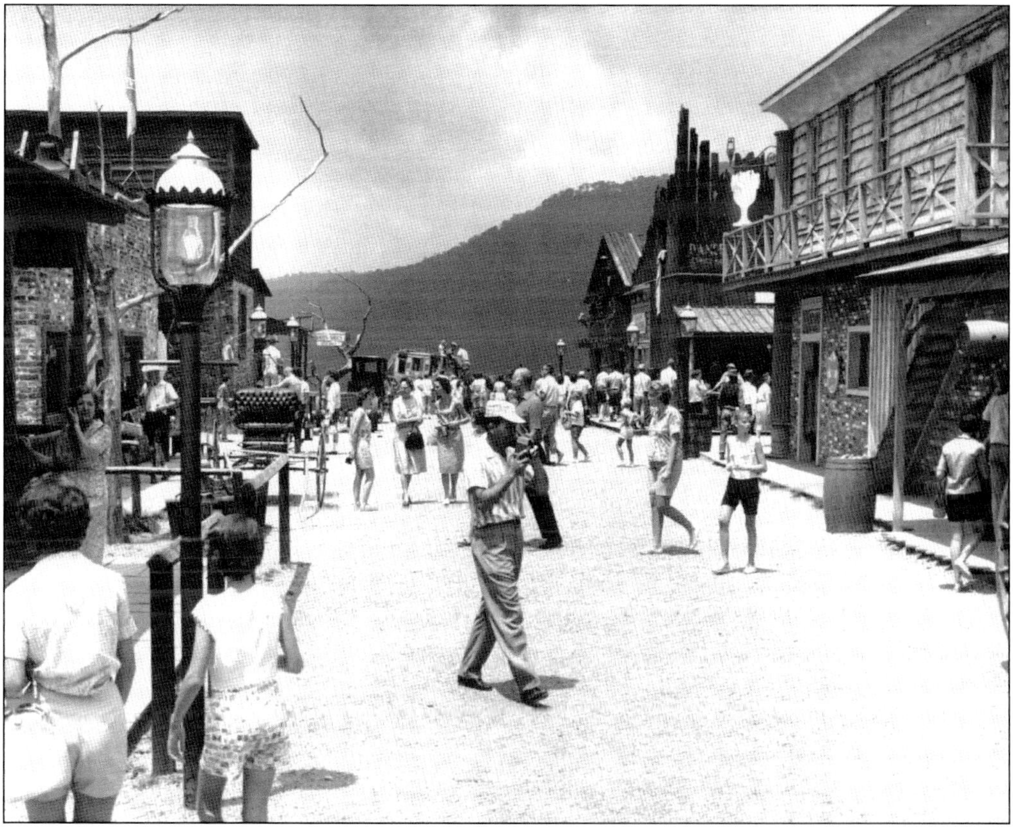

Ghost Town in the Sky. In 1960, an enterprising businessman named R. B. Coburn bought Buck Mountain above Maggie Valley and had it converted into a theme park for tourists. When it opened the following year, visitors took an incline railway up the mountainside and discovered Ghost Town, a Wild West village with roller-coaster rides, staged gunfights, and dancing showgirls. Millions came to see the spectacle. It lasted 41 years before closing in 2002 but reopened again in 2007 under new ownership. By 2009, the business was in bankruptcy. (Courtesy of the *Mountaineer.*)

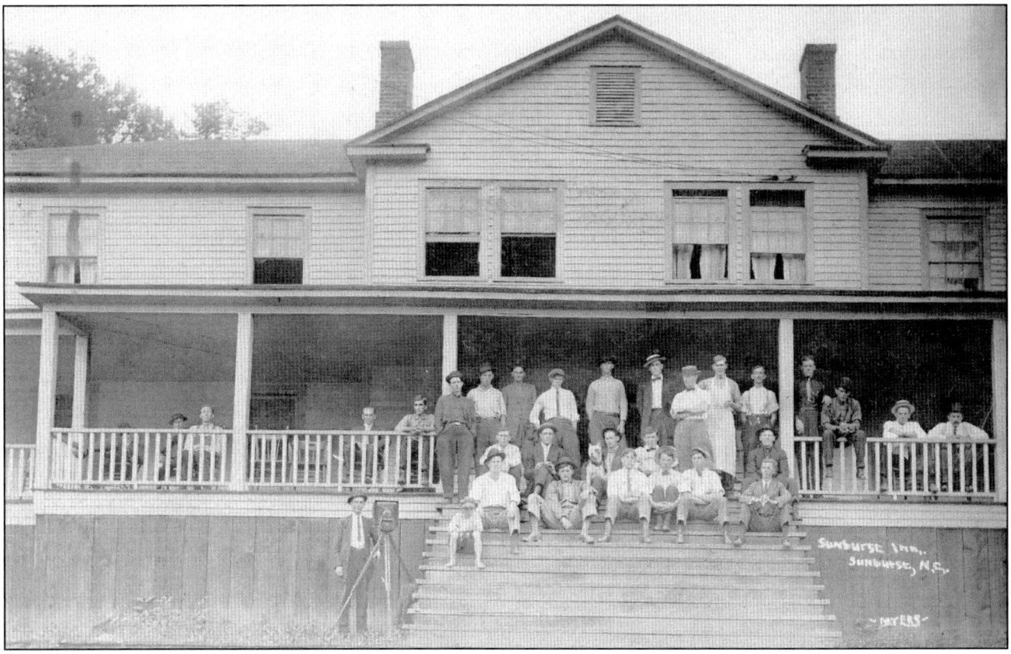

SUNBURST INN. This inn served as a boardinghouse for workers at the nearby Suncrest lumber mill in Sunburst and was given the unflattering nickname of a "Meat Skin Hotel" because of the plain food served there. This photograph, taken on August 12, 1914, offers a representation of the inn's clientele. Note the absence of women. (Courtesy of Canton Historical Museum.)

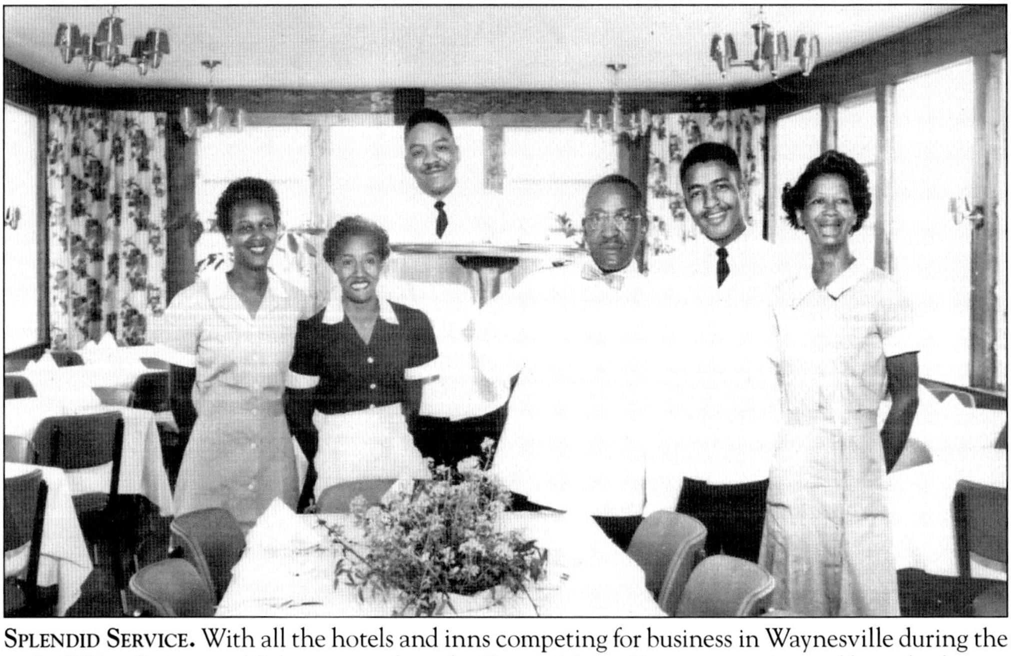

SPLENDID SERVICE. With all the hotels and inns competing for business in Waynesville during the early 1900s, dining establishments such as the Towne House Restaurant, pictured here, had to set themselves apart from the rest by offering first-class food and service, as this group of wait staff eagerly imparts. The Towne House Restaurant, which no longer stands, was located next to the present-day First Presbyterian Church of Waynesville on Main Street. (Courtesy of Henry Foy.)

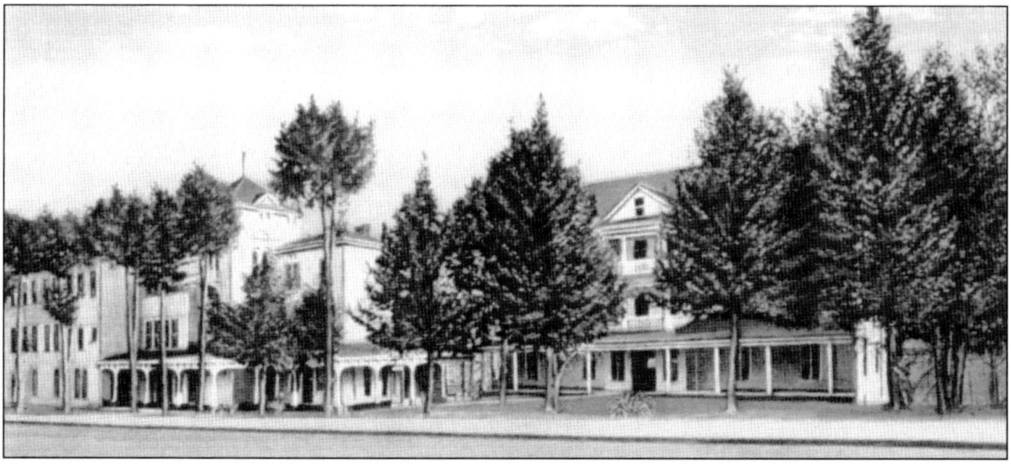

Gordon Hotel. The illustration above and the photograph below show the rise and fall of a grand hotel in the Waynesville area. Once the home of Civil War officer Capt. Alden Howell, who later became a Waynesville banker, the building was expanded on both sides (above) to include about 100 rooms, a renovated interior, and a birch wood staircase. Rooms on the second floor had private bathrooms. After a Florida hotel manager bought the Gordon in 1912, he offered guests fine cuisine, a small orchestra for their dining entertainment, a ballroom, and tea dances. Guests came from all along the Eastern seaboard. The Gordon was the most elegant hotel in downtown Waynesville. But times changed after two world wars, a Great Depression, and the rise of motels and interstate travel. In the 1950s, the Gordon suffered damage from a fire that destroyed much of its once grand frame. Below, local residents attend an auction of items at the property after the fire. (Both courtesy of Henry Foy.)

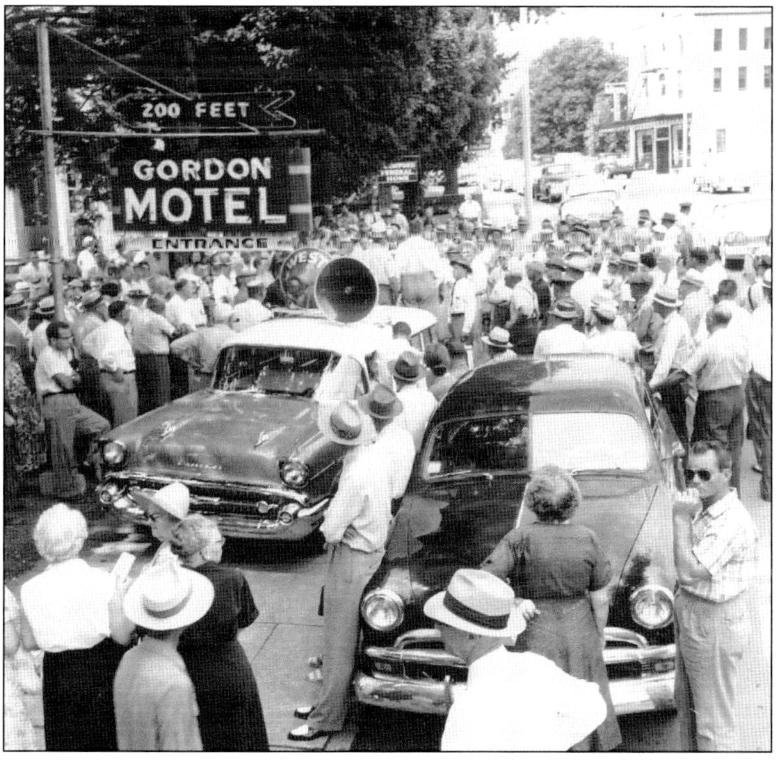

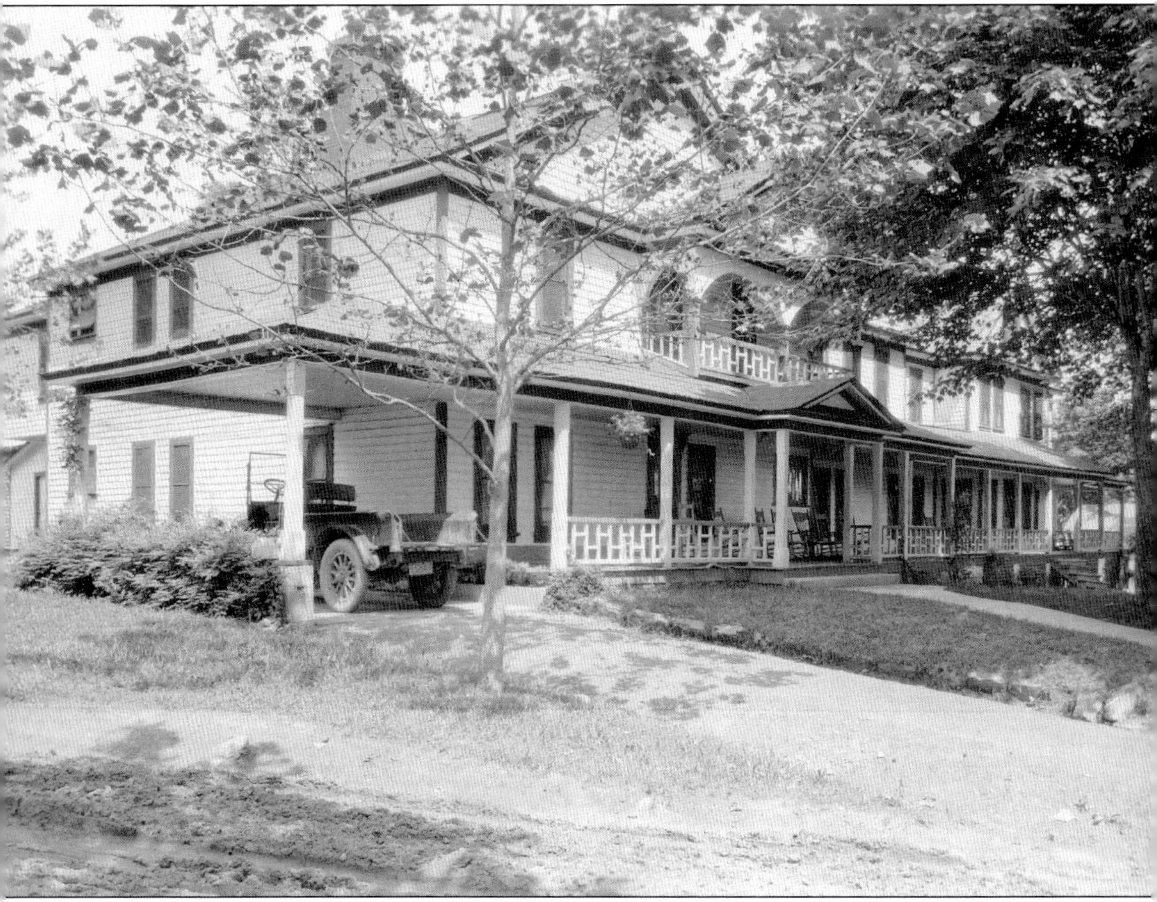

PIEDMONT INN. The Hyatt family once owned this hotel built on the base of Eagles Nest, which is the present-day site of Laurel Ridge Country Club. Originally built in the 1880s, it was expanded several times to include 75 rooms on a 250-acre parcel of land that included a dancing pavilion, lodging for summer guests, and tennis courts. Eleanor Roosevelt once stayed at the inn. However, over the years, it became less profitable, and the property was sold to Laurel Ridge Country Club in the 1980s. Though it outlasted many of its contemporary hotels in the area, it was finally demolished to make room for the golf course and country club buildings. (Courtesy of Henry Foy.)

Eight

Arts and Leisure

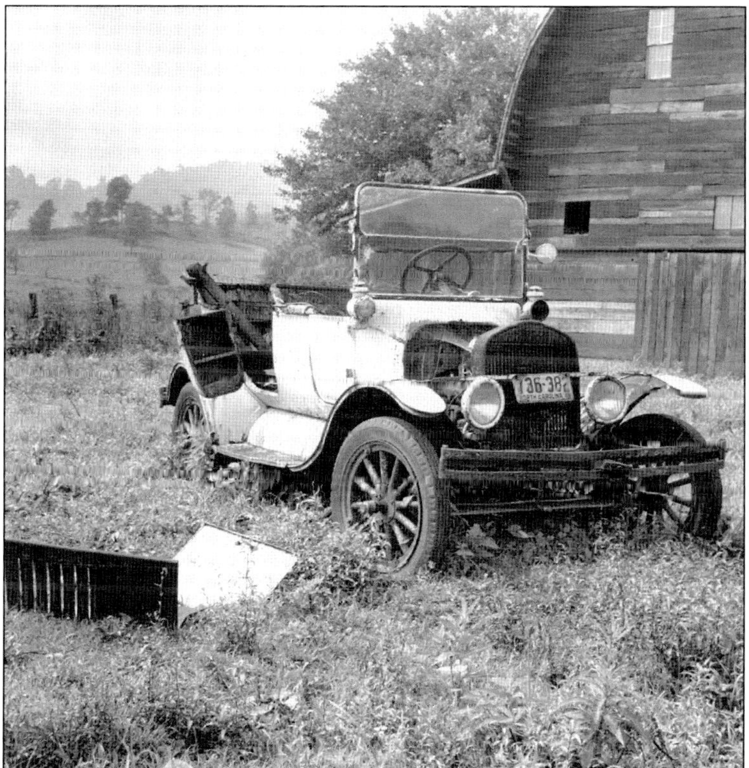

Sunday Rides. In the early 1900s, as cars became more prevalent, a popular form of weekend entertainment was the Sunday afternoon drive. Families, couples, or groups of friends would pack a picnic and go riding through the countryside. This car, which belonged to Amos Moody, would have offered just the kind of convertible experience savored by many in those days. (Courtesy of the *Mountaineer.*)

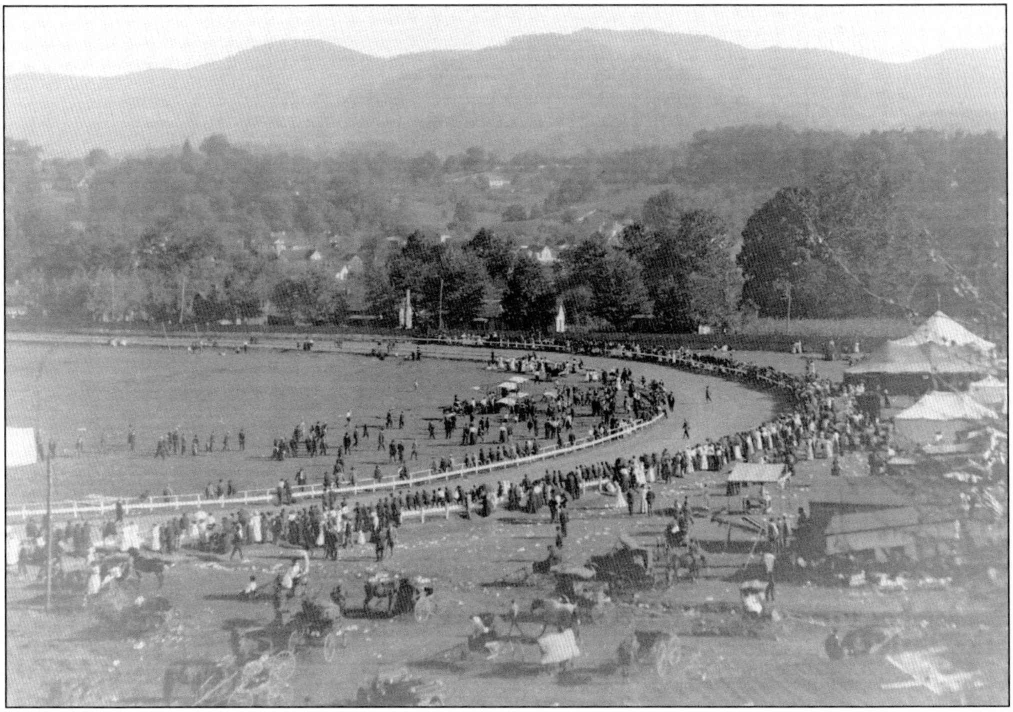

County Fair. In 1905, Waynesville hosted the Haywood County Fair, organized by the Farmers' Association and the Haywood County Stock Raisers. Local farmers showcased poultry, livestock, fruits, vegetables, and various crops. Thousands attended, and more than 750 prizes were given away for singing contests, exhibits, and various competitions. The fairgrounds site is now a residential community located near the present-day Waynesville Middle School. (Courtesy of Henry Foy.)

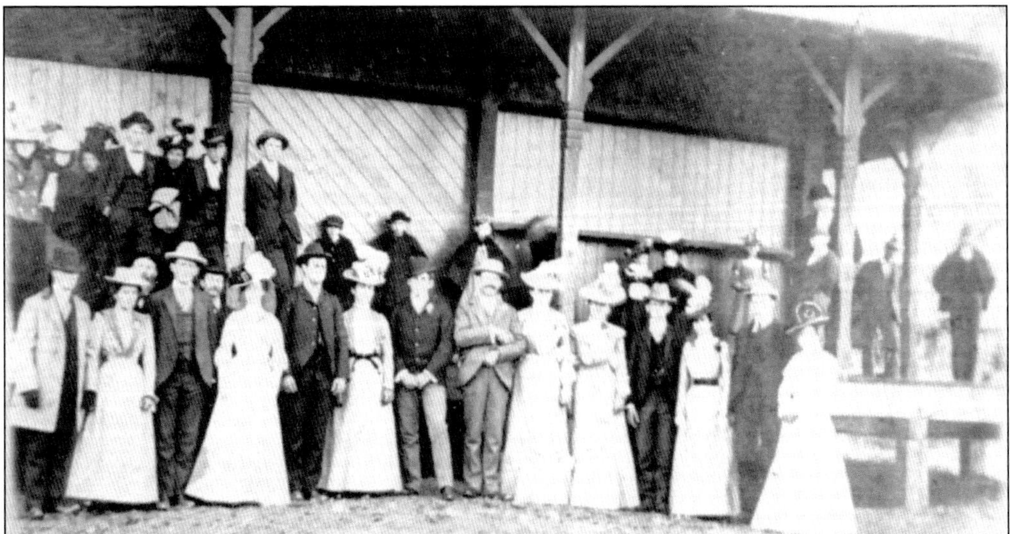

Train Rides. Weekend afternoons were often social occasions to meet new friends or go courting with a sweetheart on train rides through the countryside or to nearby towns. Dressing in their Sunday best, couples, singles, and friends would load up at the Clyde train depot to go for a ride on a service line that stretched west to Murphy or east to Asheville. (Courtesy of the Town of Clyde.)

BEEF SHOOT. Cataloochee Ranch hosted shooting contests from the mid-1940s to the late 1960s as a throwback to the days when early settlers used muzzle-loading rifles to hunt and fend off enemies on the frontier. Contestants were placed in age categories, and winners won choice cuts of beef. W. A. Bradley of Waynesville (right), who won the 1954 contest, pours black powder into a hollow bear's tooth as James Jackson Candler looks on. (Courtesy of the *Mountaineer*.)

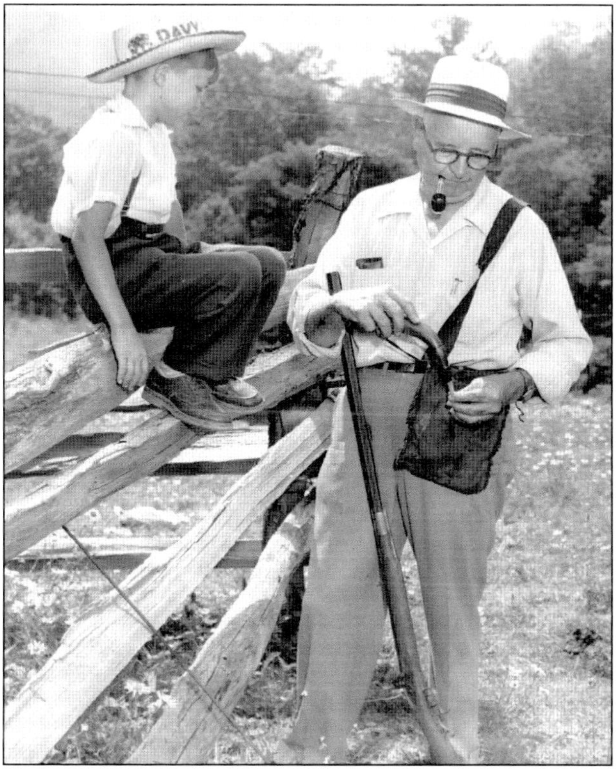

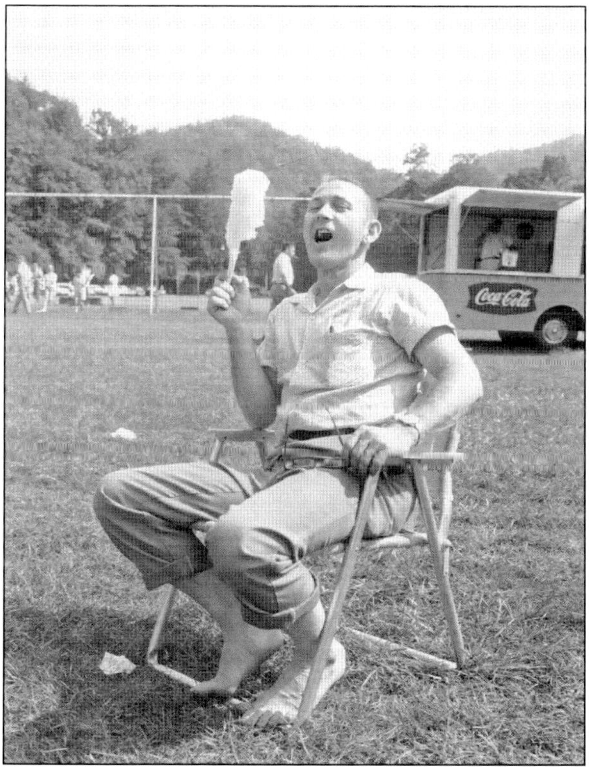

CAMP HOPE. The Champion paper mill in Canton owned a campground area known as Camp Hope in the southern end of the county. During summers, Champion employees and their families were invited to enjoy the outdoors and partake in games and entertainment at Camp Hope, which was named after the wife of Champion president Reuben Robertson. (Courtesy of Canton Historical Museum.)

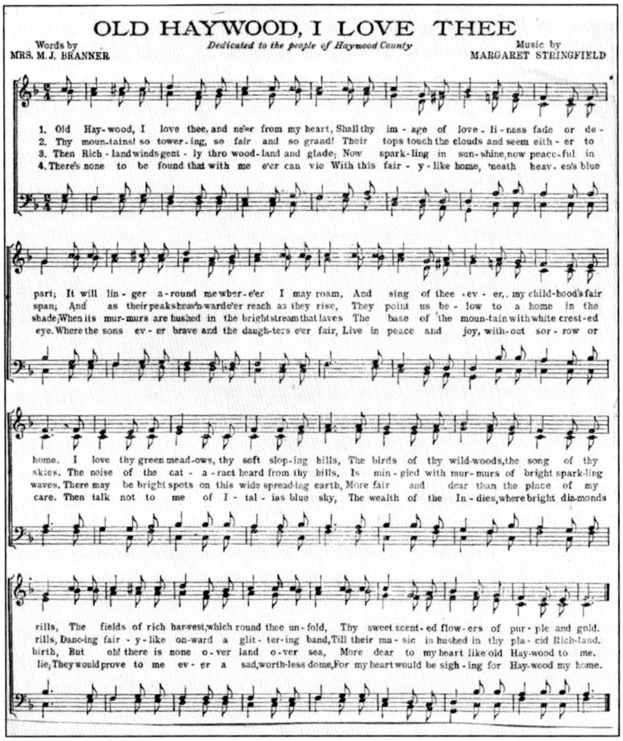

"Old Haywood, I Love Thee." Margaret Stringfield (1879–1958) penned the notes to this song in honor of Haywood County. In addition to teaching, singing, and organizing local cultural events, she worked as a music director at a Waynesville hospital for soldiers returning from World War I and composed a Cherokee-inspired opera called *Occoneechee: Fair Maid of the Forest*. (Courtesy of Henry Foy.)

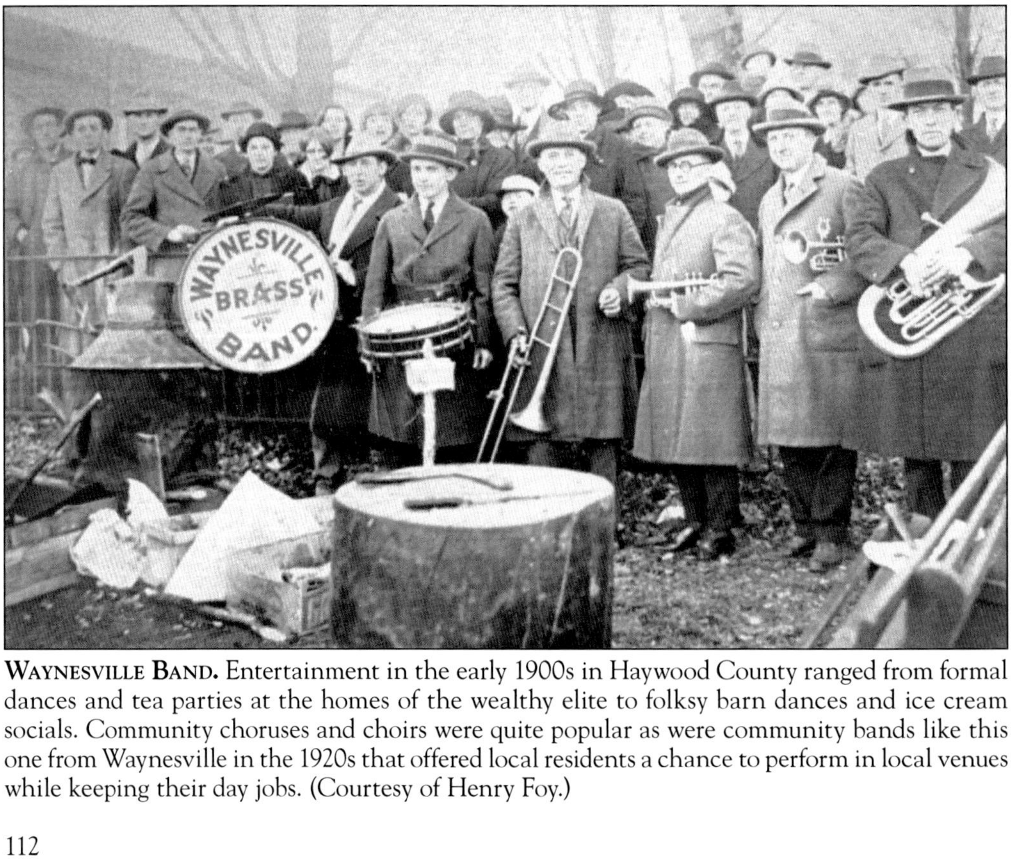

Waynesville Band. Entertainment in the early 1900s in Haywood County ranged from formal dances and tea parties at the homes of the wealthy elite to folksy barn dances and ice cream socials. Community choruses and choirs were quite popular as were community bands like this one from Waynesville in the 1920s that offered local residents a chance to perform in local venues while keeping their day jobs. (Courtesy of Henry Foy.)

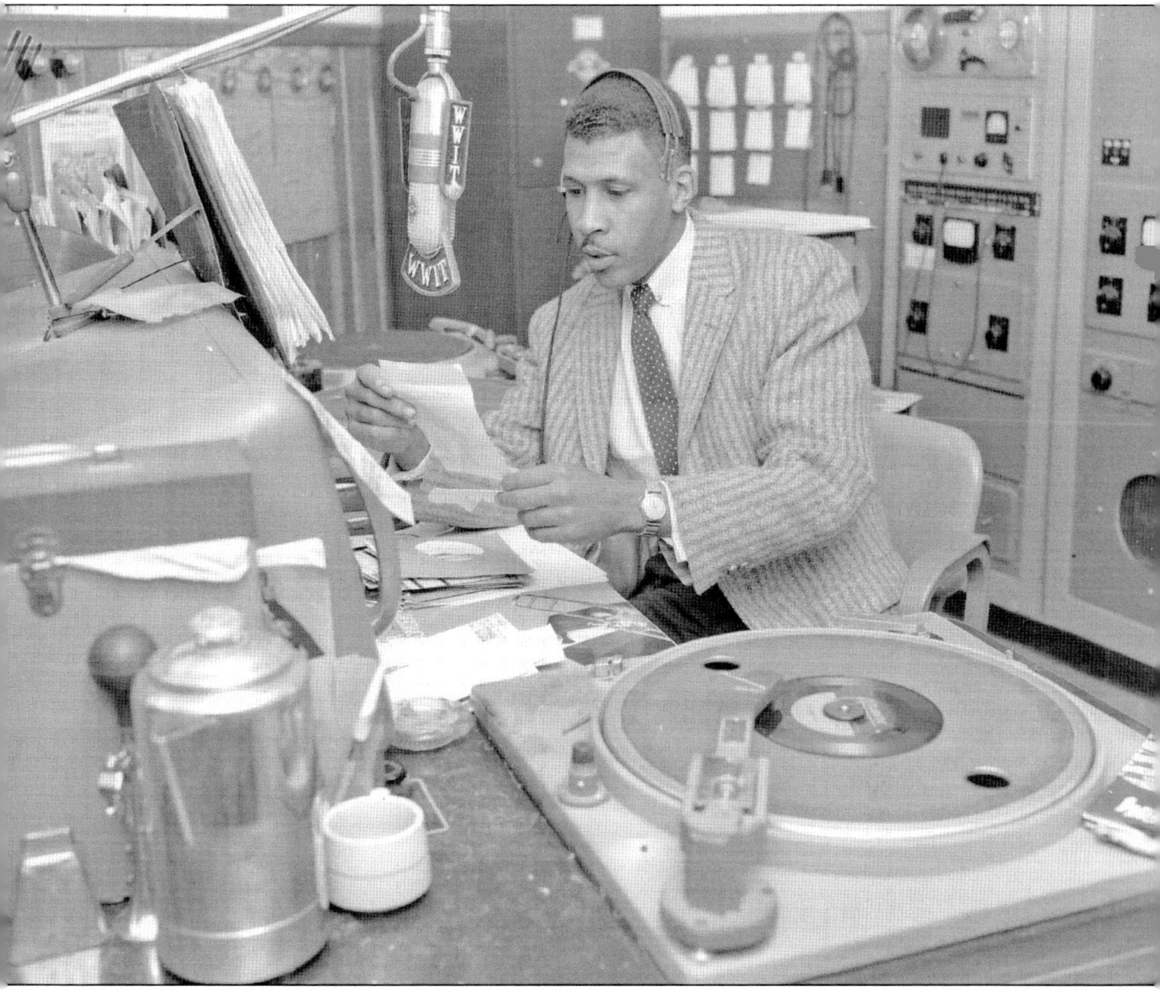

Nat the Cat. Nathaniel Lowery enjoyed a popular run as a deejay at WWIT in Canton during the 1950s and early 1960s. In the days of racial segregation, African Americans were not allowed to attend the same school as whites, so Lowery left Haywood County to get an education. After two years in the U.S. Army, he returned home and volunteered as a public address announcer for a local football game. An impressed representative from WWIT was at the game, and Lowery was soon offered a job. Using a smooth-talking radio persona known as "Nat the Cat," he would offer up lines like, "It's five past five and time to jive." While spinning the hot sounds of Motown, he continued to keep his other job at the Champion paper mill in Canton. In addition to shows Monday through Friday, he also had a 90-minute Saturday show and a Sunday gospel hour. His following of black and white fans stretched from East Tennessee across Western North Carolina, even as explosive violence erupted against protesters during the civil rights movement. (Courtesy of Canton Historical Museum.)

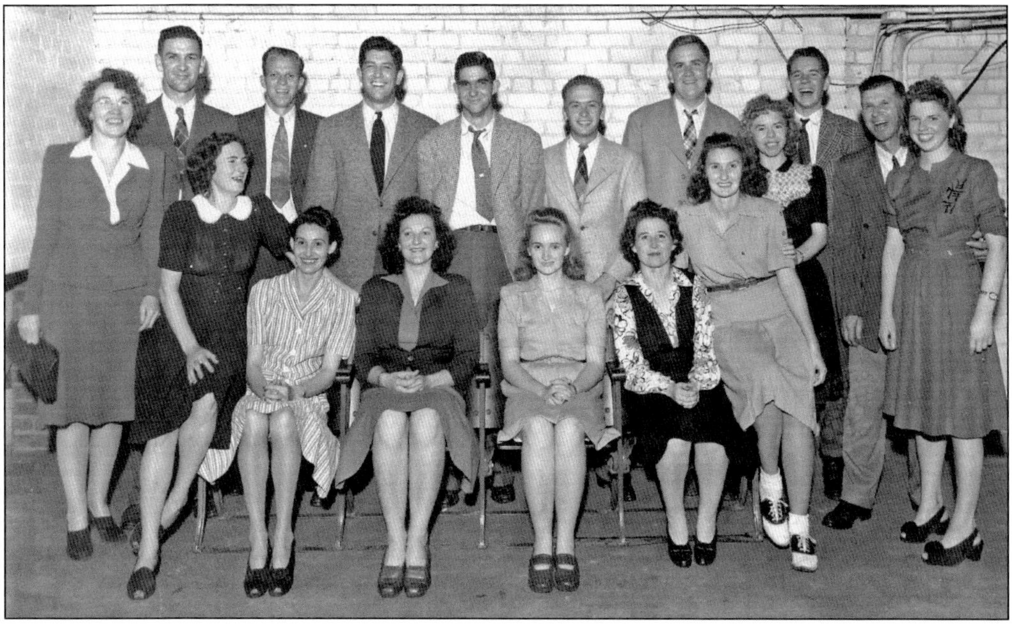

Square Dancing. The Soco Gap Square Dance Team, led by Sam Love Queen, second from right above, performed at the opening of the Dayco Rubber Plant in Hazelwood in 1941. The team organized in the 1920s and performed at numerous folk festivals and venues, including Carnegie Hall, the Waldorf Astoria, and the Smithsonian Institute. In June 1939, they were invited to perform at the White House as part of an evening entertainment program for Pres. Franklin Roosevelt, his wife, and dignitaries, including the king and queen of England. Below, one of the Soco Gap dancers, Beulah Caldwell (center), dances in the loft at Moody's Farm. (Above, courtesy of Joe Sam Queen; below, Betty Ferguson.)

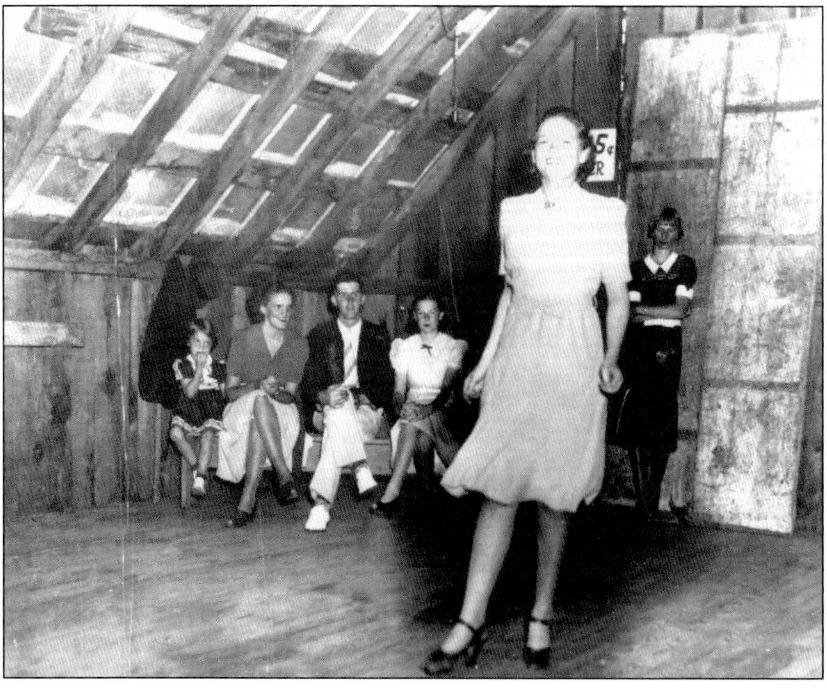

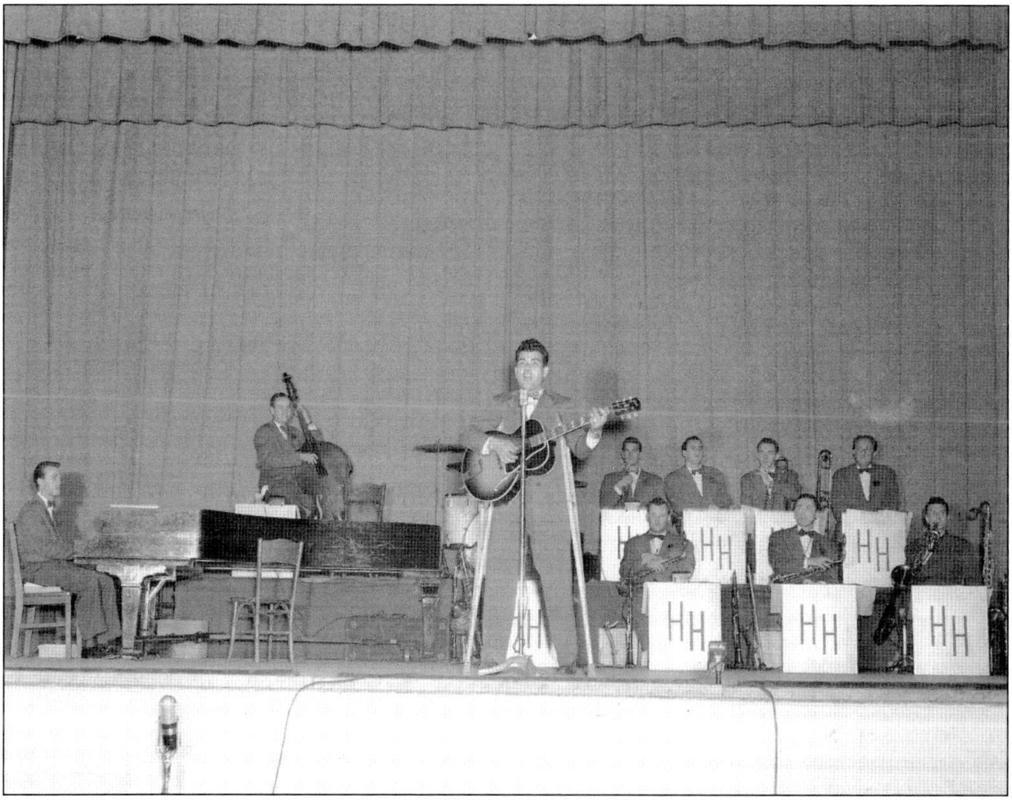

JIMMY HAYNIE. Despite losing both of his legs in a train accident at the age of 16, Canton native Jimmy Haynie went on to perform all over the country as a guitarist and singer. He won the top ballad singer prize at the 1952 National Folk Festival in Warrenton, West Virginia, and sang alongside country greats like Conway Twitty and Grandpa Jones. He later became a radio deejay at Canton radio stations in the 1960s and 1970s. (Courtesy of Canton Historical Museum.)

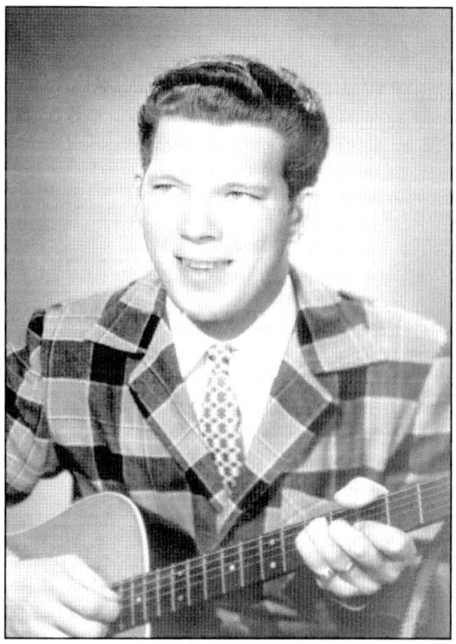

ALL IN THE FAMILY. Johnny Wiggins found fame singing with Ernest Tubb and the Texas Troubadours but left his musical career in Nashville to spend more time with his family and later helped found the Stompin' Ground, a clogging and music venue in Maggie Valley. Two of Wiggins's children, John Wayne and Audrey, went on to become Nashville recording artists and songwriters. (Courtesy of the *Mountaineer*.)

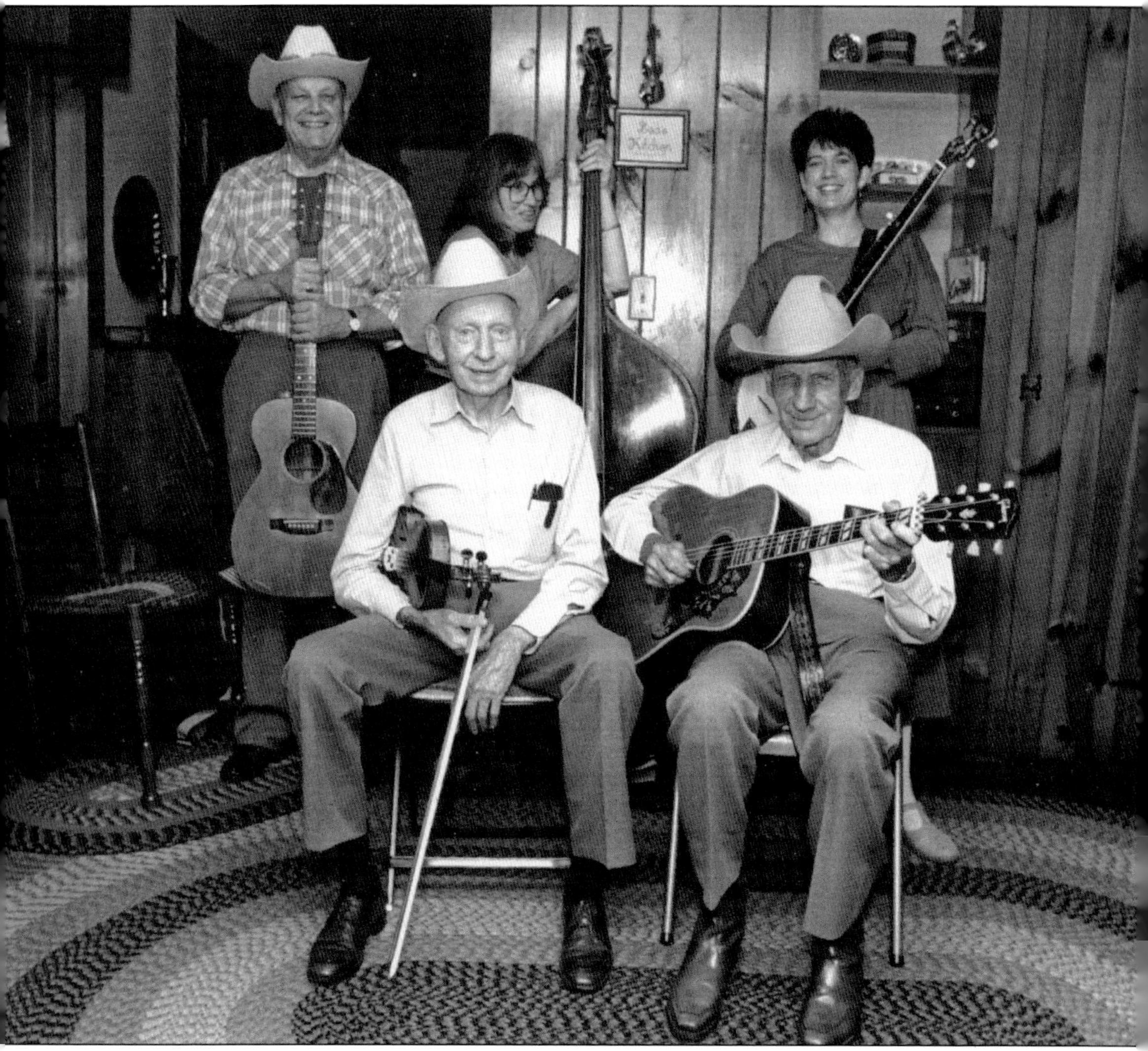

LUKE SMATHERS BAND. In the 1920s, the Smathers brothers of Canton—George, Harold, and Luke—learned to play musical instruments they had ordered from a Sears and Roebuck catalog. Luke (pictured here, front left) learned to play the fiddle while Harold and George played guitar. They formed a popular local band that played at ice cream socials. They developed a unique style called "mountain swing," inspired by old-time mountain tunes and the big band sound of that era. But then World War II came, and the band broke up. After not playing for about 25 years, a folk music revival made their brand of music popular once again. Luke formed a new family band, which included different combinations of musicians, including eventual Grammy Award–winner David Holt. They toured all over the Southeast and Midwest, recorded albums, and rehearsed in the kitchen of Luke's home—all this even after Luke lost three of his fingers in a Champion paper mill accident. Both Luke and his brother Harold (front right) were awarded the North Carolina Folk Heritage Award. Standing in this photograph, from left to right, are Charles Gidney, Hillary Dirlam, and Laura Boosinger. (Courtesy of Charles Gidney.)

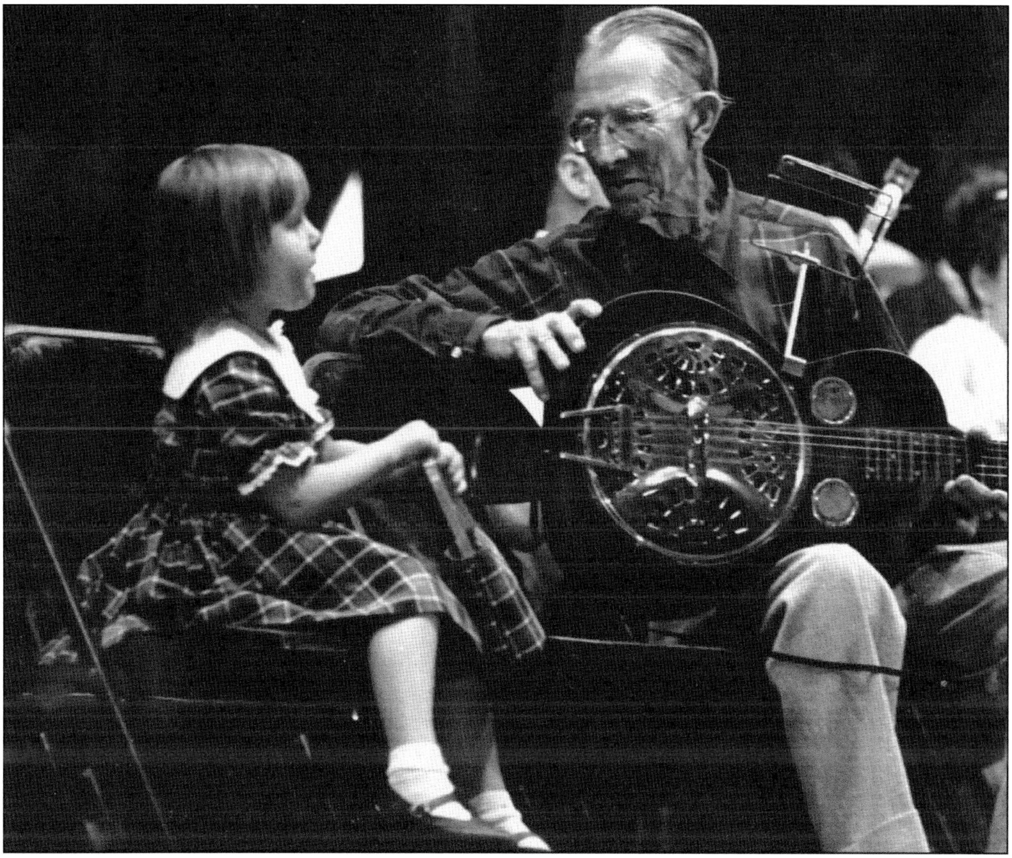

Smoky Mountain Folk Festival. Haywood County cherishes old-time mountain music and dance, bringing young and old to experience traditional music, square dancing and clogging, and a variety of family bands and veteran performers. The annual two-night festival is held at Stuart Auditorium at Lake Junaluska on the Friday and Saturday nights of Labor Day weekend. As the evening progresses, performers and fans gather under lakeside tents to jam. It is not hard to find the foot-tapping sounds of mountain music passing from one generation to the next, above. One longtime participant of the festival is award-winning ballad singer, instrument maker, and musician Jim Trantham (below). His son, Doug, and three grandchildren have also joined together over the years to perform on stage and to record their music. (Both courtesy of the *Mountaineer*.)

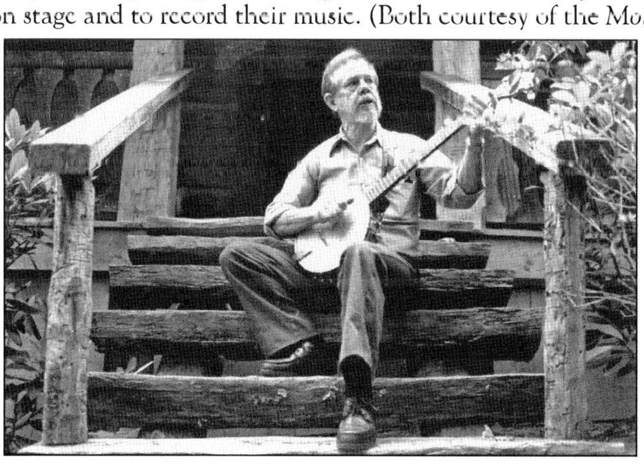

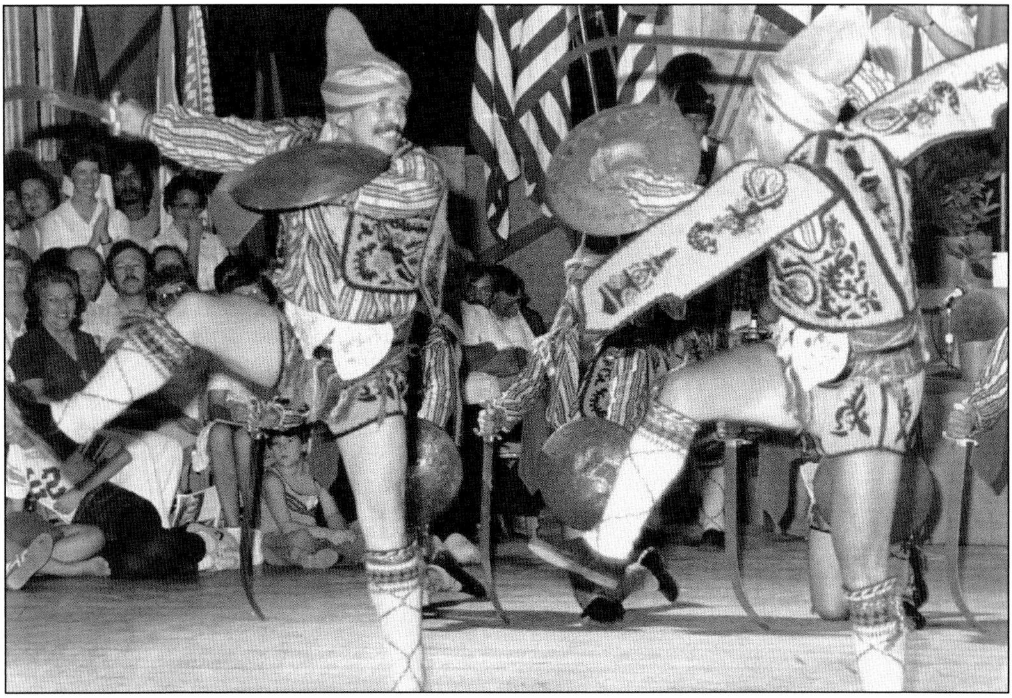

Folkmoot. In the early 1980s, Dr. Clinton Border, a physician from Waynesville, accompanied a string band and square dance team from Haywood County to take part in a folk festival in Sidmouth, England. Border was so impressed with the festival that he decided to start one up in Waynesville. After researching, raising money, and securing foreign music and dance teams, the first Folkmoot festival opened in 1984 with 10 groups that included sword-wielding dancers from Turkey (above) and a festive troupe from Mexico (below). Known by its Old English term, which means "a meeting of the people," Folkmoot has become an annual summer event ever since, promoting the exchange of music, dance, and culture with performances throughout the county and all over Western North Carolina over two action-packed weeks in July. (Both courtesy of the *Mountaineer*.)

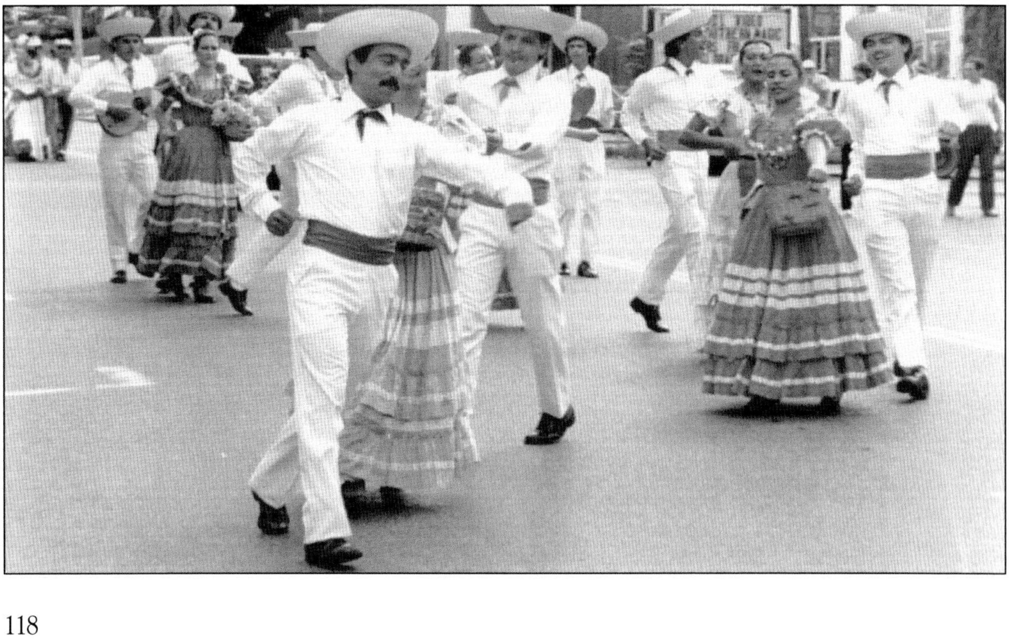

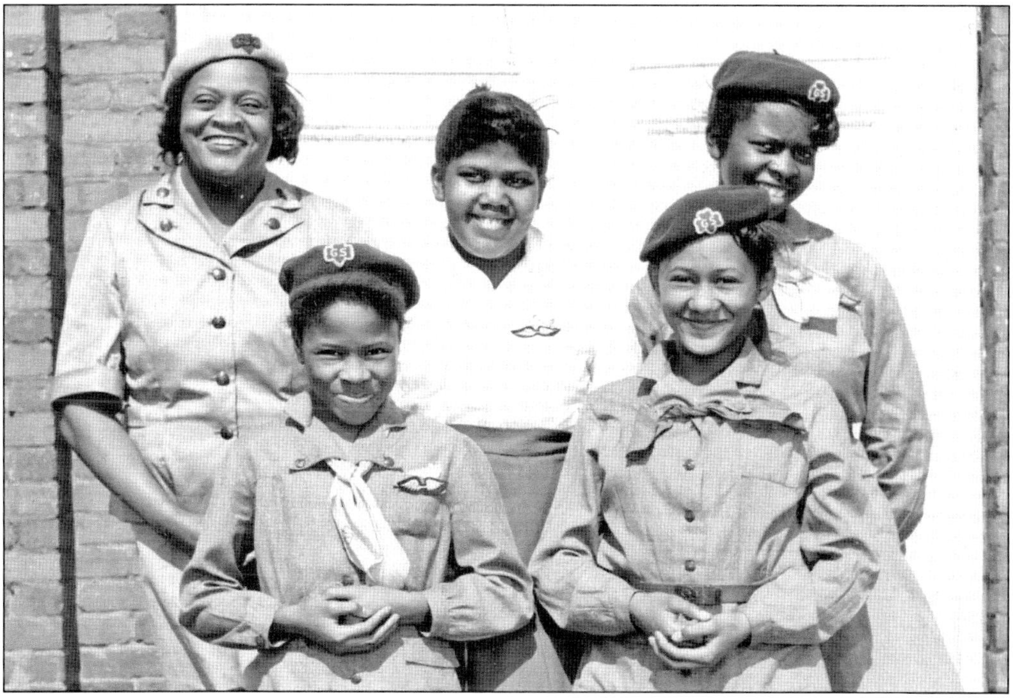

Girl Scouts. Youth groups continue to thrive throughout the county, whether they are church related, school affiliated, or organized by civic clubs. Girl Scout Troop 93 included, from left to right, (first row) Iva Jean Leigh and Mary Elizabeth Allen; (second row) Christine Allen, Ann Patton, and Mary Lee Sims. (Photograph by Town and Country Studio; courtesy of Haywood County Public Library Digital Collection.)

Flower Show. An annual flower show, sponsored by the Richland Garden Club of Waynesville and Mountain View Garden Club, features hundreds of exhibits. This show was in 1952 at the Waynesville Armory. Several garden clubs continue to beautify and maintain various gardens throughout the county and showcase their efforts in annual exhibits, including the dazzling Dahlia Exhibit held each summer at the Waynesville public library. (Courtesy of Richland Garden Club.)

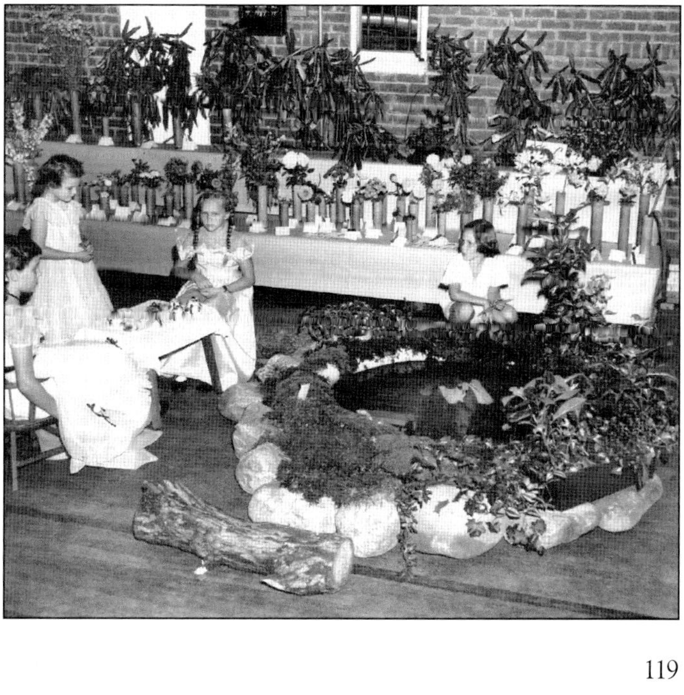

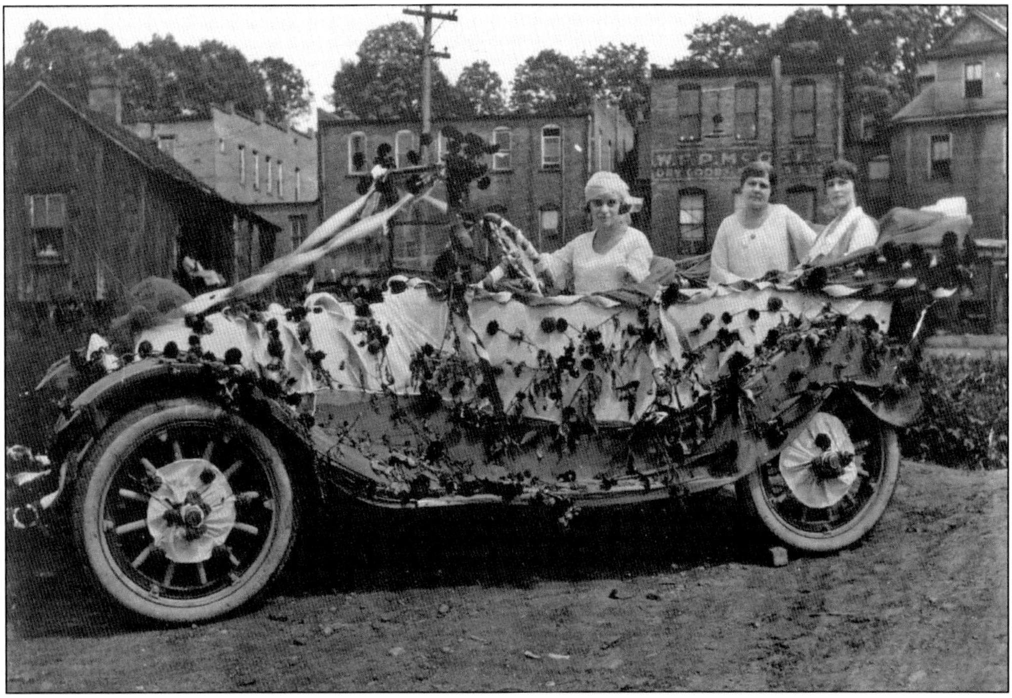

Leading Ladies. This 1921 Labor Day Parade float featured some of Canton's prominent female civic leaders in a Buick touring car decorated with roses. From left to right are Gaye Davis, Mrs. W. E. Roberts, and Mrs. Wade Hill, then the president of Canton's Women's Club. (Courtesy of Canton Historical Museum.)

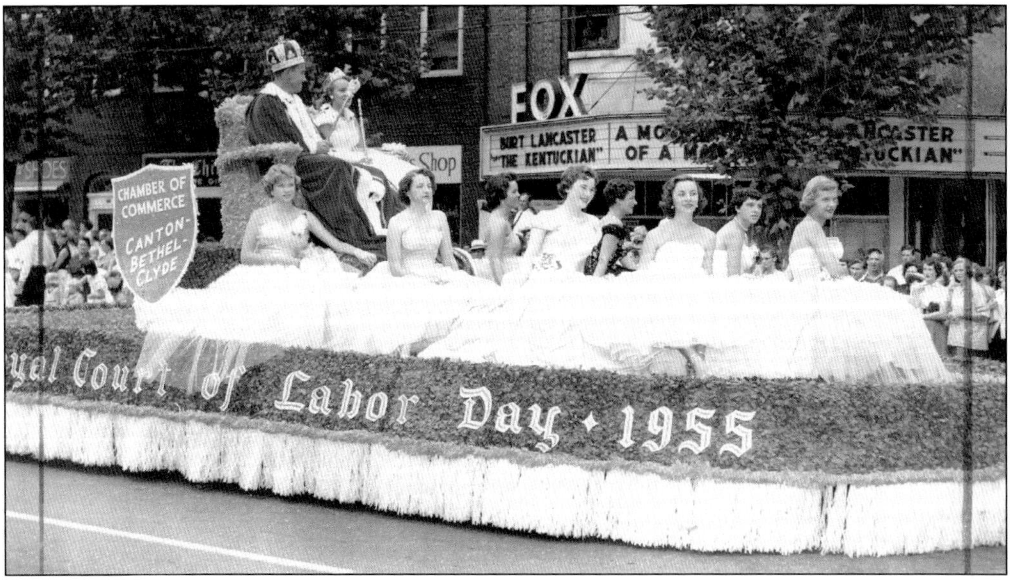

Who's the Fairest? One of the main attractions at the Canton Labor Day celebration is the beauty pageant, which once held competitions for king and queen but now only offers crowns for Miss Labor Day. Along with being crowned queen, the lucky lady these days also receives a scholarship. Once crowned, the royal court rode in local parades. This float, above, was in a parade outside of Haywood County. (Courtesy of Canton Historical Museum.)

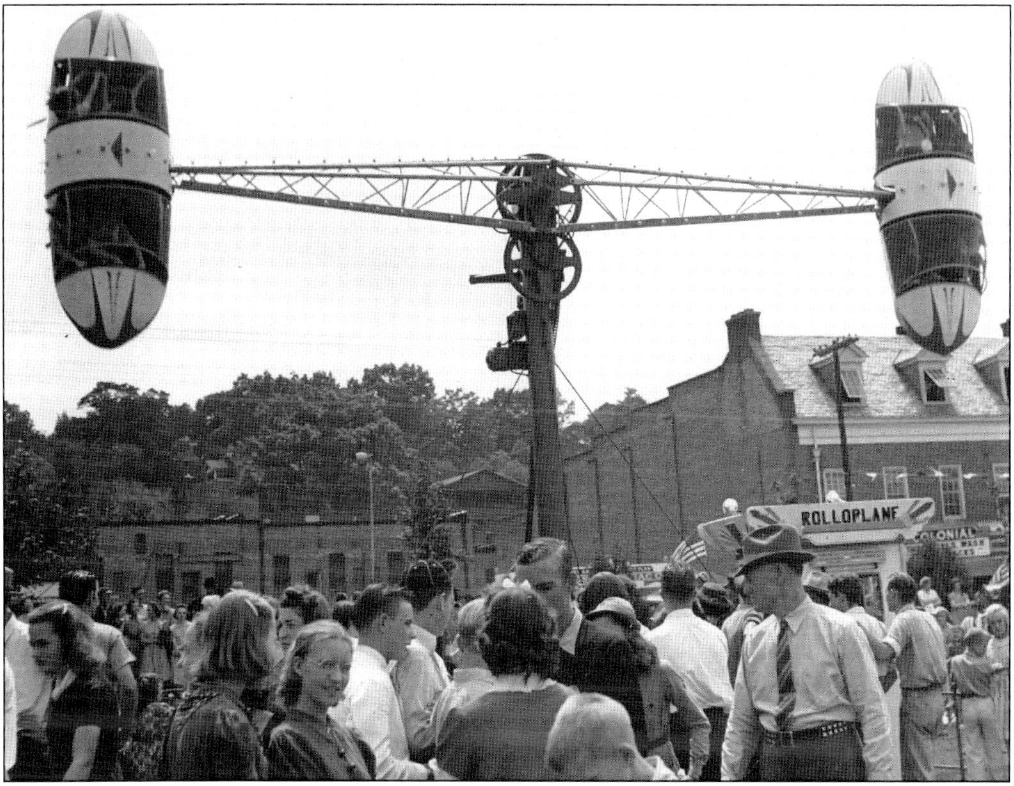

LABOR DAY RIDES. Festival-goers who came to Canton's Park Street during the annual Labor Day festivities could take advantage of all sorts of rides, including a Ferris wheel and Tilt-a-Whirl. Boat rides, a carousel, and toy plane rides were offered to the smaller children. For those a little more daring, there was the Rollo Plane (above). Buckling into the contraption, one was launched high in the air and then turned over or slung in various positions that induced plenty of screams. Canton also enjoyed a few roller coasters, below. As the speed of the cars increased, its riders were shoved to one side by the centrifugal force. (Both courtesy of Canton Historical Museum.)

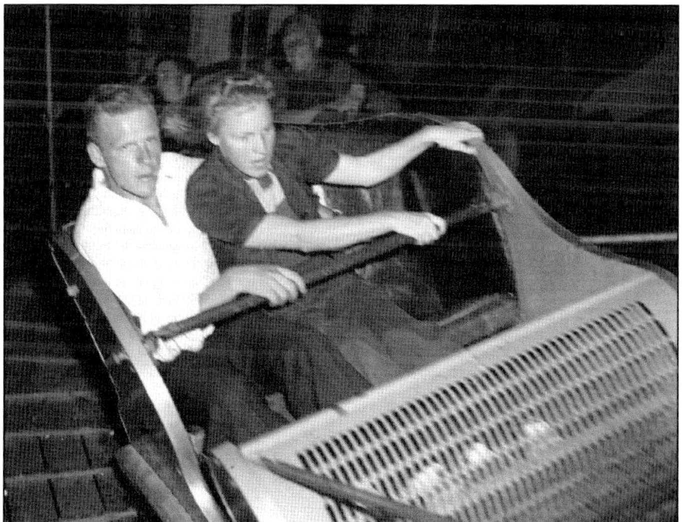

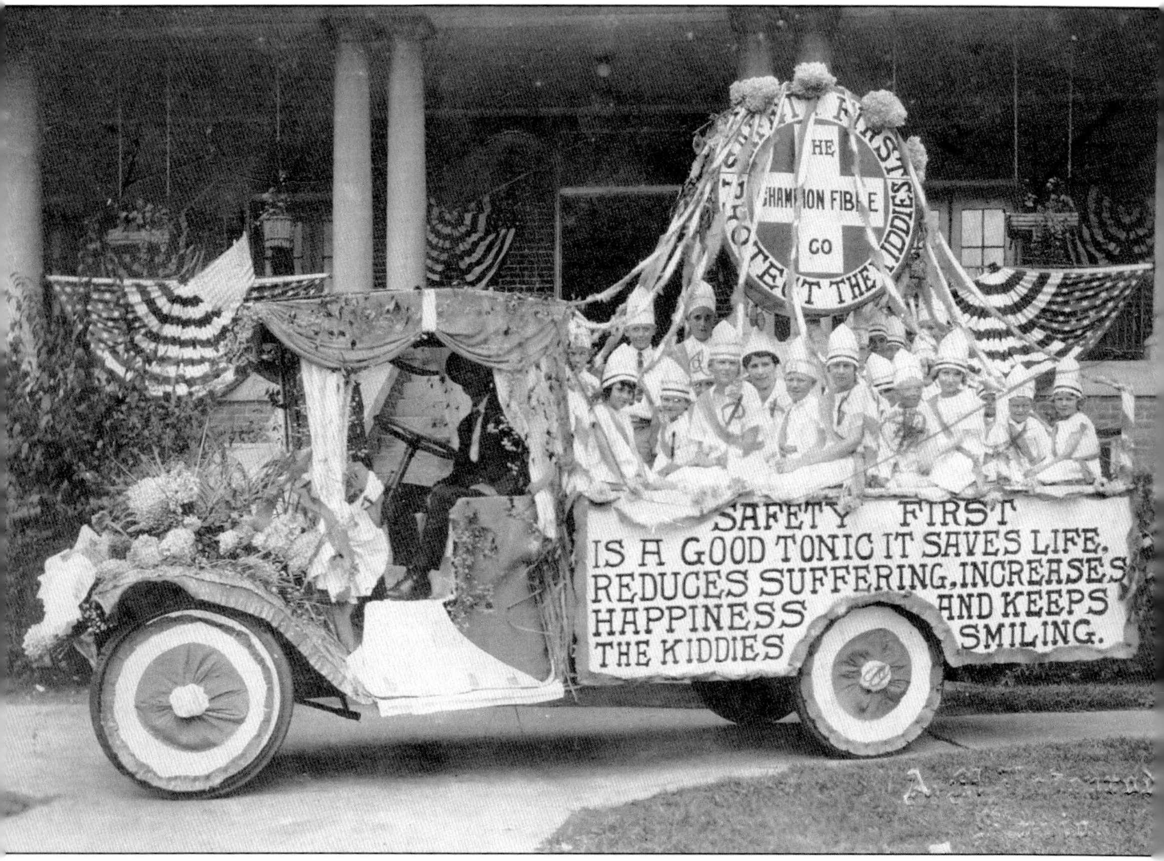

WHOLESOME FUN. The Champion YMCA, built in 1920 as a center for family-oriented exercise and entertainment, included two bowling alleys, a swimming pool, a locker and shower rooms, a library and reading room, a gymnasium/auditorium, a billiard room, a banquet room, various offices and meeting rooms, and a kitchen. Anyone over the age of 12 years was eligible for membership—and not just family members of mill employees. The building was torn down in the 1960s to make room for Champion's No. 19 machine. (Courtesy of Canton Historical Museum.)

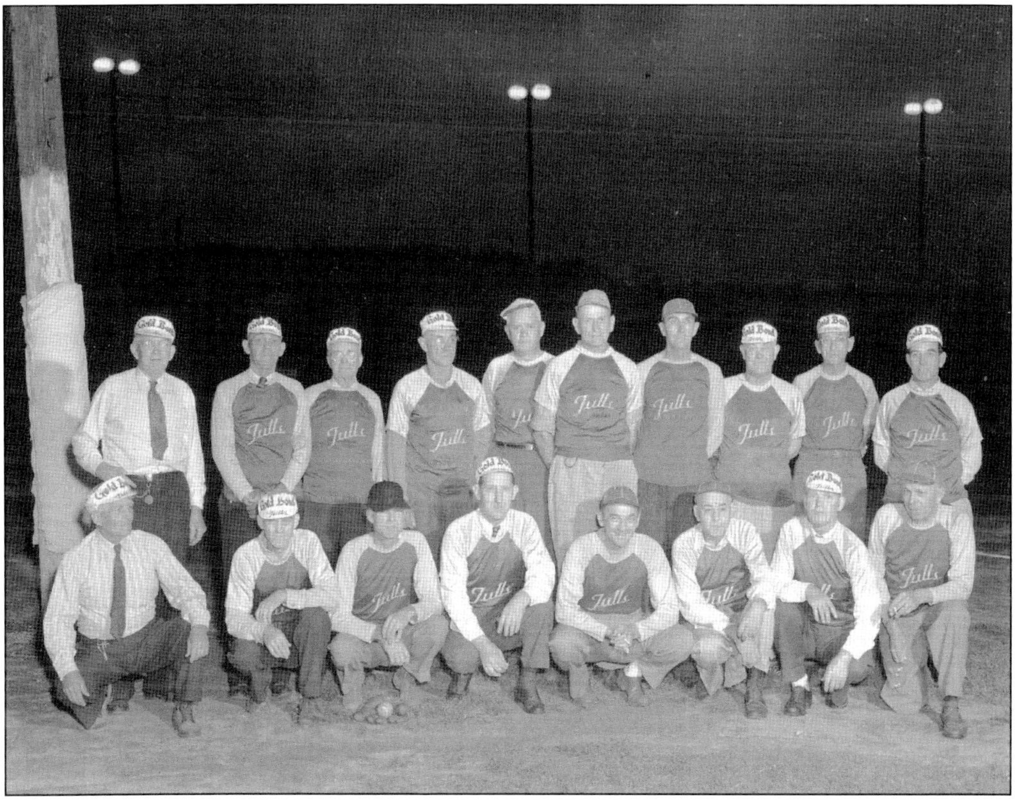

TULLS V. FRANKS. The Champion Old-Timers—older and retired members of the Champion paper mill in Canton—took part in annual softball games that pitted one group, the Franks (named after employee Frank Smathers), against another, the Tulls (named after employee Tull Jamison). The friendly rivalry featured all ranks of workers, including plant manager Dutch Helter (back row, far right). (Courtesy of Canton Historical Museum.)

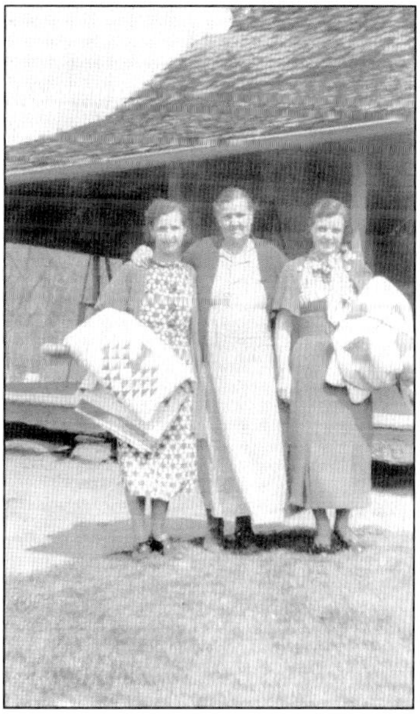

QUILTING. Some of the earliest art made in Haywood County involved quilting, which was both a social activity and a support network for women who gathered to sew and share stories. Ladies in the Palmer family on Cataloochee were quilt makers. In this photograph from the 1930s, Maria Palmer (center), who once served as a postmistress in Cataloochee, stands with two of her nieces, Beatrice Palmer Sisk (left) and Eulala Palmer Caldwell (right). (Courtesy of Cataloochee Ranch.)

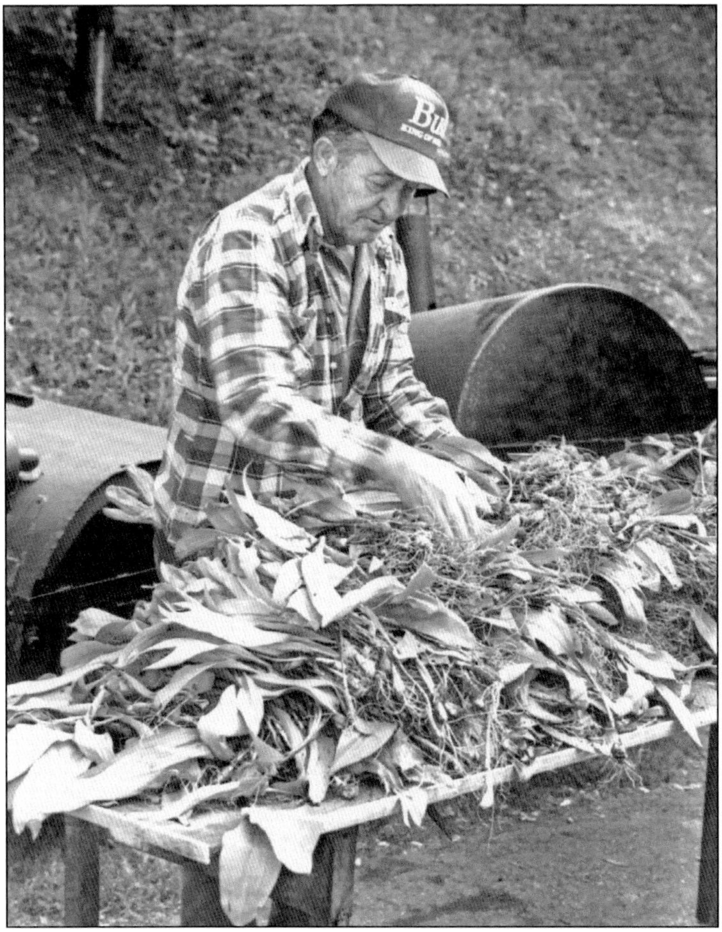

Ramp Festival. What began with local residents in Black Camp Gap harvesting the pungent cousin of the onion became an annual convention drawing hundreds, including enterprising state and local politicians looking for votes. The festival eventually relocated to Waynesville, its present-day site. Folks come to sample ramp recipes, live music, and dancing. After ramps are harvested and dried (to the left), they can be cooked or eaten raw. One of the popular draws at the event is the ramp-eating contest (below), an especially challenging feat because of the ramp's strong odor that can cling to a person for days. (Both courtesy of the *Mountaineer.*)

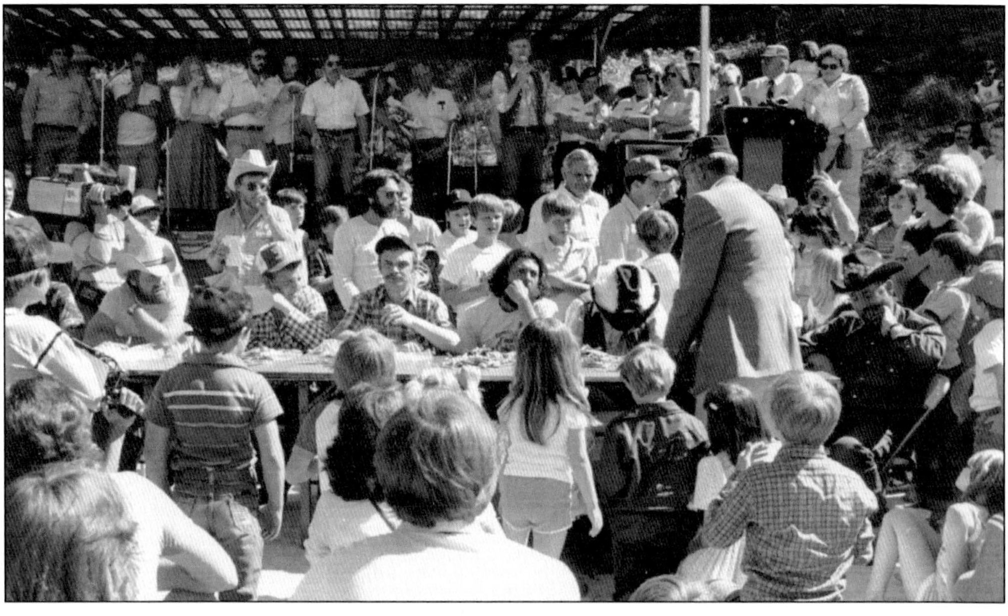

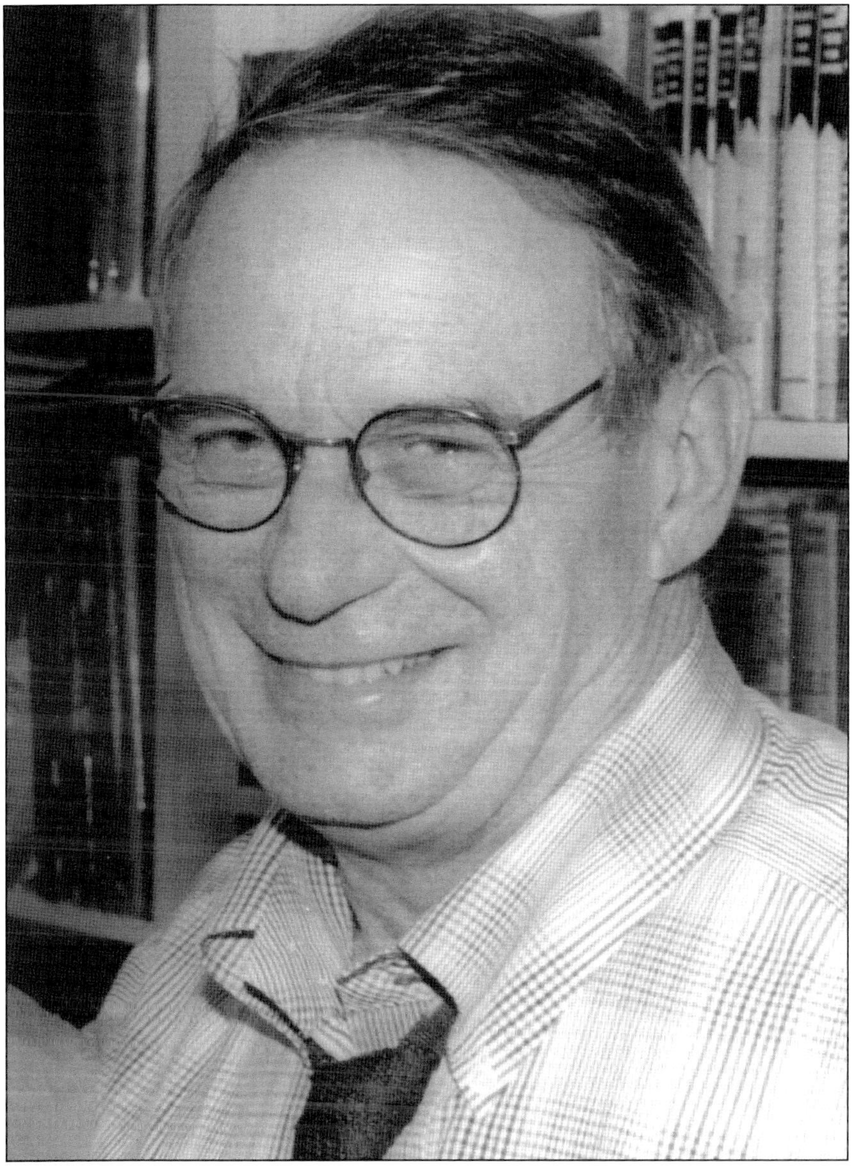

FRED CHAPPELL. Perhaps the greatest writer Haywood County has ever produced, Fred Chappell has earned a stellar reputation as a prodigious poet, novelist, essayist, and short-story author. He taught for 40 years as an English professor at the University of North Carolina at Greensboro and has written 30 books. Born in 1936 and raised in the Beaverdam community, he fell in love with writing at an early age. Schoolteachers would recall his dreamy gaze out the window as he imagined new stories and poems. He attended Duke University and studied under the legendary professor William Blackburn, who inspired a bevy of gifted writers, including Anne Tyler, Reynolds Price, and William Styron. Chappell published award-winning novels, short stories, and poetry collections that drew on his childhood experiences growing up in Haywood County. His four-part poetry collection, *Midquest*, and his four-part novels about the fictional Kirkman family (which include *I Am One of You Forever* and *Brighten the Corner Where You Are*) are among his most critically acclaimed works. From 1997 to 2002, Chappell also served as North Carolina's Poet Laureate. (Photograph by Jan G. Hensley.)

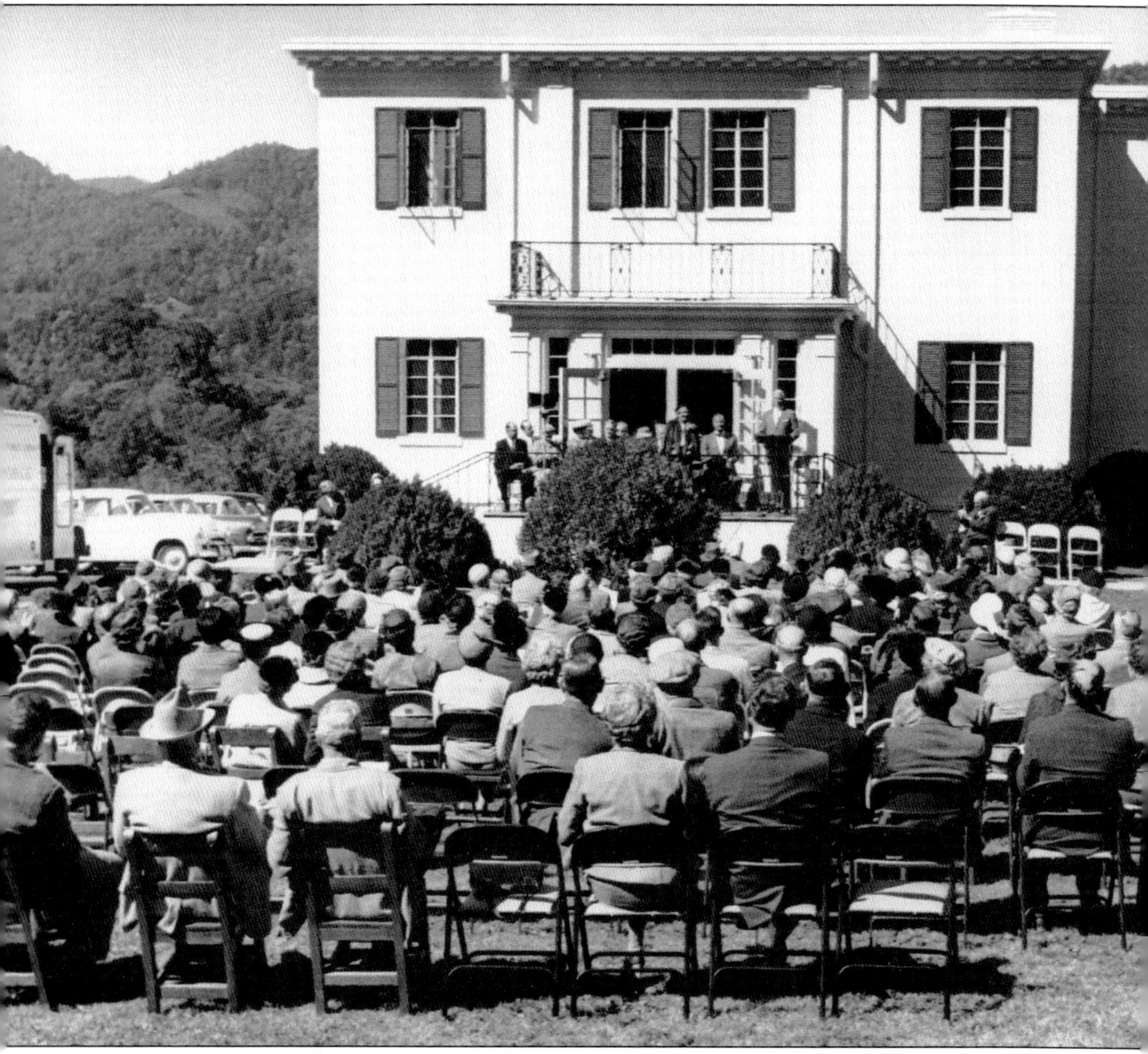

Ferguson Home. This former site of the Haywood County Public Library was located in what would now be the parking lot area of the current Waynesville public library. This photograph is believed to be the dedication ceremony for the opening of the library. Renovations to the home flattened out the roof—to the dismay of some—and reinforced the second-story floor so that heavy stacks of books could be stored there. This library also operated an elevator—not for people, but for books. Before coming to this location, the library was housed in the rock building that still stands on Main Street in Waynesville. Just down the street from the present-day library lived Caroline Miller, a Georgia native who moved to Waynesville after winning the 1934 Pulitzer Prize for her first novel, *Lamb in His Bosom*. A historical marker dedicated to her stands in front of the Waynesville library. (Courtesy of Henry Foy.)

BIBLIOGRAPHY

Alexander, Tom. *Mountain Fever.* Edited by Tom Alexander Jr. and Jane Alexander. Asheville, NC: Bright Mountain Books, Inc., 1995.

Allen, William Cicero. *The Annals of Haywood County, North Carolina.* Spartanburg, SC: The Reprint Company, Publishers, 1977.

Anderson, Nina L., and William L. Anderson. *Heritage of Healing: A Medical History of Haywood County.* Waynesville, NC: The Waynesville Historical Society, 1994.

Barnett, Phyllis Inman. *At the Foot of Cold Mountain: Sunburst and the Universalists at Inman's Chapel.* Waynesville, NC: Pigeon River Press, 2008.

Crow, Vernon H. *Storm in the Mountains: Thomas' Confederate Legion of Cherokee Indians and Mountaineers.* Cherokee, NC: Press of the Museum of the Cherokee Indian, 1982.

Davis, Hattie Caldwell. *Reflections of Cataloochee Valley and Its Vanished People in the Great Smoky Mountains.* Maggie Valley, NC: Hattie Caldwell Davis, 1999.

Medford, W. Clark. *Land O' The Sky: History, Stories, Sketches.* Asheville, NC: Miller Printing Company, 1965.

Oliver, Duane. *Mountain Gables: A History of Haywood County Architecture.* Waynesville, NC: Oliver Scriptorium, 2001.

Plott, Bob. *Strike & Stay: The Story of the Plott Hound.* Charleston, SC: History Press, 2007.

Webb, Janet Threlkeld. *Haywood County: A Brief History.* Charleston, SC: History Press, 2006.

Wood, Curtis, ed. *Haywood County: Portrait of a Mountain Community.* Greenville, SC: Southern Historical Press, 2009.